SHAKESPEARE'S POLITICAL PAGEANT

SHAKESPEARE'S POLITICAL PAGEANT

Essays in Literature and Politics

Edited by
JOSEPH ALULIS
and
VICKIE SULLIVAN

ROWMAN & LITTLEFIELD PUBLISHERS, INC.

ROWMAN & LITTLEFIELD PUBLISHERS, INC.

Published in the United States of America
by Rowman & Littlefield Publishers, Inc.
4720 Boston Way, Lanham, Maryland 20706

3 Henrietta Street
London WC2E 8LU, England

British Cataloging in Publication Information Available

Library of Congress Cataloging-in-Publication Data

Shakespeare's political pageant : essays in literature and politics / edited by Joseph Alulis and Vickie Sullivan.
p. cm.
Includes bibliographical references and index.
1. Shakespeare, William, 1564–1616—Political and social views.
2. Politics and literature—Great Britain—History—16th century.
3. Politics and literature—Great Britain—History—17th century.
4. Literature and society—England—History—16th century.
5. Literature and society—England—History—17th century.
6. Political plays, English—History and criticism. 7. Point of view (Literature) I. Alulis, Joseph, 1949– . II. Sullivan, Vickie B.
PR3017.S58 1996 822.3'3—dc20 96-19703 CIP

ISBN 0-8476-8289-7 (cloth : alk. paper)
ISBN 0-8476-8290-0 (pbk. : alk. paper)

Printed in the United States of America

∞ ™ The paper used in this publication meets the minimum requirements of American National Standard for Information Sciences—Permanence of Paper for Printed Library Materials, ANSI Z39.48–1984.

Contents

Part III: Tragedies

Preface

Literary works reveal through their very personal means of characterization—in a way a political treatise cannot—the direct effect that politics has on individuals. In displaying this effect, literature touches on the very essence of politics: the way in which individuals come together for the attainment of personal and common ends. By displaying the manner in which politics affects the lives of its characters, literature encourages one to reflect upon the way in which the distribution of power affects the good of the community and the good of the individual. Although originating from the diverse fields of philosophy, literature, and political science, the authors contributing to this volume share the conviction that the study of literature can enhance one's understanding of politics.[1]

Moreover, the contributors to this volume share the understanding that Shakespeare is the author who most effectively sets before us the multifarious spectacle of politics. Shakespeare's rich canon presents monarchy and republic, tyrant and king, thinker and soldier, and Christian and pagan. In so presenting this political pageant through poetry that touches the passions, he moves us to consider simultaneously the necessary conditions for the maintenance of different constitutions and the desirability of overturning defective ones. His poetry also raises broader political issues such as the effects of religion on regime and of regime on character.[2] In raising these questions, Shakespeare's portrait of politics provokes reflection upon the philosophical questions regarding the nature of humanity and the place of the human being in the whole. In an important sense, then, Shakespeare's reflections can be understood to transcend those arising merely from the political and social forces current in Elizabethan and Jacobean England.[3]

Because these authors look to Shakespeare for guidance in the articulation of these perennial human questions, their understanding of Shakespeare's relation to politics must be distinguished from the prominent new historicist or cultural materialist approach, which also regards Shakespeare as a political thinker. According to Jonathan Dollimore, cultural materialism refuses to "privilege" literature, to treat it, among all other activities, as exempt from the forces of the age.[4] Thus, in contrast to the understanding informing these essays, cultural materialism maintains that all political questions are to be understood strictly as matters of the material forces of particular times and places.

The approach taken by these authors must also be distinguished from an older view that regarded Shakespeare as a political thinker. The authors included in this volume are reluctant to identify any one character as the spokesperson for Shakespeare's political viewpoint.[5] Rather, the contributors attempt to examine how Shakespeare's voice emerges from the construction of the drama that necessarily entails conflict and contradiction among the characters, each of whom espouses a distinct view and possesses different concerns. Therefore, at the same time that these essays, each in its own way, proclaim the precipitousness of assuming at the outset of an investigation what is possible for a great author to write and think, they also maintain that knowledge, if it is to be had, is to be attained only with the greatest attention not only to the poet's words but also to the details of the drama. These essays, then, treat Shakespeare as a profound thinker on politics, and each essay contributes to the much greater task of assessing the character of Shakespeare's political thought as a whole.

Notes

1. See Catherine Zuckert, "The Novel as a Form of American Political Thought," in *Reading Political Stories: Representations of Politics in Novels and Pictures*, ed. Maureen Whitebrook (Lanham, Md.: Rowman & Littlefield, 1992), 167–204.

2. Allan Bloom with Harry Jaffa, *Shakespeare's Politics* (Chicago: University of Chicago Press, 1964), 11. Cf. Harry Jaffa, "An Interpretation of the Shakespearean Universe," in *Shakespeare as Political Thinker*, ed. John Alvis and Thomas G. West (Durham, N.C.: Carolina Academic Press, 1981), 290–91, 302–3.

3. Cf. Mera J. Flaumenhaft, *The Civic Spectacle: Essays on Drama and Community* (Lanham, Md.: Rowman & Littlefield, 1994), 5: "They [Aeschy-

lus, Euripides, Machiavelli, and Shakespeare] are for all times not because they can be enlisted on one side or another, but because they move us and unsettle us and make us think harder about who we are and what we ought to be, whatever the side on which we may find ourselves.'' See Paul A. Cantor's discussion of Shakespeare's understanding of Rome (*Shakespeare's Rome: Republic and Empire* [Ithaca: Cornell University Press, 1976], 7–8).

4. Jonathan Dollimore and Alan Sinfield, eds., *Political Shakespeare*, 2nd ed. (Ithaca: Cornell University Press, 1994), 4.

5. This approach is characterized by one critic as ''the old bad Tillyardian habit of giving particular characters and speeches a supradramatic significance, which is then identified with what the play or the dramatist 'really' thinks, and usually coincides with what the critic thinks'' (Graham Bradshaw, *Misrepresentations: Shakespeare and the Materialists* [Ithaca: Cornell University Press, 1993], 9).

Acknowledgments

A generous grant from the Faculty Development Committee at Skidmore College supported the production of the manuscript. Christine DeLucia provided invaluable technical help with its preparation.

Part I

Comedies

1

The New Medea: On Portia's Comic Triumph in *The Merchant of Venice*

Michael Zuckert

Partly because of its clever plot, striking characterizations, and moments of beautiful poetry, *The Merchant of Venice* has remained one of Shakespeare's best known, most often performed, and most discussed plays. It is also one of his most troubling plays. It is troubling in form because it presents a series of actions that are difficult to integrate into a coherent and unified whole.[1] It is troubling in substance because it presents a Christian society in the ugliness of its anti-Semitism, and while Shakespeare clearly has a broader view than his Venetians, his presentation of the Jew nonetheless appears to draw from the same unsavory and stereotypical prejudices that move the Christian Venetians. Moreover, among the comic resolutions of the play, the "setting to rights" of all the disruptions that have impelled the play's action, are the forced conversion of Shylock to Christianity, and the desertion by Shylock's daughter, Jessica, of both her father and her ancestral religion. Hers is a voluntary conversion to be sure, but it seems to carry the same point as Shylock's coerced conversion: Jews and Judaism are not worth the respect of Christian men and women.[2]

The focus on Shylock is not merely a product of our post-holocaust sensibilities, but seems to have been part of the reception of the play from the outset.[3] Perhaps it is the lure of thc cxotic, or perhaps it is a reaction to the character who seems to suffer most and to show the strongest and most complex passions, but it is in some ways a puzzling focus, for the play's title directs us not to Shylock, but to the merchant of Venice, that is to say, to Antonio. The focus on Shylock also contributes to the formal puzzles the play has provided, for if the play is taken to revolve centrally around Shylock and the pound of flesh pledge, then aspects of the play like the courting of Portia and the casket test seem extraneous, or at least very difficult to relate to the main story.[4]

If we follow Shakespeare's indications, we see that the focus on Shylock is largely misplaced, and the puzzlement over the formal unity of the play mistaken. Indeed, *The Merchant of Venice* is a marvel of formal coherence, and once we grasp that, we can come to a better understanding of the substantively troubling elements of this play as well. As is frequently the case in Shakespeare's dramas, he uses the opening scenes to set the problem the main action of the play attempts to resolve.[5] The problem is this: both Antonio and Portia love Bassanio; Antonio and Portia are rivals for the love of Bassanio. The play gives us the contest between the two for Bassanio. The winner of that contest, of course, is Portia, but judging from Shakespeare's title if nothing else, there is something about the losing contender that particularly requires attention. The various major events in the play are phases of the contest between Antonio and Portia. She triumphs in three stages: first, in the trial of the caskets, where Bassanio, with her help, selects the right casket and thus "wins" her; or rather, is won by her. Then in the legal trial of Antonio where Portia saves Antonio from Shylock and thereby saves Bassanio from an overwhelming and unending debt to Antonio; had Antonio lost his case to Shylock, he would therein have triumphed over Portia.[6] Finally, in the ring episode, Portia triumphs for the third and final time, achieving at last Antonio's concession of defeat.[7] Such is the story of *The Merchant of Venice*; of course the story of Shylock, the elopement of Jessica, and all the rest must find a place in this story, but this is the story in which they must find their place.[8]

With an economy suited to the chief site of the play Shakespeare quickly, if a bit subtly, establishes the problem of *The Merchant* in the opening words of each of the first two scenes. Antonio, the merchant of Venice, and therefore the central figure in Venice, the mercantile city, begins *in medias res*, in answer to a question he has just been posed: "In sooth I know not why I am so sad" (1.1.1).[9] Portia, the beautiful mistress of the "beautiful mountain," opens in a way remarkably close to Antonio's: "By my troth, Nerissa, my little body is aweary of this great world'' (1.2.1–2). Despite the great difference between Venice and Belmont, the two worlds of the play, the central figures in each of these worlds are seized by the same deep sadness.

The opening laments by Antonio and Portia set in motion the chief actions of the two opening scenes—the quest for the source of the sadness of each. Antonio's sadness is something very recent and not some abiding quality of his. Solanio has just now asked about it, and even complained of it. As Antonio tells us: ''you say it wearies you'' (1.1.2).[10] Gratiano soon after reinforces our impression of Antonio's sudden seizure by melancholy: ''Believe me, you are marvelously changed'' (1.1.76).

Antonio's sadness is apparently as mysterious as it is sudden. Antonio professes himself such a ''want-wit'' on its account that he cannot say how he ''caught it, found it, or came by it.'' As he concludes, ''I have much ado to know myself'' (1.1.3–7). Nonetheless, he thinks he knows himself well enough to reject out of hand his friends' repeated suggestions that his melancholy derives from anxiety over his mercantile ventures, a natural enough state of mind in venturesome Venice.[11] Almost like the birds of the air, or the lilies of the field, Antonio is not anxious over his worldly affairs; he has taken such care of them that he need not fear fortune (1.1.8–45, 73–75).[12] He parries his friends' other suggestions so they too come to accept the mystery of it (1.1.47–48).

The search to plumb Antonio's sadness ends when he is left alone with his friend Bassanio; here we indirectly discover the sudden source of his sadness when we discover what Antonio has been looking forward to, or rather dreading, all that day:

> Well, tell me now, what lady is the same
> To whom you swore a secret pilgrimage
> That you today promised to tell me of? (1.1.119–21)

Bassanio, a younger and ''noble kinsman,'' is especially dear to Antonio; the older man has been a regular benefactor to the younger and both speak of the love Antonio has shown toward Bassanio (1.1.57, 130–55). As is said later in the play, ''I think he [Antonio] only loves the world for him [Bassanio]'' (2.8.50). The expectation that his friend wishes to court a lady, a wish he must understand to be both rightful and inevitable, leads him to see his situation as fated, scripted, as it were, by the broader patterns and laws of life.[13] ''I hold the world but as the world, Gratiano— / A stage, where every man must play a part, / And mine a sad one'' (1.1.76–78).[14]

Portia's opening scene is much the same as Antonio's—the same world-weary sadness, the same effort by her companion to plumb her sadness. Yet there is an important difference, too: Portia is perfectly aware of the causes of her world-weariness; from the outset she is much more self-knowing than her Venetian counterpart. Her sadness derives from her father's will, according to which she may marry only the man who successfully passes the test of the caskets. Like Antonio, she feels her fate lies in the hands of external forces (1.2.22–25). Nerissa, her servant, has more confidence in the dead father's judgment than Portia does. Only "one who you shall rightly love" will choose rightly among the caskets. It is, Nerissa thinks, good protection for a very rich heiress against the wrong sort of gold-digger.[15] Portia resents her lack of autonomy, and perhaps the lack of confidence in her judgment, but it appears she also does not wish so much protection against gold-diggers. Part of her uncommon self-knowledge consists in her awareness of the conflict within herself between what we might call her head and her heart. "I can easier teach twenty what were good to be done, than to be one of the twenty to follow mine own teaching. The brain may devise laws for the blood, but a hot temper leaps o'er a cold decree" (1.2.15–19). Portia, it appears, resents the constriction, or rather nullification of her right of choice not only in the abstract, for she has her eye on someone in particular. It is none of the six suitors already come to Belmont from all over Europe (1.2.108–9). Yet there is one whom she fancies, as even Nerissa well knows: Bassanio, who, both women agree, is "best deserving a fair lady" (1.2.117–18; cf. 2.9.100).

Antonio mopes because Bassanio wishes to court Portia. Portia mopes because the casket test may keep her from Bassanio. It is unclear at this point whether she fears that another will succeed before Bassanio can, or whether she fears he will be unwilling to take or unable to pass the test himself. Antonio and Portia both suffer for Bassanio, both want Bassanio. Although neither knows the other, they are rivals for Bassanio.

I

" 'Shall I then betray my father's throne . . . ?' "[16]

In that rivalry Antonio has the first move. At first glance his move is surprising. To Bassanio's request for aid Antonio is all cooperation, all generosity. At second glance, his reaction is perhaps not so surprising. It is, after all, his habitual way to be generous, especially to Bassanio, who prefaces his request with a reminder of how much Antonio has given him in the past. As Allan Bloom observes, "Antonio . . . bases his whole life on generosity. . . . Antonio has money; it is, however, not for his own enjoyment, but rather for his friends." Along the same lines, David Beauregard identifies Antonio as the very embodiment of the Aristotelian virtue of liberality or generosity, the proper mean between prodigality and avarice, represented within the play respectively by Bassanio and Shylock.[17]

Nonetheless, the depiction of Antonio's generosity falls somewhat short of Aristotle's description of that virtue, the possessor of which "will give to the right persons the right amounts at the right times." On this criterion, Antonio must be judged deficient in virtue, for he gives to a self-professed prodigal, one who has wasted and, for all Antonio has reason to believe, will continue to waste. "He who gives to those he should not . . . is not generous but may be given another name," pronounces Aristotle.[18] The genuine virtue of generosity benefits the recipient where the pseudo-virtue does not. Antonio and Bassanio illustrate Aristotle's concern, for Antonio's repeated aid does not help Bassanio become a more responsible and self-sufficient, that is to say, virtuous, individual, but instead contributes to his lack of self-control with regard to spending and appearances, and encourages in him a tendency to view others as means toward satisfying his own pressing needs.

If Antonio's aid cannot be understood as a manifestation of the virtue of liberality, his response to Bassanio's request must be examined more carefully. Although Antonio fears Bassanio rushes to make a "secret pilgrimage" to a lady, that is to say, that Bassanio wishes to journey to the lady as to a shrine, as to one he adores or reverences, Bassanio assures him that his "chief care is to come off fairly from [his] great debts," the "most" of which are owed to Antonio. Although Bassanio speaks of Portia's beauty and virtues, he does not speak of his love for her—in marked contrast to his frequent references to the love he owes Antonio and has received from (but not given to?) Antonio (1.1.130–31, 146–47; cf. 161–76). Bassanio presents his case almost entirely as an investment opportunity for Antonio.[19] He is especially concerned to convince Antonio that further supplies would not amount to throwing good money after bad: by shooting a second arrow after the lost first arrow both men might hope to recoup what has already been lost. Bassanio has reason for hope: Portia is "richly left," and has sent him "fair speechless messages . . . from her eyes" (1.1.161, 163–64). Bassanio guessed Portia's feelings just as Nerissa did; he is adept at discerning, and quick to take advantage of, the love others have for him.

Antonio reacts not so much to the promise of repayment—no doubt he has heard such talk before—but he seems to be set much at ease by Bassanio's general approach to Portia: he is going a-courting not for the sake of his love for the lady, but for the sake of his obligation of money and love to Antonio. Antonio's feeling of relief is increased when Bassanio substitutes for the older man's image of a pilgrimage the new image of a "quest." She is not a quasi-deity but the "golden fleece," and he will become one of the "many Jasons come in quest of her" (1.1.170–72, cf. 3.2.241).[20] Bassanio, the new Jason, wishes to outfit an expedition like that to Colchis. He needs money, servants and finery, not a troop of heroes, but this, after all, is Christian, mercantile Venice, not pre–Trojan War Greece.

Under the circumstances of the quest, Antonio's reply to Bassanio's request is not surprising at all. Rather than a threat to their bond of friendship, as a marriage of love might be, it is an expression of Bassanio's deep sense of the continuing power and obligation of that bond. For Antonio to respond with his wonted generosity, moreover, is to bind anew in the very moment and in the very deed by which Bassanio attempts to discharge (some of) the bond already in place.[21]

Portia's first move is not against Antonio—she has no idea he is part of the story—but is, or seems to her to be against her father. To the new Jason, Portia is the golden fleece, but in her feelings and actions she is Medea, the daughter of King Aeëtes, the possessor of the fleece. Like Portia, Medea too falls in love with the Jason who visited her father's court.

> . . . the daughter of King Aeëtes conceived an overpowering passion . . . and when by reason she could not rid her of her madness she cried: . . . "I wonder if this is not what is called love, or at best something like this."

Like Portia, Medea sees in herself the old conflict between head and heart:

> "Come, thrust from your maiden breast these flames that you feel, if you can, unhappy girl. . . . But some strange power draws on against my will. Desire persuades me one way, reason another."

Indeed Portia even comes very close to stealing some of her lines from Medea's:

> "I see the better and approve it, but I follow the worse."

Like Portia's father, Medea's sets a formidable test between the questers and the object of their quest. Like Portia, Medea decries her father's test:

> "For why do the mandates of my father seem too harsh? They certainly are too harsh."[22]

Medea does not merely lament her situation, however. She "gave [Jason] the magic herbs, gave him instruction / In how to use them," helped him to yoke the "bronze-footed bulls, fire breathers," and to sow the serpent's teeth, and to resist the armed men who spring from the teeth, and finally, to put to sleep the dragon who guarded the golden fleece itself. All this she did for love and in exchange for a promise of marriage.[23]

But does Portia follow Medea's love-struck lead and help her new Jason overcome the barrier set up by her father? In the literature on the play this is surely one of the two or three most controverted questions. One of the strongest pieces of evidence against her acting the part of Medea to this extent is Portia's explicit vow to do no such thing: "I could teach you / How to choose right, but then I am forsworn. / So will I never be" (3.2.10–12). Yet there is some ambiguity in what she says here. Just what does it mean to "teach him how to choose right": she surely does not come right out and give the correct answer, and thus under a literalist interpretation of her oath (and we see later that Portia is quite capable of giving and taking advantage of literalist interpretations) she can avoid being "forsworn" even if, as I (and many other readers) believe, she gives Bassanio a good deal of help.[24]

Her denial is too ambiguous to settle the question whether she follows Medea this far, and thus we must consider both the casket scene and its context with greater care.[25] In marked contrast to the treatment the other suitors get, Portia does not rush Bassanio to undergo the test: "I pray you tarry; pause a day or two / Before you hazard" (2.7.1–3; 2.9.1; 3.2.1–2). As she thinks further on it, she would have him tarry even more: "I would detain you here some month or two / Before you venture for me" (3.2.9–10).

As eager as she is to be rid of the first two, she is welcoming of the company of her Venetian swain. Yet her desire for delay bespeaks even more than her fondness for Bassanio. She wishes him to wait, "for in choosing wrong / I lose your company. Therefore forbear a while" (3.2.2–3).

Portia here finally answers a question she left us with in her opening appearance in the play: she dreads the casket test not so much because she fears it will give her to another, but because she fears it will not give her to the one she favors. In a few moments Portia will project a new image for herself and Bassanio—not Medea and Jason, but Hesione and Heracles. Hesione was daughter of Laomedon, king of Troy in the generation before the Trojan War. In order to expiate the anger of the gods and the demands of his subjects, Laomedon chained Hesione to a rock on the Trojan shore as a "virgin tribute . . . / To the sea monster" (3.2.53–60).[26] Portia's new metaphor redefines the situation considerably; the casket is not something set up by a loving and wise father for her benefit, as Nerissa had urged, but is, to say the least, hostile to her best interests. It is easy enough to see how Portia can understand it so.[27] She might well envisage the intention, not just the likely effect of the casket test to be to exclude Bassanio as a suitor. The Venetian, after all, visited Belmont while the father still lived, and had he known and approved of Portia's liking, then the whole rigmarole of the caskets would make no sense. Nerissa (and Bassanio, too) knew of Portia's feelings and perhaps, she suspects, the father did, too.

Even if he did not know that Portia's affections turned in Bassanio's direction, the young Venetian seems the very sort of chap from whom he must have been attempting to guard his daughter. The wealthy heiress is a natural target for young men who are deeply in debt and without the means to continue in the style of life to which they have been accustomed. To see the application to Bassanio, we need only recall the circumstances of his quest, and his image of Portia as the golden fleece: Bassanio seeks to cut a figure in the world, or in nautical Venice, to "show a more swelling port" than he can afford (1.1.124). Marriages to such young men, a father might reason, do not promise well for young heiresses; they are anything but love matches.[28] Thus the father set the winning casket as the one about giving, not about getting, as the one that did not promise outward wealth.

So Portia-Hesione is threatened with the denial of her heart's desire by her father-Laomedon via exposure to the casket test-sea monster. Her sadness goes as deep as it does because she knows, or at least intensely fears that her father's ploy will succeed, as directly or indirectly intended, in eliminating Bassanio. Her doubts about Bassanio pop through the surface of things when he responds to her awkward but clearly heartfelt request for delay with an ultraconventional lover's image: "Let me choose, / For as I am, I live upon the rack." To which she retorts: "Upon the rack, Bassanio? Then confess / What treason there is mingled with your love" (3.2.24–27).

She speaks better than she knows, for she has not heard the earlier negotiations between Bassanio and Antonio nor has she yet experienced Bassanio's treason of the ring. She knows her man . . . and yet. . . . When Bassanio returns with another stock profession of love she again opens her troubled mind: "Ay, but I fear you speak upon the rack, / where men enforced, do speak anything" (3.2.32–33). It is all so playful, and yet she speaks her real doubts here; justifiable ones at that if we recall the "force" under which Bassanio is (at least in part) acting. He is, in Belmont, as part of his "plots and purposes . . . to get clear of all the debts" he owes. These, not the rack, are his "necessity."

The next exchange is the pivot of the whole scene, and we must therefore attend to its nuances with some care.

Bassanio: Promise me life, and I'll confess the truth.
Portia: Well then, confess and live.
Bassanio: Confess and love
Had been the very sum of my confession!
(3.2.34–36)

As many critics have noticed, Bassanio's "confession" is pretty lame: no soaring love poetry (or even love prose) here. Among the striking features of the exchange, however, is Portia's straining to allay her own doubts about Bassanio, her own suspicions about his loyalties and his sincerity. "Confess and live," she says; perhaps against her better judgment she commits herself in advance to being satisfied with the merest gesture of an answer—which is pretty much all she gets, too, as Bassanio punningly echoes back to her promise (cf. also 3.2.54). Because he builds his answer on her answer Bassanio completes the rack image by almost reversing it: "O happy torment, when my torturer / Doth teach me answers for my deliverance "(3.2.37–38). She "taught" him the answer that freed him from the rack, where she had earlier refused to teach him the answer to the casket test. But let us note how she taught him; she gave him a clue, a word ("live"), which he is able to translate into the required profession of love. Bassanio has shown her how she can "teach" him "answers for deliverance" without telling him them directly, and therefore without being foresworn.[29]

Bassanio is the third to try his wits at the caskets, and as in most fairy tales, the third time is a charm. Some critics go so far as to suggest that because he is third, he is the inevitable victor, and therefore has no need for Portia's help. This is surely a foolish argument. Even if there is something formally foreordained for Bassanio in coming third, this does not settle the issue of how or what makes him successful. That is an entirely separate matter. That Goldilocks finds that the porridge, chair, and bed are "just right" consistently on her third try does not imply, after all, that there is no significance to the fact that it was, consistently, the one that was the mean that was "just right."

As has been noticed by many previous readers, Portia's hints, if there are such, come in the form of the song she sings as Bassanio ponders the alternatives. She prefaces her song, however, with an indispensable clue: "If you do love me, you will find me out" (3.2.41). To the other contestants she gave no such guidance. Just as Bassanio had taken her comment about love as a hint in the preliminary banter that was the playful foreshadowing of the casket test itself, this hint about love proves invaluable to Bassanio.

Portia's statement about love is so important because it helps set the contrast between that and "fancy." She sings of fancy, but, she has made clear, the casket test is about something else, about love. Love is the unspoken but implicit contrast to the point she makes in her song: fancy is born in the eyes, not in the heart or head. Its birth is in the sphere of appearance, and so fragile is it that it fails to survive its in/fancy. Fine appearance, external promise—gold and silver—engender not love, but only its poor surrogate fancy. This is enough to tell the attentive Bassanio what he must do, but just in case he or some of the critics fail to get the point Portia opens her song with her oft-noted triple rhyme: "bred," "head," and "nourished."[30]

Not to worry, however, for Bassanio proves himself an exceedingly apt pupil. He picks up her thought exactly: "So may the outward shows be least themselves; / The world is still deceived with ornament" (3.2.73–74). After a longish survey of the many cases where fair, but false, exteriors conceal corrupt interiors, Bassanio draws just the point:

> Therefore then, thou gaudy gold,
> Hard food for Midas, I will none of thee;
> Nor none of thee, thou pale and common drudge
> 'Tween man and man. But thou, thou meager lead,

Which rather threaten'st than dost promise aught,
Thy paleness moves me more than eloquence;
And here choose I. (3.2.101–7)

If Bassanio has not been cued by Portia, then this chain of reasoning must be his own. But is that plausible? Is Bassanio the man to voice those sentiments? Does Bassanio really reject Midas's "hard food"? Does Bassanio turn away from external appearance and show?[31]

Bassanio's reflections are not only remarkably unlike himself, but they are altogether unlike the reasonings of the other suitors. Both Morocco and Aragon produced long speeches to justify their choices, and both reasoned entirely in terms of the legends on the caskets. Bassanio says nothing at all relating to the legends; his speech picks up entirely from Portia's song about fancy and appearance. In selecting the lead he shows neither understanding nor acceptance of the teaching about love its legend proclaims.[32]

Portia, we must conclude, extends her Medea-like behavior to helping her Jason overcome the trial established by her father to protect his treasure from adventurers like Jason. This is relatively easy for her to do because she sees herself as Hesione, the victim of her father, and not as the beneficiary of a wise and provident plan. Nonetheless, both images, Medea and Hesione, promise poorly for her. The one won by Jason, the other by Heracles, both were deserted by their respective heroes. Both images foreshadow Portia's almost fate.

II

> And when Medea saw this, Medea unsheathed her knife and cut the old man's throat; then, letting the old blood all run out, she filled his veins with her brew.[33]

The second phase of the contest for Bassanio culminates in the play's most famous scene, the trial in Venice over Antonio's forfeit of his bond. This incident is thematically important, moreover, for in it the broader significance of the love contest between Antonio and Portia begins to become clear: the struggle between Antonio and Portia is concealed here beneath a struggle between Antonio and Shylock, whose struggle in turn brings in the competing visions of the Old and New Testaments.[34]

It is not, perhaps, immediately apparent that the trial is part of the contest over Bassanio, because the antagonists are not Antonio and Portia, but rather Antonio and Shylock, with Portia as the judge who ultimately sides with Antonio. The news of the impending trial intrudes itself suddenly and violently on the scene of love; hardly have the lovers exchanged vows and rings, hardly have Nerissa and Gratiano joined the love fest than the emissaries from Venice arrive with Antonio's letter and the announcement of his default to Shylock. The letter distresses Bassanio and well it might. His friend and benefactor is to die on account of the debt Antonio incurred on his behalf. Portia notes his distress immediately.

But Bassanio's grief is not merely the grief a friend suffers at the misfortune of a friend; it is misery multiplied by guilt. As he confesses to Portia: "I have engaged myself to a dear friend, / Engaged my friend to his mere enemy / To feed my means" (3.2.261–63).

Bassanio's natural and creditable feelings are thus strong as it is, but Antonio has a knack for saying the very things that will heighten both Bassanio's misery and his guilt. Antonio's letter not only reports his situation, but refers directly to the bond of debt and guilt between them: "all debts are cleared between you and I if I might but see you at my death" (3.2.318–20). Surely there is something ironic in Antonio's wish: how can Bassanio and he be quits if Antonio goes "the last full measure" for Bassanio by dying for him? And how can Bassanio ever *feel* free of this debt if he is there to see this death for which, Antonio reminds him, he is responsible?[35] All these questions prove more than justified when we look ahead to discover what Antonio wishes Bassanio to see and, more importantly, to hear in his last moments. When it looks as though the trial will surely go against him Antonio delivers what appears to be a prepared statement. He responds to Portia's invitation to address the court as a whole, but his words are to and for Bassanio alone. He opens and closes his speech the same way: "Give me your hand Bassanio; fare you well. / Grieve not that I am fall'n to this *for you* . . ." And at the end: "Repent but you that you shall lose your friend, / And he repents not that he repays *your debt*" (4.1.264–65; 277–78).[36] Just in case Bassanio does not feel sufficiently responsible, and thus not sufficiently grateful, Antonio reminds him at this awful moment for whose sake he undergoes this fate—and how willingly at that.

He reserves the chief point of these, his dying words as he thinks, for the middle of his speech, however.

> Commend me to your honorable wife.
> Tell her the process of Antonio's end,

Say how I loved you, speak me fair in death;
And when the tale is told, bid her to be judge
Whether Bassanio had not once a love. (4.1.272–76)

This speech makes perfectly clear what Antonio is doing: why does he, after all, drag Bassanio's "honorable wife" into it? Why does he insist that Bassanio recount his death to her, and wring from her a confession that indeed Antonio loved Bassanio . . . better than she or any ordinary lover could do. Who can match, who will match Antonio's gesture of love? As Solanio once said, Antonio "only loves the world" for Bassanio. He so loves Bassanio that facing the threat of the loss of Bassanio he will lose the world, or, better yet, to prevent the loss of Bassanio, he will sacrifice the world. In the contest with Portia, Antonio has raised the stakes, infinitely, and then has played the ultimate trump card.[37]

It may seem a desperate and hopeless ploy, but in fact it succeeds, for Bassanio answers Antonio with the very declaration Antonio is seeking:

Antonio, I am married to a wife
Which is as dear to me as life itself;
But life itself, my wife, and all the world
Are not with me esteemed above thy life.
I would lose all, ay sacrifice them all
Here to this devil, to deliver you. (4.1.281–86)

Antonio is not given a reply, but this must be very gratifying to him. Where earlier on Bassanio spoke much of the debts of love he owed, he never spoke of the love he felt; now, this light young man has offered to sacrifice his own life for his friend, and, it must not be overlooked, the life of his wife as well. At least for the moment Bassanio is so overwhelmed with gratitude and guilt that he renders Antonio all the esteem and attachment the older man has sought, and declares him victor in the contest for his affection between Antonio and Portia.[38] Antonio has gained all by "giving and hazarding all he hath." Antonio is the true and proper winner of the casket test.[39]

Nonetheless, the audience can see more clearly than Bassanio and probably than Antonio himself the paradoxical, if not self-contradictory, character of Antonio's self-sacrificing love. He gives up all—to get all. His self-lessness is only a more subtle form of selfishness, for he wishes not merely to possess the object of his love, but to establish himself as the most lovable human being, as the one most worthy of love and thus as the one whose love supplants all others and lasts indefinitely.[40]

The only character in the play who seems clear-eyed about Antonio is Portia. From the moment that she observes Bassanio's reaction to Antonio's letter, she knows she does not have the full devotion of her husband. Portia shows the same wisdom in the face of Bassanio's feelings toward Antonio as Antonio showed when Bassanio resolved to court Portia. She does not in any way attempt to thwart Bassanio in his efforts to aid his friend. Indeed, her first words once she understands the situation is her offer to pay the debt, to pay double or more so that Antonio will be free from Shylock. We must see her offer in terms of her self-interest as well as her generosity. To keep her husband, or rather, to win from him the kind of loving attachment she seeks, she must save Antonio.[41] Before they can consummate this marriage, Portia insists, Bassanio must go to Antonio; the matter of Antonio must be taken care of before the marriage of Bassanio and Portia can be properly fulfilled (3.2.303–6).

Instead of paying off the debt Portia will have to preside over a trial where Shylock prosecutes Antonio to receive legal satisfaction on his contract. As most readers of the play have noticed, this trial concerns not only the two parties to it, but their respective religions and religious laws. That is to say, in the midst of this play about the rivalry between Portia and Antonio arises this most serious and far-reaching consideration of the meaning and relative merits of the two elements of what we have come to call the Judeo-Christian tradition.

We can understand the appearance of this apparently extraneous set of themes as follows. Antonio, as has often been noted, acts upon a model of human existence rooted in Christianity. He not only engages in the acts of charity prescribed by Christian precept, but, in his willingness to undergo sacrifice of his life for the sake of his love he engages in a particularly powerful form of the imitation of Christ. Antonio's justification and explanation are to be found in Christianity.[42] As Jesus says in order to explain his upcoming passion to his followers: "greater love hath no man than this, that a man lay down his life for his friends." This self-sacrificing love is not merely the extraordinary act of the extraordinary god-man, but is the model for all humanity: " 'This is my commandment, that you love one another as I have loved you.' "[43]

The New Testament authors, however, understand the life, death, and teaching of Jesus in terms of their relation to the older Jewish law, as both the completion and rejection of the old Jewish law. The defense and justification of Christianity originally appears in the form of a critique and attack on Judaism. Portia must defeat Antonio, but, strangely enough, she can do this only if Antonio can defeat Shylock; that is to say, only if Christianity can defeat or appear to defeat Judaism.

Antonio not only adheres to Christian doctrine, but, as Barbara Lewalski emphasizes, he imitates or even plays the part of Christ at various important moments in the drama. "Antonio, who assumes the debts of others . . . reflects on occasion the role of Christ satisfying the claim of Divine Justice by assuming the sins of mankind."[44] The trial is one such occasion: Antonio-Christ is once again put on trial, accused by the Jew, who seeks his life. Portia too has her part in this emblematic episode—in this case not as Medea or Hesione—but as Pontius Pilate. But she is a Pilate who prevents the passion of Christ. She is a new or reverse Pilate and thereby she will ultimately prove a new or nontragic Medea.

The tension between Antonio and Shylock obviously predates the action of the play and enters it from almost the very moment Shylock does. Upon first catching sight of Antonio, Shylock announces, "I hate him" (1.3.39). The feeling is, apparently, mutual, for Shylock complains of Antonio's extraordinarily uncivil treatment. "You that did void your rheum upon my beard / And foot me as you spurn a stranger cur / Over your threshold!" (1.3.114–16). The feelings of extreme enmity are related in both cases to the religion of the other: "I hate him for he is a Christian," says Shylock; Antonio abuses Shylock in turn as a "misbeliever" (1.3.39, 108).

Shylock mentions two other reasons, reasons that have led some critics to discount the importance of the religious issue. In addition to hating him as a Christian, Shylock also says: "But more, for that in low simplicity / He lends out money gratis, and brings down / The rate of usance here with us in Venice" (1.3.40–42). Many readers conclude from these lines that Shylock's real complaint is the economic harm Antonio does to him. However, this is to read Shylock's "But more" as though he means "a greater reason for my hatred"; a better reading, given the list of reasons Shylock is presenting, is to take "more" as "in addition." These additional points are all related: "He hates our sacred nation, and he rails, / . . . On me, my bargains, and my well-won thrift, / Which he calls interest" (1.3.45–48). Shylock attributes Antonio's practice of lending money gratis to "low simplicity," that is to say, to a base motive; he almost certainly means to accuse Antonio of acting out of enmity to Jews, specifically to harm them by decreasing their earning power (also cf. 3.1.45–47).

Shylock is thus not impressed by Antonio's pretenses to virtue and high principle. This appears to be Shylock's general perspective on the Christians and particularly on Antonio. Two issues in the play specifically divide Shylock from the Christians. They refrain from taking interest, which the Jews do not, while the Jews refrain from eating pork, which the Christians do not. The dietary laws of the Jews prompt Shylock to respond harshly to Bassanio's dinner invitation: "I will buy with you, sell with you, talk with you, walk with you, and so following; but I will not eat with you, drink with you, nor pray with you" (1.3.33–35). It is most telling that Shylock conjoins eating and drinking with praying: the dietary restraints are part of the holiness of the holy people. Those who do not keep to the dietary laws are unclean, that is to say, unfit to approach God. Shylock believes he even has the testimony of Jesus on his side, for he refers to a biblical story in which "your prophet the Nazarite conjured the devil into" a herd of swine (1.3.31–33).[45] Even Jesus understood the uncleanliness of pork, yet his so-called followers fail to.

At the same time, the Christians refrain from taking interest; yet, as Shylock makes clear, the Venetians—and especially Antonio—have no hesitation about engaging in high-flying commerce aimed at economic gain. Shylock rehearses Antonio's various ventures, argosies bound for Tripoli, the Indies, Mexico, England—all directions of the compass, all continents—all with the intention of enriching himself. The Christian attitude toward money and gain is, in a word, hypocritical. Gain from lending money is in principle no different from gain for other kinds of economic activity, and, Shylock believes, the story of Jacob the patriarch testifies to the divine favoring of enterprise and the legitimacy of gain (1.3.86–87).[46] Usury is merely a way of thriving, and all thriving is legitimate, if it is not done unjustly. Such is Shylock's view.

Antonio more than returns Shylock's feelings, and sees the latter's hateful qualities as rooted in his Jewishness. Antonio's most comprehensive statement occurs at the end of the scene: "The Hebrew will turn Christian; he grows kind" (1.3.175). Antonio is unkind to Shylock because Shylock, as a Jew, is himself unkind. The greatest evidence or manifestation of that unkindness is Shylock's practice of taking interest on the loans he makes to the Christian merchants of Venice. Contrary to Shylock's theory, Antonio does not oppose usury merely to vex and harm the Jewish money-lenders, but rather he despises the money-lenders because they take interest. As he understands it, the different practices he and Shylock stand for stem from their respective faiths. Antonio seems to understand well the Jewish law regarding usury: " 'You shall not lend upon interest to your brother. . . . To a foreigner you may lend upon interest, but to your brother you shall not lend upon interest.' "[47] Antonio makes direct reference to this law in his negotiation with Shylock:

> If thou wilt lend this money, lend it not
> As to thy friends—for when did friendship take
> A breed for barren metal of his friend?—
> But lend it rather to thine enemy . . . (1.3.129–32)

Antonio translates the law's "brother" into "friend" and "foreigner" into "enemy," but he brings out a central thought in the Jewish law nonetheless. By forbidding usury within the people, the law recognizes the evil of usury. By allowing an evil toward the "foreigner," the Jewish law indeed treats them as "enemies."

The evil in charging interest to friends remains obscure so long as attention remains exclusively focused on the essentialist issue centering on the "barren" and "non-breeding" character of metal. That is relevant only indirectly; if money "bred," that is, increased naturally, then it would not be unreasonable or unjust for the owner of the money to be able to reap the natural increase. But because money does not increase in this way, it is "unjust," because there is an "inequality" in the transaction "which is contrary to justice." The lender receives more than he gave.[48] The one who pays usury does not restore (a part of) natural increase, nor does he act voluntarily (as Shylock implies), but rather he acts "under a certain necessity insofar as he needs to borrow money which the owner is unwilling to lend without usury."[49] No wonder Antonio (and Bassanio too) treats it largely as a matter of "kindness"; the usurer is unkind, for he takes advantage of the pressing necessities of his debtor.[50] In the exchange among Antonio, Shylock, and Bassanio this last aspect is much emphasized (1.3.60, 111, 152).

Thomas Aquinas expresses Antonio's understanding with great lucidity in his discussion of the "sin of usury."

> The Jews were forbidden to take usury from their brethren, i.e., from other Jews. By this we (Christians) are given to understand that to take usury from any man is evil simply, because we ought to treat every man as our neighbor and brother.[51]

Antonio understands Christianity to involve both a broadening and a deepening of the Jewish law. It is broader because it is universal—injunctions to treat the other as neighbor or brother are not limited to one's own narrow nation. It is deeper in that the benevolence human beings owe to one another has no calculating quality to it; it is selfless. It is more sublime in that, as becomes clear later, the ultimate expression of Christian love is not merely disinterested benevolence, but self-sacrifice. Antonio is thus an apostle of Christian love, who uses Shylock and the Jews as a foil against which to define his moral vision, and uses the issue of usury as a vehicle for that moral vision.[52]

This is the abiding view each has of the other as the play opens. Yet almost immediately a new dynamic is introduced by Antonio's application to Shylock for a loan to aid his beloved friend. The Jew and the Christian agree to a loan with no interest, but with the pound of flesh pledge for collateral. This "deal" has led to one of the greatest controversies about the play: just what is Shylock up to in proposing these terms? Whatever Shylock's motives, after the elopement of Jessica, he is resolved to take advantage of Antonio's forfeiture of his bond.

Shylock and Antonio, Jew and Christian—just when it looks as though Shakespeare is setting up a contest between these two versions of the biblical religion, the terms of the relationship change. Most importantly, Shylock falls away from his status as paradigmatic Jew; the confrontation between the two in Portia's court in Venice is thus an aborted moment of judgment between those two great religions.

Shylock had raised two criteria to distinguish Jew and Christian. The Jews as the holy people, as the people of the law, are especially concerned with the clean and the unclean, sanctifying all their lives to God under the law.[53] That means, in particular, that the Jews must keep their special dietary laws; they do not eat in friendship and intimacy with other men of other nations; they are the nation set apart.[54] Shylock at first prided himself on his observance of the distinction between the clean and the unclean, the permitted and the forbidden. Yet suddenly and with little explanation, Shylock admits that he has agreed to dine with the Christians (2.5.11). We must understand this in relation to his bargain with Antonio. He has, as Antonio implied, in effect become a Christian. Just as he violates the dietary laws, so he violates the law respecting usury. True, the Jewish law legitimates interest taken from non-Jews, but it forbids what Shylock has potentially done in the "merry bond" and actually does in his resolve to collect his debt after Jessica runs off with Lorenzo:

one may not indirectly, and thus a fortiori directly take what amounts to the life of another as a pledge in loan.[55] The Jewish law recognizes (at least some) moral claims of human beings as such. Shylock has done what the Law explicitly forbids. And this is to say nothing of the commandment, "you shall not kill," a closely related provision of the law.[56] Shylock reveals himself to be a bad human being, a devil incarnate, not because he is a Jew, but because and insofar as he falls away from the Jewish law.

Portia's courtroom triumph over Antonio—that is to say, Antonio's triumph over Shylock—cannot be a triumph of Christianity over Judaism, for Shylock no longer represents Judaism, as is made perfectly clear in his most famous speech.

> Hath not a Jew eyes? Hath not a Jew hands, organs, dimensions, senses, affections, passions?—fed with the same food, hurt with the same weapons . . . ? If you prick us, do we not bleed? . . . And if you wrong us, shall we not revenge? (3.1.55–63)

This angry and moving speech must be contrasted with Shylock's earlier claim to Antonio: "sufferance is the badge of all our tribe" (1.3.107). So far as that is true, Shylock's speech about revenge, and his resolve to exact fully Antonio's pledge indicates a break with this forbearing attitude. Moreover, Shylock here speaks not as a Jew, nor even as a quasi-Christian; the standard is a purely human standard: "If a Jew wrong a Christian, what is his humility? Revenge! If a Christian wrong a Jew, what should his sufferance be by Christian example? Why revenge!" (3.1.65–68). Despite the ways or teachings or precepts of the two biblical religions, the human way is revenge. Shylock no longer even pretends to take his bearings and find his justification in the law.[57] He has, in his own way, become a political philosopher, discerning a harsh and universal nature beneath the varying laws of the nations.

The judgment Shylock undergoes at the hands of Portia is thus not a judgment on him as a Jew, or on Judaism as such. This is not to say there is no such judgment in the play—his loss of his daughter fulfills that role. Jessica enters a forbidden relation and forsakes her family, people and God (cf. 3.1.30, 32, 80–85). Her initial situation is rather like that of so many tragic lovers—Romeo and Juliet, Pyramus and Thisbe—forbidden her love by her parents or her people, yet not Jessica the lover, but Shylock the parent suffers the tragic fate in this case. Jessica lives in a community where her love is to be controlled by the laws. She is to marry inside the community and defer to her parents in choice of mate. Yet her love escapes these restraints; love cannot be so readily bidden. Like Shylock himself in his revenge, she learns and teaches something of the universality of nature in her love. The Jewish notion of a holy people, a people set apart, gives too little notice to nature, both in its higher manifestations like love, and in its lower, like revenge. No people can be simply holy; no people can be simply set apart. This is Shakespeare's judgment on Shylock. The perspective of that judgment shares something important with the Pauline Christian condemnation of Judaism as particularistic, but it is not necessarily the same as that perspective and surely not the same as Antonio's virulent anti-Jewish pronouncements.

Shylock is a Jew who violates his own law, the observance of which would at least have saved him from the inhumanity to which he sinks in his hatred for Antonio. Likewise, just as Shylock's defeat cannot stand for the defeat of the Jewish way, so Antonio's triumph does not represent a triumph of Christian principles. Although the disguised Portia delivers a lovely speech on mercy, the outcome of the trial does not in fact depend upon mercy, Christian or otherwise. Shylock's suit fails in two respects, on two legal technicalities. Both of these derive from the Jewish law, whence Portia has imported them into Venetian law. She first grants Shylock the right to his pound of flesh, but "in the cutting of it" he is allowed not "one drop of Christian blood" (4.1.305–9). Now this literalism is frequently decried as contrary to the reasonable meaning of the law: if Shylock has a right to the flesh, he must have a right to any necessary appurtenances of the flesh. Yet this fine-honed distinction is not of Portia's making; it derives instead from the Jewish dietary laws: " 'However, you may slaughter and eat flesh . . . Only you shall not eat the blood.' "[58] If the distinction between the flesh and the blood is valid, as the Jewish law insists that it is, then the conclusion Portia draws is valid as well. No wonder Shylock cries out "Is that the law?" (4.1.313).

The second part of Portia's verdict comes when she turns the tables on Shylock: an alien may not directly or indirectly attempt the life of a citizen. Shylock has quite openly done that very thing, and thus must pay the penalty for it. But as we have noted above, this law, especially as applied to the circumstances at hand is part of the Jewish law as well: one may not take " 'a life in pledge.' "[59] One may supply various theological interpretations of Portia's legal maneuverings—interpreting her as attempting to illustrate, for example, the Pauline principle that righteousness under the law is not possible for sinful man. Although that interpretation resonates with Portia's speech on mercy, it does not fit so well the way the scene develops: the insistence that the Jewish law is perfectly sufficient to produce the just—and merciful—outcome.

One must instead view the trial as a reenactment of the trial of Jesus, with Antonio in the title role, Shylock in place of the Jews prosecuting Jesus, and Portia taking the part of Pontius Pilate.[60] Shylock insists on the law ("I stand here for the law") under which Antonio must pay the penalty of his default, i.e., must die; his predecessors urged much the same: "The Jews answered [Pilate], 'We have a law, and by that law he ought to die . . . ' "[61] In the trial of Antonio Portia urges Shylock to recognize that if he presses his claim, "this strict [code] of Venice / Must needs give sentence 'gainst the merchant there," to which Shylock replies, "My deeds upon my head" (4.1.203–5). Wittingly or unwittingly, he thus echoes the very thought of his predecessors, who responded to Pilate's resolve to "wash his hands" of the matter, " 'His [Jesus'] blood be on us and on our children.' "[62]

Antonio casts himself as decisively in the role of Jesus as Shylock does in the role of Jesus' Jewish accusers. From his opening lines in the scene until the moment when Portia's verdict goes against Shylock, Antonio takes the part of one who suffers a fated martyrdom, a martyrdom, as we have seen, of self-sacrifice motivated by love.

> I do oppose [says Antonio]
> My patience to his fury, and am armed
> To suffer with a quietness of spirit
> The very tyranny and rage of his. (4.1.10–13, cf. 83)

He calls himself "the tainted wether of the flock, / Meetest for death," like the scapegoat on whom the community heaps its sins, and which is an image of Jesus' redemptive mission (4.1.114–15).

Yet the trial of Antonio does not end as did the trial of Jesus, because Pontius-Portia plays her part differently. Two things are particularly striking in the behavior of the original Pontius Pilate. First, he repeatedly proclaims his conviction of Jesus' innocence. "And Pilate said to the chief priests and the multitudes, 'I find no crime in this man,' " a conclusion he repeats twice more after further inquiry.[63] Judging Jesus under the relevant law, the Jewish law, Pilate found no grounds to condemn him. Yet he gave in to the repeated urgings of the Jews: "But they were urgent, demanding with loud cries that he should be crucified. And their voices prevailed. So Pilate gave sentence that their demand should be granted. . . . Jesus he delivered up to their will.''[64]

Portia, the new Pilate, breaks with her predecessor on one central point: unlike Pilate, who sacrificed his judgment of the law to fear of the mob or concern for politics, she sticks to the law, the Jewish-become-Venetian law.[65] Under that law Antonio is free from Shylock's bond. Portia gives Antonio a victory of sorts, although it is also a most telling defeat, by sticking to the letter and spirit of the old law. She thus doubly thwarts the new Jesus: she neither vouchsafes him his longed-for martyrdom, nor does she appeal to specifically Christian principle to do so.

III

> I am abandoned; I have lost my throne, my native soil, my home, my husband—who alone for me took the place of all![66]

The trial is a great triumph for Portia, and yet she is never closer to suffering the tragic fate of Medea—abandonment by the one she loves, by one who has sworn eternal and complete devotion to her. Despite the fact that she has prevented Antonio from rendering that ''last full measure'' of his devotion to his beloved, Bassanio has yet been deeply affected by Antonio's gesture. He confesses to esteeming Antonio more highly than her and would sacrifice her life (and his own) in order to save Antonio's. Bassanio apparently has taken to heart the injunction to love as Antonio has loved him.[67] Although Portia has defeated Antonio, it yet might appear that he has gotten all he could have hoped for from the episode. He has won Bassanio's love with his offer to sacrifice his life, without needing to carry through on his offer.[68]

Feeling victorious, Antonio provokes the third round in his contest against Portia by intervening in the post-trial exchange between Bassanio and the disguised Portia over the ring Portia has requested from Bassanio as a reward or remembrance for her service to the two friends. Bassanio is most reluctant to part with the ring:

> Good sir, this ring was given me by my wife,
> And when she put it on she made me vow
> That I should neither sell nor give nor lose it. (4.1.440–43)

Should he do any of these things, Portia had meaningfully observed earlier, "Let it presage the ruin of your love . . ." (3.2.171–73). As soon as he hears the reason for Bassanio's refusal to surrender the ring Antonio enters the discussion in order to loosen his friend's resolve.

> My lord Bassanio, let him have the ring.
> Let his deservings, and my love withal,
> Be valued 'gainst your wife's commandment.
> (4.1.448–50)

A more calculating move can hardly be imagined. Both to register the implications of Bassanio's declaration at the trial and to reinforce his supreme position Antonio prods Bassanio to do the thing that most concretely symbolizes his triumph. He makes the point perfectly explicit: his "love" is to be weighed against Portia's "commandment."[69] In accord with his declaration Bassanio accedes. What Bassanio said at the trial was thus not idle talk—he is more devoted to Antonio than to his wife.

Here then is Portia's greatest moment of crisis. She must act decisively in order to restore her love, a need with which the audience are in full sympathy, for we cannot willingly accept an Antonian victory in this contest.[70] Portia has our sympathies because we have seen the less attractive underside to Antonio's love. The claim he raises is the claim of sacrifice and selflessness, yet we see this to be largely fraudulent; beneath the selflessness is a deep and potent self-seeking. The deficient character of Antonio's love is visible in at least two of its effects. First is his "spoiling" of Bassanio: he seeks to render Bassanio dependent rather than good. His "selfless" love is selfish in that it does not produce the good of the beloved, but of the lover.[71] Secondly, we see, perhaps with surprise, the virulence of his hatred for Shylock. While Shylock is not entirely attractive either, his most vicious acts are the consequences of the attitudes of the Antonios of the world. Antonio is a genuine anti-Semite, a genuine hater. He displays what Machiavelli had earlier denounced as "pious cruelty." His philosophy of love ironically issues in acts of hatred.

Portia returns from Venice to Belmont in a darkly melancholy mood. Her melancholy is foreshadowed in a remarkable dialogue between Jessica and Lorenzo, in which these two newlyweds celebrate the night and their love by recounting the tales of ill-fated lovers of note from the past. These reminders of failed and betrayed loves reflect both on their own love and on the unfolding betrayal of Portia by

Bassanio. It is probably no coincidence that the central item in this exchange concerns Medea: "In such a night / Medea gathered the enchanted herbs / That did renew the old Aeson" (5.1.12–14). Aeson was Jason's father, a very old and dying man to whom Medea brought new youth and salvation through her magic. Nonetheless, Jason's gratitude did not prevent his subsequent abandonment of Medea. The parallel to Portia and Bassanio is clear: as Medea saved Aeson, so Portia saved Antonio.

"In such a night as this . . . ," a moonlit night, a night for lovers, and yet a night that reveals the unsteadiness, the evanescence, the unreliability of love. A night for recalling disloyal lovers. Even Lorenzo's famous and quite lovely rapture on the music of the spheres fits the mood. Even though: "There's not the smallest orb which thou behold'st / But in his motion like an angel sings," nonetheless this heavenly

> Harmony is [only] in immortal souls,
> [And] whilst this muddy vesture of decay
> Doth grossly close it in, we cannot hear it.
> (5.1.60–65)

Perhaps it is Jessica's keen appreciation of how far earthly love falls below Lorenzo's heavenly harmonies that leads her to confess, "I am never merry when I hear sweet music" (5.1.69). In this comic celebration of love, Shakespeare comes to the very brink of exposing love in its lunar, that is, false and fleeting, cold and changing character.

By the time Portia arrives, the brightness of the moon, which so impressed Lorenzo and Jessica, is shown for what it is—unsteady and unreliable. Not the moon, but a "little candle" from her own hall, is all she can see now. By her yet lesser light, Portia stands much deeper in her despair of love than Lorenzo and Jessica.

> That light we see is burning in my hall;
> How far that little candle throws his beams!
> So shines a good deed in a naughty world. (5.1.89–91)

Can there be any doubt that she is the "little candle"—Portia reduced to a little candle!—casting little light, having little good effect in herself and yet shining brightly by contrast with the "naughty world," the betrayers, the self-promoters, adventurers and hypocrites—the Jasons and Antonios—around her. Despair gnaws at her heart; all the world empties itself of meaning and goodness. "Nothing is good, I see, without respect" (5.1.99), that is, but by contrast. The good is merely what appears better by contrast to something worse or less.[72]

Despair gnaws at Portia, yet she does not give way to it. On hearing of the approach of her husband, she resolves, "Let me give light."[73] In this now dark night, the moon obscured, "the sun . . . hid," Portia will attempt to bring the world back to light. But this requires something of her as well: "Let me give light, but let me not be light" (5.1.129). Portia requires a certain weightiness, a moral seriousness, in order to bring the world back into light. One is tempted to say that she must repent her earlier lightness, that lightness that did not, for example, take sufficiently seriously her father's warnings and her father's efforts to help her find a suitable husband. Both she and Bassanio must grow beyond where they were at the opening of the play in order to be worthy of love—solar rather than lunar love, let us say. She must grow to transcend her alter-ego Medea; Medea the enchantress, associated with the moon, must give way to Portia, the Sun, source of illumination.[74] Portia resolves to be the light by being weighty; not Antonio, but she, is to be "the true light."[75]

From the moment Portia greets Bassanio on his arrival at Belmont, the delicate negotiation between them commences. Bassanio once again signals how things stand with his curt return of Portia's greeting ("I thank you, madam") and his far more expansive introduction of Antonio: "This is the man, this is Antonio, / To whom I am so infinitely bound" (5.1.133–35).[76]

Portia, however, quietly corrects him: "You should be . . . much bound," but not apparently, "infinitely bound" (5.1.136). If Bassanio is infinitely bound to Antonio, then, of course, he has no bond left for Portia. She is less forthcoming to Antonio, however, than Bassanio would apparently have her be: she "scants this breathing courtesy," that is, elaborate words of welcome. How welcome he is "must appear in other ways than words," in part because he is welcome in order to be part of the final showdown over Bassanio, and in part because just how welcome he is will depend on subsequent events (5.1.139–41).

Before Portia even mentions Bassanio's infidelity, Nerissa and Gratiano erupt into an argument over their parallel situation. This proves most useful to Portia (did she preconcert it with her maid?), for it allows her to accuse Bassanio, indirectly at first in the guise of accusing Gratiano, of the great violation of trust he has committed.

> You were to blame—I must be plain with you—
> To part so slightly with your wife's first gift,

A thing stuck on with oaths upon your finger,
And so riveted with faith unto your flesh. (5.1.166–69)

Her lines echo earlier images of the almost crucified Antonio, but it is Bassanio she casts now as the central actor in the moral drama. It is he who is "riveted"; it is he who receives "faith." Bassanio needs to see himself as a serious moral agent in a serious moral relationship with Portia. Before the trial he was little given to this kind of moral seriousness in any form, because of the general levity of his character. In the wake of Antonio's gesture, Bassanio is equally little given to the kind of moral agency Portia calls forth, for he sees Antonio as the center and himself as the merely reflected image, infinitely bound to the original.

Bassanio at first inclines to defend himself in terms that reflect the very Antonio-centeredness she must overcome.

Sweet Portia
If you did know to whom I gave the ring, . . .
And would conceive for what I gave the ring . . .
You would abate the strength of your displeasure. (5.1.192–98)

Although many critics are entirely appeased by this defense—indeed some see it as a sign of Bassanio's understanding and acceptance of the burden of love—Portia is not in the least satisfied—and rightly not.

If you had known the virtue of the ring,
Or half her worthiness that gave the ring,
Or your own honor to contain the ring,
You would not then have parted with the ring.
(5.1.199–202)

In giving it away, Bassanio has undervalued the ring itself and what it means—"a thing held as a ceremony," a symbol of their love and its hoped-for abidingness. As such a thing, no reasonable person would demand it and no service can be commensurable with it. It was, of course, Antonio, who prevailed on him to present the ring to Balthazar/Portia, precisely to get Bassanio to make the point Portia now blames him for. Thus Bassanio also undervalued Portia relative to Antonio in giving up the ring, whereas, she implies, she is more worthy than Antonio. Bassanio is guilty of disloyalty, but also of poor judgment; he does not see through the character of Antonio's "selfless" love, but is flattered by the appearances he does discern. He thereby misses the true source of human value. Accordingly, she also accuses him of undervaluing himself by so lightly setting aside his own oath; a man's oath and his resolve to keep it are tokens of his true dignity as a moral agent. To be bound by one's own word is to legislate for oneself and to commit oneself to being the kind of human being that can determine itself to its own commitments, to its vision of its own future. But in the shadow of Antonio Bassanio takes himself as little seriously as he took his love or the character of his wife.[77]

Bassanio takes up only part of the immediate challenge posed by Portia's accusation: it was not a smirch upon his honor to give away the ring but a requirement of it (5.1.218–19). So much was this a demand of his honor that had Portia, who now claims to speak on behalf of his honor, "been there [he] thinks [she] would have begged / The ring of [him] to give the worthy doctor" (5.1.221–22). He replies to her charge about his honor, but she no doubt notices that he has said not a word about the other two points of her accusation, that he slighted both their love as symbolized by the ring, and herself. She is therefore not in the least appeased by his defense.

If he will stand on his honor as a thing apart from their marriage, then she will threaten his honor in a way that will remind him that his honor is now at least in part in her keeping:

> Let not that doctor e'er come near my house.
> . . . I will become as liberal as you;
> I'll not deny him anything I have,
> No, not my body nor my husband's bed. (5.1.223–28)

This is not merely a threat to his honor, but an expression of hers: "Now by mine honor, which is yet mine own, / I'll have that doctor for mine bedfellow" (5.1.232–34). If Bassanio attempts to treat his honor as his own, that is, independent of her and their marriage, then she can treat her honor in the same way. But, of course, the premise of her speech is precisely the opposite, that both their honors are now inseparably bound up with the other's; her first need is to get Bassanio to see and understand at least this much. By standing up for her own honor, she at the same time attempts to make him see and understand something of her undervalued worth.

Before Bassanio can reply, Nerissa, Gratiano, and Antonio intervene. Antonio's brief interjection—"I am th' unhappy subject of these quarrels"—is especially important, because the discussion between Portia and Bassanio has been moving in the direction of the recognition of Antonio's role in the incident. At first Bassanio defended himself for giving the ring away "unwillingly," constrained by the "civil doctor's" unwillingness to accept anything but the ring (5.1.196, 210). After Portia reminds him of the unreasonableness of such a gift, Bassanio subtly shifts ground. In his next speech he refers to the "enforced" character of his gift, but no longer is the doctor implied to be the source of the compulsion. It is left at the vague admission, "I was enforced to send it after him" (5.1.216). But the audience knows and Portia knows or suspects that the compulsion came from Antonio. This is just what Portia is attempting to make Bassanio see and to truly understand. She can free Bassanio from the bond of Antonio's love only by exposing its grasping underside.

As in the casket scene, Bassanio proves a remarkably apt pupil of Portia's subtle instruction. She brings him to the self-knowledge he has thus far almost completely lacked: "I swear to thee, ever by thine own fair eyes, / Wherein I see myself" (5.1.242–43). He sees himself and his situation in her eyes, that is to say, he sees himself as she does; as Portia puts it, he sees himself as a double-dealer: "In both my eyes he doubly sees himself, / In each eye one" (5.1.244–45). Because of this newly acquired self-knowledge, he capitulates completely. He no longer protests that Portia would have willed he do as he did, but twice within ten lines he asks her pardon. The first time he continues to speak of it as an "enforced" deed, but he now calls it a "wrong." The second time he drops all reference to compulsion, and calls it not merely wrong, but a "fault" (5.1.240, 247).

Bassanio at one and the same moment has broken Antonio's spell and become a man, responsible for himself and the moral character of his actions. He has finally become worthy of Portia, who has herself become worthy of the love of another mature adult by facing her own errors and despair. By this last scene she is no longer the talented, beautiful, wealthy but spoiled heiress of the opening of the play and the casket scene, just as he is no longer the fortune-hunting adventurer. Neither Medea nor Jason, Portia and Bassanio become fit heroes of a comic world where love thrives.[78]

In order to recognize his deed as a "fault," Bassanio must see in Portia's eyes not only himself, but his susceptibility to Antonio and the character of Antonio's love game. She helps him to see both by making him relive and ponder deeply his own and Antonio's deeds, but also by making him look into himself and reconsider the nature of love. He discovers not only the underlying will to power in Antonio's professed selfless love, but he discovers a core of selfishness in love itself.[79] The lover seeks an exclusive possession—sexual, but more than sexual—of the beloved. Love is of and for the other, but it is of and for the self, as well. This was true even of Antonio's love, but only illicitly so. By becoming more self-consciously selfish in his understanding of love, Bassanio also becomes more genuinely loving. He gives up not only Antonio, but that pride that prevented him from admitting fault and asking pardon. To paraphrase a much less insightful, more modern statement, Bassanio discovers that love is learning to say you're sorry. Bassanio comes to understand the kind of risk and hazard that, according to the lead casket, love entails.

Contrary to first impression, Antonio's kind of love does that much less well. Bassanio and Portia learn that love has an indissolubly exclusive character. It can never be the foundation for society as a whole. Human beings cannot build their lives on the purely selfless or sacrificial love which Jesus and Christianity command. In the final analysis, *The Merchant of Venice*, while not overtly a political play, has deep political implications. Those implications are emblematized most of all in the outcome of the trial: the law provides a solider basis for just and decent social life than the replacement of the law with love can do. A humanely just society is far more the achievement of good laws than of love.[80]

The promise of *The Merchant of Venice* nonetheless is the promise of love, through which pleasure, duty, and honor can find harmonious reconciliation. In love and the responsibility it breeds lies the good of the soul and whatever of eternity human beings can attain.[81] The culminating moment of the decisive scene is Bassanio's final apology and acceptance of the meaning of his marriage. "Pardon this fault, and by my soul I swear / I never more will break an oath with thee" (5.1.248–49). In that "never more" lies the real moral of this lovely tale of love and marriage: and they lived happily ever after.

Notes

I am grateful for helpful suggestions on earlier drafts by Joe Alulis, Vickie Sullivan, Ruth Weiner, Catherine Zuckert, and Rachel Zuckert. I would also like to acknowledge a general debt to the excellent essay by Barbara Tovey on *The Merchant of Venice* (see below, n. 6).

1. David N. Beauregard, "Sidney, Aristotle, and *The Merchant of Venice*: Shakespeare's Triadic Image of Liberty and Justice" *Shakespeare Studies* 20 (1988): 33, 48; John Lyon, *The Merchant of Venice* (Boston: Twayne, 1988), xi, xv, 1–17, 95–96; Barbara K. Lewalski, "Biblical Allusion and Allegory in

The Merchant of Venice," *Shakespeare Quarterly* 13 (1962): 328; Joan Ozark Holmer, "Loving Wisely and the Casket Test: Symbolic and Structural Unity in *The Merchant of Venice,*" *Shakespeare Studies* 11 (1978): 53; Herbert S. Donow, "Shakespeare's Caskets: Unity in the *Merchant of Venice,*" *Shakespeare Studies* 4 (1968): 86.

2. On *The Merchant of Venice* as "the most scandalously problematic of Shakespeare's plays," and "the only one of Shakespeare's plays . . . which a sizable body of sane people might consider unfit to be seen or read," see Lawrence Danson, *The Harmonies of The Merchant of Venice* (New Haven: Yale University Press, 1978), 2–3; Derek Cohen, *Shakespeare's Motives* (London: Macmillan, 1988), 104–18; Lewalski, "Biblical Allusion," 333–34; Lynda E. Boose, "The Comic Contract and Portia's Golden Ring," *Shakespeare Studies* 20 (1988): 241.

3. On the stage history, and Shylock's role in it, see Lyon, *Merchant*, xiv–xvi, and more generally, ibid., 43; on Shylock as "the play's strongest and most discussed piece of characterization," see 106. Marion D. Perret, "Shakespeare's Jew: Preconception and Performance," *Shakespeare Studies* 20 (1988): 263–64.

4. See, e.g., Harley Granville-Barker, "*The Merchant of Venice*," in *Prefaces to Shakespeare* (Princeton: Princeton University Press, 1947), ii, 89, 91.

5. *Contra* Lyon, *Merchant*, 31.

6. Barbara Tovey, "The Golden Casket: An Interpretation of *The Merchant of Venice*," in *Shakespeare as Political Thinker*, ed. John Alvis and Thomas West (Durham, N.C.: Carolina Academic Press, 1981), 228; Donow, "Shakespeare's Caskets," 87.

7. Thus Lyon is quite mistaken to say that the ring incident represents "a new and independent plot [that gets] fully underway only in [the] last act" (*Merchant*, 117); or to call it "the tangential ring plot" (118).

8. The clearest account heretofore of the structure is in Lawrence Hyman, "The Rival Lovers in *The Merchant of Venice*," *Shakespearean Quarterly* 21 (1970), 109–10.

9. Quotations are from the Signet edition, ed. Kenneth Myrick (New York: Penguin Books, 1965).

10. *Contra* Allan Bloom, *Shakespeare's Politics* (New York: Basic Books, 1964), 19: "Antonio is sad, and life does not mean much to him" because of his Christianity. Also *contra* Danson, who associates Antonio's sadness with the "moral failure" of his treatment of Shylock (*Harmonies*, 32). Neither Bloom nor Danson account for the sudden onset of Antonio's sadness. (Also *contra* Thomas Fujimara, "Mode and Structure in *The Merchant of Venice*," *PMLA* 81 [1966]: 509.)

11. Though cf. Lars Engle, "Thrift Is Blessing: Exchange and Explanation in *The Merchant of Venice*" *Shakespearean Quarterly* 37 (1986): 21–22 and Allan Haladay, "Antonio and the Allegory of Salvation," *Shakespeare Studies* 4 (1968): 111.

12. Cf. Lewalski, "Biblical Allusion," 328–29.

13. Cf. Lewalski, "Biblical Allusion," 329; Thomas Cartelli, "Shakespeare's *Merchant*, Marlowe's *Jew*: The Problem of Cultural Difference," *Shakespeare Studies* 20 (1988): 257–58.

14. Danson rejects the conception that Antonio's love for Bassanio underpins his melancholy because this is "not coherent with the play's overall shape and tone" (*Harmonies*, 36, 38, 40). This is, of course, a circular argument. Lyon, *Merchant*, 47, accepts Antonio's love for Bassanio as the cause of sadness, however, as does Keith Geary, "The Nature of Portia's Victory: Turning to Men in *The Merchant of Venice*," *Shakespeare Survey* 37 (1984): 58–59.

15. See Holmer, "Loving Wisely," 54.

16. Ovid *Metamorphoses* 7.38; Frank Justus Miller, trans., Loeb Classical Library, 345.

17. Beauregard, "Sidney, Aristotle, and *The Merchant of Venice*," 33–39, 47–48; Bloom, *Shakespeare's Politics*, 19; Danson, *Harmonies*, 51–55; Lyon, *Merchant*, 45; Geary, "Nature of Portia's Victory," 60.

18. Aristotle, *Nicomachean Ethics*, ed. and trans. Hippocrates G. Apostle (Grinnell, Iowa: The Peripatetic Press, 1975), 1120, 1126–130.

19. Cf. Geary, "The Nature of Portia's Victory," 59: "Bassanio . . . describes his projected journey to Belmont less in terms of intended marriage than as if it were a business venture . . ."; also Engle, "Exchange and Explanation," 25.

20. Boose, "Comic Contract," 248.

21. Tovey, "Golden Casket," 221, 223; cf. Geary's statement: "The scene is tense with an unspoken loosening of ties" ("Nature of Portia's Victory," 59).

22. Ovid *Metamorphoses* 7.9–21, Loeb Classical Library, 343.

23. On the comparison of Portia and Medea, see Donow, "Shakespeare's Caskets," 87-88.

24. Danson rejects in the strongest terms the notion that Portia can have hinted at the right answer: "The imputation . . . that Portia through the most blatant trick makes her . . . father's dying inspiration nugatory—is one which . . . would make the rest of the play inexplicable." In other words, it conflicts with Danson's sense of the larger patterns and meanings in the whole (*Harmonies*, 117–18). This is a perfectly reasonable approach, but its circularity must again be noted. The position Danson merely takes for granted is that there is no plausible construal of the whole consistent with this "imputation." That, I believe, is false, and indeed, to go further, it is Danson, I will suggest, who ignores many elements of the play that are not only consistent with this imputation, but insistently point toward it. A more balanced approach to the question is in Lyon (*Merchant*, 92–97). Lyon also contains a good discussion of the scholarly to and fro on the issue.

25. *Contra* Geary, "Nature of Portia's Victory," 62.

26. On the story of Heracles and Hesione, see Robert Graves, *The Greek Myths* (Harmondsworth, Middlesex: Penguin Books, 1966), 2:168–73.

27. So far as I know, Lewalski is the critic to pay the most attention to the Hesione image, but she does not much analyze what this implies about Portia's stance toward the casket test ("Biblical Allusion," 336).

28. Cf. Geary, "Nature of Portia's Victory," 62. Bassanio is a "fortune-hunter."

29. Cf. Olivia Delgado de Torres, "Reflection on Patriarchy and the Rebellion of Daughters in Shakespeare's *The Merchant of Venice* and *Othello*," *Interpretation* 21 (Spring 1994): 343; Bloom, *Shakespeare's Politics*, 24–27.

30. Tovey, "The Golden Casket," 217.

31. *Contra* Holmer: "Only Bassanio, his wisdom revealed in his soliloquy over the caskets, is capable of loving wisely, and therefore his character guarantees the right choice . . ." ("Loving Wisely," 59); and Donow, "Shakespeare's Caskets," 91.

32. Cf. the contrary reading in Lewalski, "Biblical Allusion," 335. She does not note Bassanio's complete failure to attend to the legends or to show any signs of absorbing their point. Also *contra* Hyman, "Rival Lovers," 114.

33. Ovid *Metamorphoses* 7.285–87, Loeb Classical Library, 363.

34. Cf. Tovey, "Golden Casket," 229.

35. Cf. Tovey: "Such a letter is calculated to make Bassanio spend the rest of his life in remorseful remembrance" ("Golden Casket," 225).

36. Emphasis added.

37. Hyman, "Rival Lovers," 112; Geary, "Nature of Portia's Victory," 63, 65.

38. Cf. Tovey: "Bassanio's preference for Antonio could hardly be stated in starker terms" ("Golden Casket," 229).

39. Holmer, "Loving Wisely," 60.

40. In his portrayal of Antonio, Shakespeare has come very close to Nietzsche's understanding of self-denying love in 1.13 of *The Gay Science*: "Even if we offer our lives, as martyrs do for their church, this is a sacrifice that is offered for *our* desire for power or for the purpose of preserving our feeling of power" (trans. Walter Kaufmann [New York: Random House, Vintage Books, 1974], 87); also cf. 1.14. Cf. Tovey, "Golden Casket," 224–225, 233; Bloom, *Shakespeare's Politics*, 19–21; Geary, "Nature of Portia's Victory," 64.

41. Cf. Tovey: "As soon as she hears of Antonio's predicament, Portia clearly recognizes the threat that his imminent martyrdom poses to her married life." ("Golden Casket," 228); cf. Bloom, *Shakespeare's Politics*, 29; Delgado de Torres, "Reflections on Patriarchy," 343; Geary, "Nature of Portia's Victory," 64; Boose, "Comic Contract," 250.

42. See Lewalski, "Biblical Allusion," 329, 338.

43. John 15.12 RSV. Martin Luther, *The Freedom of a Christian*, in *Three Treatises*, trans. W. A. Lambert, revised by Harold J. Grimm (Philadelphia: Fortress Press, 1960), 302–9.

44. Lewalski, "Biblical Allusion," 334, cf. 339; Tovey, "Golden Casket," 227.

45. Cf. Mark 5.1–13.

46. On Shylock's use of the story of Jacob, see Engle, "Exchange and Explanation," 32.

47. Deut. 23.19–20; cf. Deut. 28.12. Note that Deut. 23 joins the very two issues that Shylock joins—usury and uncleanness.

48. Thomas Aquinas *Summa Theologica* 2–2 Q. 78, A1 Resp.

49. *Ibid.* A1, ad obj. 7.

50. On Shylock, see 1.3.110; on Bassanio, see 1.3.140; cf. 139, 150, 165, 175.

51. *Aquinas* 2–2 Q.78 A1 ob. 2.

52. On Antonio's Christian vision see St. Paul, *Letter to the Galatians*, who sees Christianity as a counter-movement to Judaism along three dimensions:

Jewish	*Christian*
Particularistic	Universalistic (cf. esp. Gal. 3.28)
Worldly Prosperity (Flesh)	Spiritual Prosperity
Law	Faith-Love (cf. Gal. 3.13; 5.13–14)

According to Antonio's lights at least, Shylock embodies all three of the Jewish traits, and he the Pauline triad.

53. Cf. Deut. 14.

54. Cf. Deut. 14.2, 21, 28–29.

55. Deut. 24.6.

56. Deut. 5.17 RSV.

57. *Contra* Bloom, *Shakespeare's Politics*, 23–24, 27.

58. Deut. 12.15–16 RSV.

59. Deut., 24.6 RSV.

60. See Tovey, "Golden Casket," 232.

61. John 19.7 RSV.

62. Matt. 27.24–25 RSV.

63. Luke 23.4, 14, 22 RSV; cf. John 19.6.

64. Luke 23.23–25; cf. John 19.12–16 RSV.

65. *Contra* Tovey, "Golden Casket," 237.

66. Ovid *Heroides* 12.161–63; Grant Showerman, trans., Loeb Classical Library, 155.

67. Cf. esp. 5.1.47: Bassanio's "horn full of good news."

68. Thus Tovey considerably understates the situation when she says all that remains for Portia is a "chastising" of her unfaithful husband ("Golden Casket," 230). Cf. Hyman: "The climax of the play, Portia's turning the tables on Shylock, is also the high point of Portia's victory over Antonio" ("Rival Lovers," 112).

69. Cf. Hyman, "Rival Lovers," 112.

70. This is quite independent of any suggestion of a homoerotic character of Antonio's feelings for Bassanio. Given the echoes of Christianity in the

play, I do not believe this is the point Shakespeare is attempting to explore. Cf. Hyman, "Rival Lovers," 110; Geary, "Nature of Portia's Victory," 59–60, 66. Note that even though Antonio is denied his Christlike sacrifice, he continues to cast the situation in Christian (love) vs. Jewish (commandment) terms.

71. Cf. Plato *Symposium* 177–185; Tovey, "Golden Casket," 233.

72. Boose misses Portia's near despair and near failure in her presentation of Portia as the source of "the castrating manipulations of the benefactress who has strategically orchestrated all such acquisitions" ("Comic Contract," 249).

73. Cf. Gen. 1.3 RSV.

74. Robert Graves, *Greek Myths*, 1:335, 2:253, 258; but cf. Ovid *Metamorphoses* 12.208–9.

75. Cf. John 1.9 RSV.

76. Cf. John 19.5 RSV.

77. Thus Holmer seems to miss almost entirely what has happened in the ring episode when she says that in giving away the ring "Bassanio is as firmly devoted to Portia as ever; . . . the bond is still intact" ("Loving Wisely," 71).

78. See Donow, "Shakespeare's Caskets," 92.

79. Consider Hyman, "Rival Lovers," 115; in his otherwise fine treatment of the play, Geary misses the real dynamic of this episode when he puts its weight on the revelation of Balthazar's identity ("Nature of Portia's Victory," 66). The decisive things have happened before that revelation occurs. Also see Aristotle *Ethics* 1170b30–1171a21.

80. *Contra* Boose, who sees the ending of the play as showing "an anxiously defensive hostility directed against . . . the social bond itself" ("Comic Contract," 251).

81. *Contra* Tovey's identification of Belmont and Portia with Platonic philosophy. At this point this otherwise excellent essay loses touch with the play, as in the judgment that Portia acts "to emancipate the potential philosopher [Bassanio!] from the religion of his city" ("Golden Casket," 234–37).

2

Fathers and Children: Matter, Mirth, and Melancholy in *As You Like It*

Joseph Alulis

Midway through *As You Like It,* in act 3, scene 4, there occurs a passage that, taken in context, is very amusing and, as Duke Senior might say, "full of matter." Rosalind speaks to her "coz" and confidant, Celia, of a chance encounter with her father in the Forest of Arden. She brings her account to an abrupt close by saying, "But what talk we of fathers, when there is such a man as Orlando" (3.4.34–35).[1]

Part of what makes this line so attractive is that it captures the spirit of the comedy. We laugh because of the pleasure we take in the sight of young love. Granted, one might criticize Rosalind for a lack of filial piety. She seems inconsiderate of a father from whom she has been long separated.[2] But in her defense it might be said there is a natural justice in the daughter's neglect of the father for the sake of the lover: for every old father was once a young lover. This equation is made explicit just after Rosalind has fallen in love with Orlando. Celia, seeing her cousin absorbed in thought, asks her if she is thinking of her exiled father. Rosalind replies that that is only partly true; part of her thought is for her "child's father" (1.3.11).[3]

The significance of Rosalind's line in act 3, scene 4 is, first, that it reflects the structure of the play. The play literally begins with the children talking of the fathers; first, Orlando talking of his father, Sir Rowland de Boys, then Celia and Rosalind talking of their fathers, Dukes Frederick and Senior. The latter two fathers dominate acts 1 and 2 respectively. Then, in the center of the play, the fathers are forgotten. Through all of act 3, save a short first scene, the fathers are gone from the stage and this is true of all of act 4 as well and nearly all of act 5. It is only at the end, in the last scene of the play, that the fathers are recalled.

This structure, in turn, points to the play's "matter," that is, what the play is about.[4] The great division in the play is between the court and the Forest of Arden. This division, as has often been noted, is not one between a corrupt state of society and an idyllic state of nature but rather between two different social states or ways of life: one a way of wealth and brilliance, the other, of simplicity and freedom.[5] But the contrast between these two ways of life, by raising the question of which is better (cf. the conversation between Touchstone and Corin, 3.2.11–83) suggests the idea of nature, not as a possible human state distinct from society but as a standard by which different social states may be evaluated. In this way, the theme of the relation of nature and convention emerges. This theme is then readily associated with the relations of fathers and children. For it is the fathers who make the rules, thereby defining a way of life, and it is the children who encounter these rules as an alien imposition upon their own natural impulses. But nature in this sense is not a standard but the human given, which must be shaped to conform to the standard. Thus nature appears in two lights. If the fathers represent "the right way of life," then nature is both child and "super" or "first" father.[6] In the play, Rosalind personifies both senses, as teacher and lover, judge and daughter.

The argument of this chapter is that the matter of the play is the relation between nature and convention, the former understood as both standard and native impulse, the latter understood as a society's accepted ideas of right and wrong and the mechanisms by which such ideas are made to govern our lives. The play explores the different standards of justice supplied by nature and convention and the different ways in which the children, or nature, are dependent upon and independent of the fathers, or convention. What makes this play the delightful affair it is, is that while it affirms an essential goodness of nature, hence the deficiencies of convention that depart from nature's standard, it also shows the necessary role of convention in relation to natural impulses, both in curbing those that are harmful and in protecting and fostering those that are beneficial. It rejects the melancholy view, occasioned by the spectacle of human injustice, that both nature and convention are meaningless, respectively teaching and serving only the pursuit of selfish ends by the most powerful. Shakespeare invites us to see our condition in nature and the world rather as an occasion of mirth. Whether we wish to accept that invitation is another question.

Matter: Nature and Convention

The matter of a tension between nature and convention, that is, between what is simply good and what is so because it is our own, is presented most plainly in the scene that introduces Rosalind, in the conversation between her and Celia that opens the scene. Celia's father, Duke Frederick, has taken from Rosalind's father, Duke Senior, the dukedom to which the latter possesses conventional title as "senior." Celia complains that Rosalind's sadness at her father's exile proves that Rosalind does not love Celia as much as Celia loves her. Had their situations been reversed, Celia says, she would have taught herself to take Rosalind's father as her own (1.2.7–13). But while the two men are equally fathers, they are not equally worthy of love: Duke Frederick is an unjust man and Duke Senior, his brother, is not. Celia loves her father as her own, not as good, and so cannot expect another, lacking this motive, to love him as she does.

That Celia understands this, act 1 makes clear. In her initial conversation with Rosalind, she tacitly censures her father's usurpation by assuring Rosalind that when she, Celia, inherits the dukedom, she will restore it to Rosalind (1.1.16–19). The censure is merely tacit because of filial piety: Celia honors her father as good because he has been good to her.[7] This piety is reflected in her anger at Touchstone later in this scene when he makes an observation that reflects badly upon Duke Frederick (70–79). At the same time, Celia honors what is good simply, that is, what is just, even though counter to her father's will. This is expressed in her commitment to restore the dukedom to Rosalind. In one sense, here, too, the good is merely conventional: the dukedom belongs to Rosalind as heir of the conventionally sanctioned possessor. But Celia's commitment seems to spring primarily from her "affection" for Rosalind for her personal qualities and as such may be said to reflect a love of justice as determined by nature. Rosalind should have the dukedom because she can make the best use of the office.[8] For Celia's love for Rosalind is a tribute to Rosalind's superior merit (cf. 1.3.67–68). In fact, Celia does love Rosalind more than Rosalind loves Celia because Rosalind is more worthy of love.[9] Though it is "natural" for Celia to protest against this inequality, it also appears that she accepts it and this, too, may be described as natural. In this way Celia is to be distinguished from her father.

Before scene 2 ends Celia does explicitly express her distress at her father's actions. When Duke Frederick refuses to reward Orlando for his victory in the wrestling match, Celia comments to Rosalind: "My father's rough and envious disposition / Sticks me at heart" (1.2.230–31). Here, too, a dual loyalty is expressed. A natural love of justice binds Celia to condemn the action while the tie of blood makes this necessity painful. In the third scene of act 1, in which Duke Frederick commits his third act of injustice, banishing Rosalind, Celia breaks with her father. But she does not seek to undo his actions or even openly reproach him; she removes herself from his dominion. Celia freely renounces all the goods associated with her father's rule: "Let my father find another heir" (1.3.95). Even more to the point, making clear the real meaning of her first speeches in the play, Celia seeks Rosalind's father for her own. After Duke Frederick leaves, having pronounced his sentence of banishment, Celia says to Rosalind, "Wilt thou change fathers? I will give thee mine" (1.3.87). Then, when the two plan their course of action in banishment, it is Celia, not Rosalind, who suggests that they seek out Rosalind's father in the Forest of Arden (102–3). Children love and need their fathers, just as all human beings need and love some rule that orders their collective life. But while they honor their fathers, all children wish that their fathers might be good, just as human beings desire that their collective way of life may be one that most closely conforms to what is simply good for humankind.

In order to distract themselves from melancholy reflections, occasioned by the presence and absence of fathers, Celia makes the following suggestion: "Let us sit and mock the good hussif Fortune from her wheel, that her gifts may henceforth be bestowed equally" (1.2.30–32). Celia's chief complaint against fortune, it seems, is the accident of her birth, that she should have the father she has rather than another. But whether this is a complaint against fortune or nature remains a question.

The way in which Rosalind takes up Celia's invitation offers a further development on the relation between nature and convention: "I would we could [mock fortune into bestowing her gifts equally]; for her benefits are mightily misplaced, and the bountiful blind woman doth most mistake in her gifts to women" (33–35).[10] Unlike a comparison of particular individuals, like Duke Frederick and Duke Senior,

Rosalind speaks of women as a class being unjustly treated by fortune. She cannot mean that the distribution of worldly goods among individual women is mistaken because there is no reason to think this is any more mistaken among women than among men. The context suggests why this thought should be present to her mind. Fortune has deprived her father of his dukedom and in so doing has imposed a burden upon her as well. But fortune's blow to Duke Senior is assuaged as hers is not. As Duke Senior tells us in his first speech in act 2, the forest, being free of the ills inescapably associated with the life of the court, offers some compensation for his loss of office (2.1.1–17). Rosalind, however, detained at court, is denied that compensation. Her detention by her uncle reflects the fact that generally women, as the weaker sex, are denied the freedom men enjoy. Rosalind's thought, then, is that, in general, because women are weaker than men, fortune treats them less well. But Rosalind does not make her complaint against nature for making women physically weaker. Nature, presumably, has supplied ample compensation for the difference in bodily strength. For Rosalind, what is at issue is not nature but how we respond to nature; that is, the conventional arrangements that govern the relations of men and women. The natural physical weakness of women does not dictate that they be accorded an inferior status: that is the work of convention, the will of the fathers. If "the good hussif Fortune" is especially unjust in her treatment of women, it is only because of the antecedent injustice of the fathers.[11]

In directing her complaint against fortune rather than the fathers, Rosalind may be understood as shielding Celia from a harsh truth. Indeed, Celia is herself engaged in a kind of salutary self-deception insofar as her complaint against fortune on account of her father is, in fact, a complaint against nature. By substituting fortune for nature she succeeds in redirecting her complaint away from a provident deity, as nature's author, and toward a goddess of notoriously unreliable character. Rosalind's superiority to Celia is evident in her clear-sighted recognition of what belongs to each, nature and "fortune," and her ability to bear with equanimity the spectacle of the unequal distribution of their gifts. In particular she is able to bear the injustice to which she as a woman is subject. This capacity for bearing results from a recognition of a kind of necessity: because men are physically stronger, they *can* impose rules that are more advantageous to themselves and so *will* do so.[12] But it seems also to be related to a recognition that the natural relations of men and women also serve to moderate the degree of injustice that the former naturally do the latter.

When they are searching for some sport to make themselves merry, it is Celia who suggests that they sit and mock fortune. Rosalind makes a different suggestion: "What think you of falling in love?" (1.2.24). Love softens the harshness of the dictates of the fathers.[13] Further, if convention unfairly forecloses from us the enjoyment of some of the pleasures that nature affords us as human beings, it does not necessarily foreclose all. One measure of the degree to which the conventional idea of justice departs from a natural standard is the quantity and quality of the natural pleasures it leaves within the power of those capable of enjoying them. In turning her thoughts to love in the fullest sense of the idea, Rosalind turns to what is the preeminent good available to her and, perhaps, the preeminent good available to any human being as such.[14]

The next stage of the conversation confirms the idea that Rosalind's account of fortune directs our attention to the relation between conventional and natural goods. Celia agrees with Rosalind that fortune treats women unjustly but she apparently misunderstands Rosalind's meaning.

> *Celia:* 'Tis true, for those that she makes fair, she scarce makes honest; and those that she makes honest, she makes very ill-favouredly.
> *Rosalind:* Nay now thou goest from Fortune's office to Nature's; Fortune reigns in gifts of the world, not in the lineaments of Nature. (36–41)

Celia is, at least in part, making a little joke: the "fair," being the object of so much attention, have a greater need for chastity than the ill-favored, while it is precisely the lack of opportunity that makes the ill-favored "honest." (Hamlet, in a less playful way, also comments on the relation between beauty and honesty.[15]) By making beauty a gift of fortune, Celia again begs the question of what belongs to nature and what to fortune. Rosalind distinguishes between the gifts of nature, beauty and just parents, and those of the world, wealth and, apparently, honesty. Celia responds to Rosalind by seeking to reassert fortune's rule even in nature's realm: "No? When Nature hath made a fair creature, may she not fall into the fire?" (42–43).

This idea of the power of accident, however, does not lessen the utility of Rosalind's distinction between nature and "the world." Rather it clarifies the relation between the two. Because the good things that nature gives us may, in a contingent universe, suffer harm, the fathers should arrange things in the world to protect them. The role of convention is to protect and foster nature's goods. The fathers are entrusted with the responsibility to take care of things in the world for the common good. They do this best when their ideas of justice and right and wrong conform most closely to what nature dictates in these matters.

An important way in which convention protects and fosters nature's goods is by education, especially moral education. When Celia speaks, in the context of beauty and chastity, of a fair creature's "fall into the fire," the primary significance of "fire" is not literal but metaphorical. Fire is a common Shakespearean usage for "sexual ardor" or lust and from this takes on the additional meaning of the burning of venereal disease.[16] In this sense, it is "honesty" that saves one from the "fire" and Rosalind, in reply to Celia, makes honesty a gift not of nature but of the world. Honesty is the product of the education ordained by the fathers for the protection of the children.[17] Here is a convention that conforms to nature's rule, an instance in which the fathers' will is simply benign.

If we now turn to the first scene of the play, we see that it concerns the issue of education as, in both a literal and legal sense, the dictate of a father's will. Moreover, the issue here is precisely the distribution of material goods so as to protect and cultivate nature's gifts. The play opens with Orlando lamenting the fact that his education or, rather, lack of it, "mines [his] gentility" (1.1.20). His father, Sir Rowland de Boys, upon his death, provided for Orlando's education but his eldest brother, Oliver, in whose hands it rests to execute Sir Rowland's will, has deprived Orlando of his due. The old father's will is frustrated by his successor, the new father. Such gentility as Orlando possesses is not a product of education but a gift of nature. He is "gentle, never schooled yet learned, full of noble device" (1.1.164–65). Insofar as "gentility" includes virtue (cf. Touchstone's play with the different meanings of "manners," 3.2.39–43), one sees another sign of it in Orlando's native sense of justice.

In complaining to Adam of his plight, he shows he is able to weigh carefully what is due himself and what is due others: "I will no longer endure it [the injustice Oliver does him], though yet I know no wise remedy how to avoid it" (1.1.23–25). Though the victim of injustice, Orlando will not be so unjust to others, or to himself, as to embrace a remedy that he cannot approve as wise. Orlando is, so to speak, naturally virtuous. And yet one may perhaps detect a slight weakening of his disposition in the desperate remarks he makes to Rosalind and Celia before the wrestling match. He claims to have no friends, which is unjust to Adam; declares himself willing to die in a frivolous cause, which is unjust to himself; and opines that the world will suffer no injury by his loss because he has no place in it, which is unjust to the world. For we already know from his brother how much he is "in the heart of the world" for the sake of his natural gifts (1.2.177–80, 1.1.165–67). In short, as he says to his brother, he is in danger of being "marred" by his fortune (1.1.31–34).

Like Duke Senior Orlando is the victim of injustice at the hands of his brother. But by a natural standard he is a victim of injustice at the hands of Sir Rowland as well. For Orlando clearly possesses greater natural gifts than his brother, Oliver, and therefore can be expected to make better use of the world's gifts. But convention, the will of the fathers, dictates that the eldest son be favored before the youngest. In Shakespeare's source, Thomas Lodge's *Rosalynde,* Orlando's counterpart, Rosader, though the youngest, is awarded by the father the largest share of the estate because of his natural virtue.[18] Shakespeare alters his source to place Orlando in a situation where he can be described as suffering injustice at the hands of convention. In scene 2, when Rosalind makes a gift to Orlando to compensate for Duke Frederick's poor treatment of him, she speaks of herself as "one out of suits with fortune" (1.2.236). We recognize this description as appropriate to both young people because of the particular injustices they have suffered. But, as Shakespeare has taken care to suggest, it fits them also as members of classes of persons who are disadvantaged by the fathers generally.[19]

To women and youngest sons we may add as a third class of persons who are "out of suits with fortune": those of mean birth, like Adam.[20] Though we see Adam only as an old man, he recalls a time when he was Orlando's age. He tells us he was seventeen when he began service to Orlando's father and shows us by his account of his prudence (his temperance and his savings) that he is not unintelligent (2.3.71–72, 38–39, 47–51). Nonetheless, fortune decreed that he should lead the life of an "ox" and in age, be treated like a "dog" (1.1.10, 81). And yet Adam accepts his position and we are invited to admire his loyalty to the master who treats him well within the limits of the relation in which fortune has placed them both.

Here then is the question of the relation of nature and convention in its most troubling form. We have considered three characters "out of suits with fortune," Rosalind, Orlando, and Adam. Each represents a class—women, youngest sons, persons of mean birth—that suffers by convention or the will of the fathers. Each by reason of personal merit deserves better at the world's hands. But not one condemns the fathers or seeks to reverse the fathers' will by force or fraud, justifying such expedients by an appeal to a natural standard. Shakespeare dramatically endorses their self-restraint by portraying each favorably and then ratifies this endorsement by portraying unfavorably a similarly situated character who does violate convention's dictate. This is Duke Frederick, who, like Orlando, is a younger son. In the persons of Frederick and Orlando Shakespeare presents two contrasting understandings of nature and convention and the relation of the two.

Like Orlando, Frederick appears superior to his brother in certain natural gifts. Clearly Duke Senior is superior morally: lords follow him into exile in devotion to his character and we see him in the forest of Arden bearing his exile without bitterness (1.1.100–104; 2.1.1–17). But the very fact that he is in exile may be taken as a sign of his weakness as a ruler. He has been taken unawares by his brother and deprived of his dukedom. Moreover, unlike Prospero in *The Tempest,* Duke Senior does not recover his state by his own actions. This suggests that Frederick, at least in a kind of practical sagacity, is superior to his elder brother. But Orlando, occupying a similar position of superiority vis-à-vis his brother, does not even think of justifying usurpation on that ground. He is wary of acting too rashly even in advancing his strictly conventional claims (1.1.23–35). The ground of this wariness is suggested by the way he characterizes that conventional arrangement that accords the greater share to the eldest. Orlando calls it the "courtesy of nations" (1.1.46). By contrast, Frederick's disregard for the same convention bespeaks a view of it as the "curiosity of nations," an arbitrary arrangement not worthy of respect. Frederick, like Edmund, mocks courtesy; Orlando respects it.[21]

The rules of courtesy prescribe those practices by which human beings curb their egoism in their interactions with others so that society may be peaceable. The idea of the courtesy of nations reminds us of the constant danger of an appeal to force in human intercourse. In his first encounter with Duke Senior, when Orlando appears sword in hand to demand satisfaction of his needs, the older man asks him if he is "a rude despiser of good manners" (2.7.93). Of course, Orlando is just the opposite and, at the hands of one like himself, secures his needs by courtesy rather than force. In despising courtesy Frederick implicitly embraces an appeal to force to decide differences among egoistic human beings. He does so confident that his superior ability will reward him with success regardless of harm to others.

It is the most powerful, the fathers, who set down the rules of courtesy as a restraint upon themselves as well as the less powerful.

But it is more than an egoistic desire for peace that prompts respect for the imperfect rules of justice they dictate. When Orlando confronts Oliver over the injustice Oliver does him within the limits of convention, he tells us twice in the space of fifty lines that he is prompted to do so by "the spirit of [his] father" (1.1.21–22, 70). The spirit of his father aims at justice even if the father's will is defective.[22] One submits to the will of the father, though it sometimes be unjust by nature's standard, because the spirit is true. That spirit is itself a gift of nature. It is that disposition to justice that we all have to a greater or lesser degree by nature. In the case of Orlando and Rosalind the formula "spirit of my father" applies literally. Sir Rowland de Boys and Duke Senior are both men who love justice, hence the tie of love between them (1.2.224; 1.3.27; 2.7.198–99).[23] But Celia, who we have noticed loves justice, is the daughter of a father who does not, just as Sir Rowland has a son, Oliver, who does not. Each case casts some light upon the other. As a just Sir Rowland had two sons, one just and one unjust, so one might imagine that Duke Senior and Duke Frederick had a father who was just.

The love of justice in Celia is the spirit of her father's father. The generational scheme Shakespeare presents us in the two families leads the (traditional) mind backward to the first father, Adam, whom God made in his image. The conversions of Oliver and Duke Frederick at the play's end depend ultimately upon the triumph in them of the spirit of the first father, a triumph the possibility of which is thus suggested in the opening scene of the play. By the same token, reliance upon God is a reliance upon the spirit God places in man. Thus, in venturing forth with Orlando, Adam, the old servant, trusts that "He that doth the ravens feed, / Yea providently caters for the sparrow, / [Will] be comfort to may age" (2.3.43–45). When Adam is saved from starvation in act 2, scene 7 by Duke Senior, we are invited to think his faith is rewarded.[24]

Frederick's scorn for courtesy, his appeal to force to attain his title and to secure it for his heirs, suggests a radically different vision of nature and convention. In this view nature ordains no good but personal advantage, the will of the fathers seeks no more than this, and the spirit of the father aims only at power. If convention only serves the advantage of the more powerful, why shouldn't Frederick scorn it when it is disadvantageous to him, especially if he has the force and wit enough to do so successfully?[25] In this view the world is a place of "stern alarums" rather than "delightful measures" and life is to be encountered with vigor as a bracing struggle to get to the top of the heap by fair means or foul.[26] To one who does not share this view, however, this vision is an unattractive one. It is the world described by Duke Senior and the lords who surround him in the forest of Arden, a world that the egoism of individuals fills with "peril" and "ingratitude," in which "most friendship is feigning, most loving mere folly" (2.1.4; 2.7.176, 181). Love in this view is not the preeminent good but a snare and a weakness (cf. 3.2.277–78).

Surely there is peril, ingratitude, and falseness in the world, but that these things are dominant is a vision of the world that Shakespeare encourages us to reject as false. By and large, the world appears very well in this play. The world loves Orlando for his natural virtue (1.1.162–69) and one surmises it is for the same reason that it loved his father (1.2.224–25). Each day men of power give their allegiance to Duke Senior in preference to his usurping brother (5.4.153–54). Moreover, though Frederick is temporarily successful, it is the very nature of the world that dooms his usurpation to ultimate failure. The people are devoted to Rosalind for her virtue, which raises the likelihood that they will support her restoration at the earliest opportunity. It is this natural bent of the world that Frederick attempts to counter by banishing Rosalind (1.3.76–78).[27] But we know that his effort to secure the title to his heirs is fruitless because Celia has already promised to restore the dukedom to her cousin.

Finally, Shakespeare portrays the ground of Frederick's view and action as ugly. His action arises from something like a resentment of nature's goodness—resentment that nature's goodness does not yield to his will. Duke Frederick treats Orlando unjustly at the wrestling match because Orlando's father, Sir Rowland de Boys, was his enemy (1.2.213–19). Sir Rowland's enmity presumably sprang from the fact of Duke Frederick's injustice. By means of that injustice Duke Frederick attained the power, in terms of the world's gifts, that he must have thought would make him esteemed. Yet nonetheless, "all the world" loved Sir Rowland for his goodness while even those who pay court to Duke Frederick do not respect him (1.2.224–25 and Le Beau's remarks to Orlando in the same scene, 256–57). Frederick hates Sir Rowland and thereby Orlando because of their goodness and because the world in esteeming them more highly for their goodness than him for his "worldly" success is not as craven as he is.[28]

If the world were really such as Frederick imagines it, that would be an occasion for melancholy for anyone who loved the idea of justice as something more than the egoism of the strongest. It is that thought which accounts for the presence in the play of one of Shakespeare's most memorable characters, Jaques. Nature looks to Jaques as it does to Frederick; it is the scene of a cruel struggle for power by selfish individuals. But while this spectacle fills Frederick with ambition and resolve, it fills Jaques with dismay. He is, in Orlando's phrase, "Monsieur Melancholy" (3.2.288–89). Jaques represents, by reflection, the idea of nature as incapable of recognizing a good understood as independent of human will for its being. Shakespeare's depiction of Jaques, then, constitutes a further exploration of the matter developed in the first act of the play and to that depiction I will now turn.

Melancholy

Jaques is not merely a memorable character; we tend to like him and Shakespeare gives us some good reasons for doing so. He belongs to the circle of Duke Senior, which puts him in the camp of the just. He is one of those Lords of whom Charles spoke who have sacrificed their property out of love for Duke Senior (1.1.99–104). Jaques, not present on Duke Senior's first appearance, is spoken of by the Duke and other lords with evident goodwill (2.1.25–69); his melancholy is treated as a harmless, even amusing, disposition. If he is somewhat excessive in his criticism, still there is much in the world of which to be critical. He does not appear to be depressing company. And who has not sometime or other sucked melancholy out of a song (2.5.11–13)?[29]

It remains, however, that Shakespeare censures Jaques. Successively, in acts 2, 3, and 4, Duke Senior, Orlando, and Rosalind respectively, rebuke, reject, and ridicule Jaques's melancholy. One must feel the full force of this repudiation to appreciate the play's meaning.

The occasion for Jaques's melancholy seems to be the wickedness of the world (cf. 2.1.25–63). But in his consciousness of this Jaques is not unique. All in Duke Senior's party comment upon the same theme. In the speech that opens act 2, Duke Senior describes the court as "envious" and favorably compares the "icy fang . . . of the winter's wind" to the "flattery" of "counsellors" (2.1.6–11).[30] The idea is echoed by the song the Lords sing in the last scene of this act, which concludes: "Heigh-ho, sing heigh-ho, unto the green holly, / Most friendship is feigning, most loving mere folly" (2.7.190–191).

But while the other lords observe and comment upon the injustice of humankind they do not take pleasure in the contemplation of it the way Jaques does. More important, for Jaques the wickedness men do suggests that nature is utterly corrupt. In describing his melancholy to Ganymede, he tells "him" that it results from "the sundry contemplations of my travels" (4.1.17–18). What prompted Jaques to travel and what he saw he does not say. But we can surmise the answers to these questions from what we already know about Jaques. From the first, Jaques is presented as a witness to the folly, misery, and wickedness of human beings. As the First Lord reports to Duke Senior, in his moralizing, Jaques "invectively" pierces through "The body of country, city, court" (2.1.58–59). The manners of men differ from one sphere to the other but are no less wicked. We are led to the thought that Jaques went abroad to see if there was any place where men were wise, happy, and just and discovered that no such place exists.[31]

The melancholy of Jaques suggests that the will of the father is hopelessly corrupt. Whatever good nature may be said to intend for humankind, convention does little to foster it and much to undermine it. But the fathers are themselves products of nature. If their wills are hopelessly corrupt, then so is nature. One conforms to the will of the fathers, adopts manners, to escape the brutality of unchecked egoism but does not thereby escape the more refined egoism of social life in which manners merely cloak our indifference to or even hatred of each other (cf. 3.2.249–54). The choice for the individual seems to be between the savagery of anarchy or the injustice of the fathers' rule. Jaques presents this melancholy view most fully in the last scene of act 2 and it is in the same scene that it is most effectively rebutted.

In the third scene of act 2 we see Orlando flee Oliver for fear of his life, accompanied by Adam. They have no clear destination. In scene 6 we see Adam on the verge of collapse from hunger. Orlando settles him in some shelter and goes in search of food. In the next scene he comes upon Duke Senior's group and attempts to extort food from them by the threat of force. He has recourse to force because he thinks he is no longer in the realm of the fathers but in a Hobbesian state of nature: "I thought that all things had been savage here" (2.7.107). Duke Senior responds in such a way as to make him doubt this judgment. Orlando then applies the following test to determine whether these strangers are civil rather than savage. Here is what he asks his unknown host:

> If ever you have look'd on better days;
> If ever been where bells have knoll'd to church;
> If ever sat at any good man's feast;
> If ever from your eyelids wip'd a tear,

And know what 'tis to pity and be pitied,
Let gentleness my strong enforcement be. (2.7.113–18)

To this Duke Senior replies in kind:

True is it that we have seen better days,
And have with holy bell been knoll'd to church,
And sat at good men's feasts, and wip'd our eyes
Of drops that sacred pity hath engender'd;
And therefore sit you down in gentleness,
And take upon command what help we have
That to your wanting may be minister'd. (120–26)

The effect is a kind of litany, chanted by the new father and the old father, of the way of the fathers when that way is designed to foster and cultivate nature's goods. The first institution characteristic of this way is the family. When Orlando, surveying a group of men separate from women and children, asks them if they have seen "better days," he is inquiring if they have known the gentling experience of family life. The second institution is that of religion, that is, the means by which we express our love of God who alone is good. Beyond this, his speech describes mores that encourage liberality and compassion. These are the means to tame egoism and foster nature's goods.

Just before Orlando entered Jaques had described a different way to deal with the wickedness of humankind. Given his vision of our moral incorrigibility, the aim would not be to make us good so much as to hold wrongdoing in check. He addresses the Duke: "Give me leave / To speak my mind, and I will through and through / Cleanse the foul body of th' infected world" (58–61). Now around the time this play appeared satire was very much in fashion. In 1598 John Marston published a work in this genre entitled *The Scourge of Villainy*. This is exactly what Jaques is proposing: to scourge men, verbally by raillery and mockery, to curb their wrongdoing by calling attention to the ugliness of their wickedness.[32] This is a very different approach from that which Orlando describes and Duke Senior echoes. Shortly after Marston's book appeared, the Bishop of London banned all works of satire.[33] The thought behind this action may have been the same as that which prompts the Duke to reply to Jaques with a rebuke.

Most mischievous foul sin, in chiding sin.
For thou thyself hast been a libertine,
As sensual as the brutish sting itself,

> And all th'embossed sores and headed evils
> That thou with license of free foot hast caught
> Wouldst thou disgorge into the general world. (64–69)

The result of Jaques's proposed railing would be the opposite of what he intended. One whose ability to expose wickedness to mockery depends upon his own intimate acquaintance with it may rather put ideas in the heads of the innocent than correct the erring.[34] More important, Jaques would corrupt because his scourging would be seen by many, especially the young, as a cynical portrait of the way men inescapably are. In the end, what Jaques would inculcate, to use one critic's description of Marston's view, is "a dark pessimistic weariness that falls little short of complete despair."[35]

When Orlando leaves to fetch Adam, Jaques delivers his "seven ages" of man speech (2.7.139–66). This is, probably, the most often noted speech of the play. But given the context, it is a mistake to read this as intended by Shakespeare as a simply true or complete picture of human experience. Rather, the speech perfectly expresses Jaques's melancholy by portraying its cause. It depicts life as low and meaningless, dominated by senseless passion and corrupt motives. James Smith likens it to Macbeth's more famous comparison of life to the part acted by "a poor player": "a tale / Told by an idiot, full of sound and fury, / Signifying nothing."[36]

Though he has just rebuked Jaques for his melancholy vision of humankind, the Duke does not object to this speech. He is silent, I think, because it is well for us to be reminded of our foibles as long as the reminder is offered in a manner that reduces the likelihood of corruption. Jaques's scourge of villainy here is not "as free as the wind" but is restricted to a small circle; it is a rebuke to the ruler, the Duke, not to forget himself.[37] In addition, as has been often noted, all who hear it see something contrary.[38] They see a young man, "the lover" of Jaques's "seven ages," moved by "sacred pity" to care for an old man whose known worth marks him as a venerable being not a "pantaloon" and these two greeted by a "justice" whose wisdom we know is not a matter of "saws" drawn from books but something "feelingly" acquired in the Forest of Arden.

What makes Jaques attractive to us is precisely his goodness. He is not simply hopeless. His travels may have shown him that most men are corrupt and yet he knows some who are not: himself and those friends of the Duke who sacrificed material goods out of loyalty to virtue. In act 2, scene 5 where he improvises his "*ducdame*" stanzo, he mocks those who leave "wealth and ease/ A stubborn will to please" (49–50) meaning, surely, those he addresses with his "Greek invocation," the followers of the Duke. But he is one of their number. Here he is like the Fool in *King Lear,* noting what the wicked think wise without himself following their opinion.[39] But he is less wise than the Fool because too doubtful of his own goodness. By suggesting that his action springs less from decency than "a stubborn will" he does himself, and nature, an injustice.[40] By the same token, we can let our perception of the world's injustice distort our vision. There is reason to be more hopeful about nature than Jaques. This reason is suggested in the persons of Rosalind and Orlando, the children, and it is to them, especially Rosalind, that I turn for my discussion of mirth.

Mirth

The word mirth occurs only twice in the play, but these two instances frame the action of the drama. It occurs in the second scene of the play and in the last. In the first case Rosalind is the speaker; in the second, Hymen. But insofar as Rosalind controls Hymen, it is she who speaks both times (cf. 5.2.58–62). The first time she comments that she is without mirth; the second time, the scene of the weddings that conclude the play, there is mirth in abundance. Both usages suggest a single meaning: mirth is occasioned by a union of two things that belong together, fathers and children, men and women. In the first scene, Rosalind is without mirth because of the forced separation between her and her father (1.2.2–6). In the last scene, there is mirth because she has been united, not only with her father but with "her child's father." Here is what Rosalind gives Hymen to say on the latter occasion: "Then is there mirth in heaven, / When earthly things made even / Atone together" (5.4.107–09).[41] The proper relation of fathers and children, that is, when nurture looks to and accomplishes the good of nature, is an occasion for mirth. Mirth is the sentiment proper to the comedic resolution of the matter of the play; it is the state to which a comedy about fathers and children, nature and convention looks as its conclusion.

But Hymen adopts a heavenly perspective. There is another kind of mirth on earth occasioned by just the opposite phenomenon: discord between things that belong together. Much of the humor of the play involves this earthly mirth: discord between nature and convention and discord within nature itself. Hymen's speech in the last scene serves as our point of departure. The point of view in these lines is explicitly divine and the divine teaching of the Judeo-Christian tradition, the tradition the play evokes in the person of Adam and in the word "atone" in the above speech, is that nature is good, albeit fallen.[42] These two ideas, the essential goodness of nature and our fallen condition, underlie both kinds of mirth stirred in us by the events in the Forest of Arden.

If heavenly mirth is occasioned by the redemption of nature, earthly mirth is occasioned by the disjunction between its essential goodness and its fallen condition.

Fallen nature establishes conventions that do not nurture but mar nature's goodness. An earthly mirth is then occasioned by nature's escape from convention seen as something alien and inferior.[43] When the children are free of the fathers' discipline, seen now not as care but as constraint, the experience is mirthful. We experience this escape in contemplating Orlando free of his brother's tyrannic will but even more so in contemplating Rosalind in disguise. Given that it is Rosalind who raises the issue of the injustice convention does to women, it is not surprising that it is she who volunteers to adopt the role of the man in her flight with Celia from the court (1.3.110–12). For in pretending to be a young man she not only escapes the unjust constraint of convention but heartily mocks that convention. In her account of the natural weakness of women, as "changeable," "proud," "shallow," and the more witty, the more "wayward" (3.2.398–400 and 4.1.152–53), she presents the justification offered for the inferior status convention assigns to women. But she thinks this justification false since she thinks women are treated unjustly. In presenting it seriously now to Orlando, whom she loves and who she knows loves her, she accomplishes an important object. In drawing from Orlando a defense of women, or at least of his Rosalind (4.1.60–61), she educates the future father of her child, freeing him from the corruption of unjust convention.

But if nature is essentially good, it is also fallen and contemplation of our fallen condition may also be a source of mirth so long as no serious harm results.[44] Atonement is the act by which humankind is pardoned and spared the ultimate penalty of the fall, the penalty of death. But humankind continues to suffer the penalty that Aquinas likens to a demotion in social status in a hierarchical society, in which a person born to one rank is made subject to the laws of an inferior rank.[45] From the perspective of our birth rank as rational beings the control the body and human passion exercises over our judgment is very amusing: it is an occasion of mirth. Nowhere is this control more tyrannical than when we fall in love. It is funny to see Silvius's infatuation, still funnier to see Phoebe, who scorns him for it, herself smitten. But best of all, it is delightful to see Rosalind in love.

When Rosalind first encounters the poems written for her by Orlando, not knowing their author, she mocks them for their technical crudeness. To Celia, who reads her one of them, she replies "what tedious homily of love have you wearied your parishioners withal" (3.2.152–53). When Celia first hints of the identity of the author, however, Rosalind adopts a different tone. Up till now she had loved Orlando without knowing that he loved her as well. The possibility that he does has, by Celia's testimony, a physical impact: "Change you colour?" (179). Rosalind is, by her own description, powerfully moved: she begs Celia "with most petitionary vehemence," to tell her plainly who the author is (186–87). When Celia does so, Rosalind's pleasure at the news is such that she showers Celia with a multitude of questions she does not allow her to answer (215–47). Love, as Rosalind says, is a kind of "madness" (388) and the actions it compels, so long as they cause no harm, fill us the spectator with mirth just as the experience of love, on the same condition, occasions mirth in the lover.

But the experience of another pair of lovers in the play, Touchstone and Audrey, suggests that fallen nature uncorrected by convention may lead to harm. Touchstone's love for Audrey is utterly egoistical and in his intentions he is careless of any harm he may do her (3.3.81–85). For himself, he could not honestly echo Silvius's account of love, that it is "all made of faith and service" as do Orlando and, tacitly, Rosalind (5.2.88, 91–92). Fallen nature as manifest in Touchstone must be checked by convention. Appropriately enough, it is Jaques who discovers Touchstone's designs upon Audrey. Jaques, we may imagine, by reason on his own experience as a libertine, is well acquainted with such expedients as Touchstone's proposed "bush" marriage. In his self-assumed role of chastiser of human wickedness he prevents it: "Get you to church, and have a good priest that can tell you what marriage is" (3.3.75–77). For Jaques, love is little more than the "brutish sting itself" (2.7.66). It is a piece of folly, that is, a "fault," something to be mocked as he does in his "seven ages" speech, not enjoyed as it clearly is by Orlando and Rosalind (3.2.277–78; 4.1.195–98). Conventional arrangements like marriage check the fault or limit the damage. For the other pairs of lovers, however, love has a deeper meaning, it is as much made of "patience" as "impatience," of "duty and observance" as of "passion" and "of wishes" (5.2.94–96).

But for them, too, the conventional arrangement of marriage is necessary. Their love impels Rosalind and Orlando to marriage, first to the mock wedding of act 4 and then to the formal ceremony of act 5. For what Rosalind says of woman is characteristic of humankind's fallen state in general: passion has learned to reason and will outface reason itself.

> You shall never take her without her answer, unless you take her without her tongue. O that woman that cannot make her fault her husband's occasion, let her never nurse her child herself, for she will breed it like a fool. (4.1.162–67)

Rosalind here personifies nature as a beautiful woman who tells the truth about her own capacity for deceit so that convention, in the person of her child's father, may be better able to protect that beauty and the good it occasions from harm. The convention of wedlock protects what is good in nature from the harm nature might do itself. It may be seen as a check to something vicious but this is a one-sided view. It is as much an "honoured" crown to what is good in nature, a means by which that good may be brought to fruition (5.4.140–45).

This image of Rosalind as personifying nature, a nature that knows her own essential goodness as well as her fallen state, takes us back to the passage with which I began in act 3, scene 4: "But what talk we of fathers." Rosalind has mentioned to Celia an encounter with her father the day before. Her father did not recognize her in her disguise, which she took as an occasion for a joke. The Duke asked her what her parentage was and she replied it was as good as his at which, she reports, "he laughed and let me go" (3.4.33–34). Now both father and daughter laugh for a similar reason. Rosalind laughs because she knows the remark is true but also knows that it does not appear to be true to her father. The Duke laughs because he thinks he knows that the remark is not true but also thinks that it must appear to be true since he bears no marks of his noble birth. Though the joke is similar on both sides, it is the daughter who has the better laugh because she laughs twice: once at her father's failure to recognize who she is and a second time at his confidence that he understands the situation better than she does. The encounter is symbolic of the meaning of the play. Convention, seeing the waywardness of fallen nature, mistakenly thinks itself superior. Nature, however, as essentially good, knows its own worth; but it knows as well its debt to convention for protection and nurturing. Finally, however, insofar as convention is true, both nature and convention have a common author. To paraphrase Rosalind's laughing response to her father, Duke Senior's parentage is as good as hers.

Notes

This paper was originally prepared as a talk for the University of Chicago's Basic Program Spring Weekend, April 22–24, 1994. I am grateful to Chris Colmo and Vickie Sullivan and to the readers for Rowman & Littlefield for their comments on earlier drafts of this essay.

1. All references to *As You Like It* are to the Arden edition, ed. Agnes Latham (London: Methuen, 1975; reprinted, London: Routledge, 1989).

2. Coleridge comments on this scene that "Rosalind is not a very dutiful daughter." While he grants that her neglect of her father "though not quite proper, is natural enough," he concludes that "she might, at any rate, have shown more interest in her father's fortunes," *A New Variorum Edition of Shakespeare: As You Like It,* ed. Horace Howard Furness (Philadelphia: J. B. Lippincott Co., 1891), 195.

3. Rowe in his second edition (1714) altered this to read "father's child" and while Theobald (1733) restored Shakespeare's language, Pope (1723), Johnson (1765), and other editors accepted Rowe's emendation. Coleridge comments of the unemended passage, "Who can doubt that this is a mistake . . . ?" (Furness, *New Variorum Edition,* 49).

4. See the entry for "matter" in C. T. Onions, *A Shakespeare Glossary,* enlarged and revised by Robert D. Eagleson (Oxford: Oxford University Press, 1986).

5. Cf. Alfred Harbage, *William Shakespeare: A Reader's Guide* (New York: Farrar, Straus and Co., 1963), 229; Michael Taylor, "*As You Like It:* The Penalty of Adam," *Critical Quarterly* 15 (1976): 76; Russell Fraser, "Shakespeare's Book of Genesis," *Comparative Drama* 25 (1991): 122.

6. Cf. C. L. Barber on the dual attitude toward nature in Shakespeare's festive comedy: In these plays "the poetry about the pleasures of nature and the naturalness of pleasure serves to evoke beneficent natural impulses; and much of the wit, mocking the good housewife Fortune from her wheel, acts to free the spirit as does the ritual abuse of hostile spirits. A saturnalian attitude assumed by a clear-cut gesture toward liberty, brings mirth, an accession of wanton vitality." But at the same time the saturnalian attitude brings "the clarification of limits which comes from going beyond the limit." "The plays present a mockery of what is unnatural," that is, whatever restrains "wanton vitality" at the same time that "they include another, complementary mockery of what is merely natural" (*Shakespeare's Festive Comedy* [Princeton:

Princeton University Press, 1959], 7, 13, 8). See also Barber's discussion of Rosalind in *Ibid.*, chap. 9, "The Alliance of Seriousness and Levity in *As You Like It.*"

7. Cf. Aristotle *Nicomachean Ethics* 1162a5f.

8. The classic statement of this view of what nature dictates as regards rule is the idea of the philosopher king, *Republic* 473a–e. The modern critique of this view is probably best expressed by Hobbes, *Leviathan,* chap. 10, section on "Worthinesse, Fitnesse."

9. Cf. Aristotle *Ethics* 1158b23–28.

10. Harbage fails to see much significance in this conversation: "The logic chopping about Nature and Fortune will do as a sample of small talk between lively and cultivated girls, but it seems to come from the top of their heads" (*Reader's Guide,* 225). John Shaw, on the other hand, sees in this conversation between Rosalind and Celia, 1.2.30–53, "on one level . . . the plot of *As You Like It* in epitome," "Fortune and Nature in *As You Like It,*" *Shakespeare Quarterly* 6 (1955): 46. He argues that "behind the gay romancing of the characters throughout *As You Like It* there is a basic philosophical strife between Fortune and Nature that would be obvious to the Renaissance" (45). In this reading Rosalind, Orlando, and the Forest of Arden are associated with nature understood as wisdom and virtue and Frederick, Oliver, and the court are associated with fortune and the use of "policy and cunning" to win her gifts (48).

11. Cf. John Stuart Mill, "As for vicissitudes of fortune, and other disappointments connected with worldly circumstances, these are principally the effect either of gross imprudence, of ill-regulated desires, or of bad or imperfect social institutions," *Utilitarianism* in *On Liberty and Other Essays*, ed. John Gray (Oxford: Oxford University Press, 1991), 146.

12. Cf. Plato *Republic* 458c–d.

13. Cf. David Hume, *An Inquiry Concerning the Principles of Morals,* Library of Liberal Arts, ed. Charles W. Hendel (New York: Macmillan, 1957), 21–22.

14. See the discussion of the observations of Aristotle and Tocqueville on the place of women in the polity in Mary Nichols, "The Good Life, Slavery, and Acquisition: Aristotle's Introduction to Politics," *Interpretation* 11 (1983): 28–54 and Delba Winthrop, "Tocqueville's American Woman and the True Conception of Democratic Progress," *Political Theory* 14(1986): 239–59. When I speak of love "in the fullest sense of the idea" I have in mind the notion of love as an ascent to the highest as expressed in its classic form by Socrates in the *Symposium.*

15. *Hamlet*, 3.1.103–15. All references to other plays by Shakespeare are to *The Complete Works,* ed. Alfred Harbage (Baltimore: Penguin Books, 1969).

16. Eric Partridge, *Shakespeare's Bawdy,* 3d ed. (London: Routledge, 1968), 106; cf. *Hamlet*, 3.4.83–86.

17. Cf. Fraser's treatment of this passage where safety from the fire is the

product of fortune understood as grace, "Shakespeare's Book of Genesis," 125–26.

18. Geoffrey Bullough, *Narrative and Dramatic Sources of Shakespeare,* 8 vols. (London: Routledge & Kegan Paul; New York: Columbia University Press, 1957–1975), 2:161.

19. In an excellent article, " 'The Place of a Brother' in *As You Like It:* Social Process and Comic Form," *Shakespeare Quarterly* 32 (1981), Louis Montrose argues that Orlando's plight as a younger brother disadvantaged by primogeniture is the source of conflicts, generational and social, the resolution of which give the plays its comic form (29). He views the play through the lens of the social anthropologist as a dramatization of a successful "transition" from youth to manhood, from poverty to gentility and the reconciliation of classes of persons divided into superior and subordinate by a patriarchal social order. This transition is brought about not by dissolving that order but by translating it "into a quiet and sweet style" (29–30, 35, 41).

20. It may be worth noting in passing that according to a tradition first recorded in the seventeenth century, Shakespeare played the part of Adam: Samuel Schoenbaum, *William Shakespeare: A Compact Documentary Life* (Oxford: Oxford University Press, 1967), 202. And like Adam, Shakespeare as a player was, at least technically, a servant of the Lord Chamberlain, obliged, in order to enjoy the law's protection, to "carry [his] patron's livery as [one of] his personal retainers," Andrew Gurr, *The Shakespearean Stage, 1574–1642* (London: Cambridge University Press, 1970), 20.

21. *King Lear*, 1.2.4. I think Montrose errs in reading into Orlando's speech the sentiments of Edmund simply because their place is similar, namely, that of younger brother (" 'The Place of a Brother,' " 30–31). For, first, Orlando's response to their similar plight is so different from Edmund's and second, Shakespeare has introduced Frederick, who does act as Edmund does, as a foil to Orlando. Cf. 41–42, 47–48. See my "Wisdom and Fortune: The Education of the Prince in Shakespeare's *King Lear*," *Interpretation* 21 (1994): 373–90.

22. Cf. Aristotle *Politics* 1269a1–2.

23. It is noteworthy that three times it is said that Duke Senior loved Sir Rowland but nowhere is it said that Sir Rowland loved Duke Senior. Sir Rowland, it may be supposed from this, is the superior of the two, the goodness of Duke Senior being reflected in his love for the best man. It may be taken as a sign of Sir Rowland's superiority that, unlike Duke Senior, he was not dispossessed of his property and, moreover, that as subordinate in rank to Senior he did not himself attempt to usurp the latter's office. The idea of such a usurpation of duke by knight is suggested by Oliver's conduct. When in scene 1, Oliver asks Charles for news of "the new court" he specifically asks about Rosalind: "can you tell if Rosalind the Duke's daughter be banished with her father?" (1.1.105–6) It is significant that he here speaks of Rosalind's father as the Duke without qualification. Charles speaks of "the old Duke"

and "the new Duke" and Oliver in his next two speeches also employs this language. But it remains that he has insinuated that the new Duke's claim to the title is less good than the old Duke's claim and thus Celia's claim as heir is less good than Rosalind's. Oliver's inquiry suggests a scheme to attain the Dukedom by marrying Rosalind and using her claim to unseat Frederick, not with a view to justice but to personal advantage.

24. Cf. Aristotle *Ethics* 1165a21–24.

25. Cf. *Hamlet*, 1.2.103–4. Arguing that Hamlet's grief at the loss of his father is excessive, Claudius says it is "To reason most absurd, whose common theme / Is death of fathers." Reason, indeed, questions the rules of the fathers and may see their deaths as an opportunity to reform; in the eyes of Claudius, however, one feels that reason's theme is less the death than the murder of "fathers" and that for strictly personal ends: Claudius is not himself a father.

26. *Richard III*, 1.1.8. In the BBC production of *Richard III* the last image offered to the viewer is one of Richard, literally, "on top of the heap," the heap being a pile of corpses with Richard's corpse in the arms of a madly cackling Queen Margaret.

27. Cf. *Pericles*, 4.3.28–39; see also, 4.Cho.5–40.

28. Cf. *Othello,* 5.1.18–20; see also, 1.3.311–14.

29. Latham offers a generally positive account of Jaques, which highlights his most attractive qualities and defends him from those critics who have seen him in the harshest light ("Introduction" to Arden Edition, xlvii and lxxvi).

30. Cf. *King Lear,* 3.2.14–18.

31. Though Harold Jenkins sees Jaques as expressing "a jaundiced view of life" and thinks it "strange that some earlier critics should have thought it might be Shakespeare's," nonetheless he links this view of life with what he takes to emerge from the conversation of Touchstone and Corin of act 3, scene 2: "In city or country, *all* ways of life are at bottom the same, and we recognize a conclusion that Jaques, by a different route, has helped us to reach before" ("*As You Like It*," *Shakespeare Survey* 8 [1955]: 45, 48). Speaking of Touchstone then as the author of this "realistic" view, he comments: "Whether he is wiser or more foolish than other men it is never possible to decide, but Touchstone is, as well as the most artificial wit, the most natural man of them all; and the most conscious of his corporal needs" (48). Cf. 50–51.

32. Latham notes that a number of critics have commented on the way in which Marston may be seen as the model for Jaques ("Introduction," xlviii–li).

33. Latham, "Introduction," xxvii; *The Poems of John Marston,* ed. Arnold Davenport (Liverpool, UK: Liverpool University Press, 1961), "Introduction," 3.

34. Cf. Robert Pierce, "Moral Language of *Rosalynde* and *As You Like It,*" *Studies in Philology* 68 (1971): 172.

35. Davenport, "Introduction" to *The Poems of John Marston,* 17; cf. Helen Gardner, *"As You Like It,"* in *Shakespeare: The Comedies,* ed. Kenneth Muir (Englewood Cliffs, N.J.: Prentice-Hall, 1965), 70.

36. *"As You Like It," Scrutiny* 9 (1940): 16; *Macbeth,* 5.5.24, 26–28. Cf. Barber, *Shakespeare's Festive Comedy,* 266, who describes it as a speech in "praise of the folly of living in time."

37. For a different account of Duke Senior's silence see Harbage, *Reader's Guide,* 234.

38. For example, see Jenkins, *"As You Like It,"* 49; Harbage, *Reader's Guide,* 235; Gardner, *"As You Like It,"* 67.

39. 2.4.65–73.

40. Cf. Davenport, "Introduction" to *The Poems of John Marston,* 18: "This corruption Marston sees as universal, and he certainly recognizes it in himself. Unlike Hall and the earlier satirists, . . . who took the standpoint of being right-minded, moral men righteously lashing the base wickedness in others, and applying in their judgments criteria of unquestionable soundness, Marston is not certain of his own criteria, and is clearly aware 'that he is part of what he is attacking. The position of superior and aloof satirist he leaves to Hall.' " Davenport here quotes Hallett Smith, *Elizabethan Poetry.*

41. As regards Rosalind's authorship of this speech, note that she uses similar language in her own name: 5.4.18, 24–25.

42. Cf. Gardner, *"As You Like It,"* 70–71.

43. Clearly this view is not that of Calvinist Christianity, the view which Davenport attributes to Marston, that "fallen man is wholly corrupt and if he is virtuous it is solely by the grace of God" ("Introduction" to *The Poems of John Marston,* 20). By introducing Jaques into the play, Shakespeare underscores the difference between a Calvinist Christian vision of nature and the Christian vision implicit in the story of Rosalind in the Forest of Arden. Russell Fraser appears to opt for a Calvinist reading of the play: "The joker in the pack and a puzzle to modern readers, grace, an absolute despot, complicates the relation between cause and effect" ("Shakespeare's Book of Genesis," 125.) For another discussion of the role of grace in the play see Taylor, "The Penalty of Adam," *passim.*

44. I wish to reserve the word mirth, both heavenly and earthly, for a positive emotion. But one might speak of a splenetic mirth that is indifferent to the harm caused by the disjunction between an original and fallen nature. Cf. *Measure for Measure*, 2.2.117–23.

45. St. Thomas Aquinas, *Treatise on Law* (Chicago: Henry Regnery, 1970), 28.

3

Wisdom and the Law: Thoughts on the Political Philosophy of *Measure for Measure*

Barbara Tovey

The opening lines of *Measure for Measure* and *The Tempest* are remarkably similar. In both plays a superior summons a subordinate, calling him by name or title and giving him commands.

> *Master*: Boatswain!
> *Boatswain*: Here, master. What cheer?
> *Master*: Good, speak to th' mariners; fall to't yarely, or we run ourselves aground. Bestir, bestir! (*Tempest*, 1.1.1–4)[1]

> *Duke*: Escalus.
> *Escalus*: My lord.
> *Duke*: Of government the properties to unfold
> Would seem in me t'affect speech and discourse,
> Since I am put to know that your own science
> Exceeds, in that, the lists of all advice
> My strength can give you. Then no more remains
> But that, to your sufficiency, as your worth is able,
> And let them work. . . .
> There is our commission,
> From which we would not have you warp.
> (*Measure for Measure*, 1.1.1–14)[2]

Thus at the very outset of these plays Shakespeare suggests that they will be concerned with the theme of rulership. In the case of *Measure for Measure* this is made fully explicit. It would be inappropriate, Shakespeare may be suggesting, for a dramatist to present a "discourse" unfolding the properties of government, but the play, which explores some of the most fundamental problems of political philosophy, will perhaps be a substitute for such a discourse.

It may be helpful to begin with a consideration of the similarities and differences between the central figures of the two dramas. Both Prospero and Duke Vincentio control the actions of their respective plays in a way that has no parallel, I believe, elsewhere in Shakespeare's plays. Each may be said to play the role of a nearly omnipotent and omniscient God, guiding and directing all of the other characters to a providentially foreordained end. It is noteworthy that at the end of *Measure for Measure* the repentant Angelo explicitly attributes godlike qualities to the duke:

> O my dread lord,
> I should be guiltier than my guiltiness.
> To think I can be undiscernible,
> When I perceive your grace, like power divine,
> Hath looked upon my passes. (5.1.364–68)

Despite his divine, or semidivine attributes, it is clear that Vincentio, like Prospero, had been far from a perfect ruler prior to the opening of the play. By his own admission he had been lax in enforcing the laws designed to curb vice, especially sexual promiscuity. The result is that Vienna became a corrupt city in which prostitution flourished and venereal disease was rampant. There was a general defiance of authority. "And Liberty plucks Justice by the nose, / The baby beats the nurse, and quite athwart / Goes all decorum" (1.3.29–31).

Why was the duke such a poor ruler? Prospero's fault was that he was a contemplator rather than a statesman; bored by the task of ruling he neglected his city in order to study the liberal arts. This element of repugnance toward political life is also present in the duke.[3]

> I'll privily away. I love the people,
> But do not like to stage me to their eyes;
> Though it do well, I do not relish well
> Their loud applause and *Aves* vehement;
> Nor do I think the man of safe discretion
> That does affect it. Once more, fare you well.
> (1.1.67–72)

> My holy sir, none better knows than you
> How I have ever lov'd the life remov'd,
> And held in idle price to haunt assemblies,
> Where youth, and cost, witless bravery keeps.
> (1.3.7–10)

Perhaps the most important single statement about the duke is that made by Escalus, describing the duke as "One that, above all other strifes, contended especially to know himself" (3.2.266–67). In the classical tradition, to come to know oneself is to acquire the highest wisdom. It is synonymous with the activity of philosophizing. There seems to be a natural tension between the quest for wisdom and the obligations of political rule. Thus Plato, recognizing this problem, stated that the philosophers must be forced back into the cave of political life, for those most fitted to rule least desire the office.

The duke's inadequacies as a ruler, then, stem in large measure from his philosophical nature. A philosophical nature may unfit a person for political rulership in at least two distinct ways. First, as in the case of Plato's philosophers, the philosopher or potential philosopher may be distracted from the task of governing by his desire to devote himself as completely as possible to contemplative activity. This desire may cause him to pay insufficient attention to the needs of the state and hence to be negligent in carrying out his political duties. Clearly something of this sort occurred in the cases of both Prospero and the duke.

There is a second way in which philosophy may limit a ruler's effectiveness. In *The Republic* Plato suggests that political rulership requires an element of harshness or, one might say, susceptibility to anger in the soul of the ruler. This is supplied by the spirited part of the soul. It is no accident that Plato's presentation of this element of the soul is embedded in the context of a discussion of the *polis*. Rulership requires a willingness on the part of the ruler to inflict some degree of pain upon at least some of his subjects, that is, to enforce the law by providing suitable penalties for law breakers. The person who devotes himself to the acquisition of self-knowledge, as is said of the duke, is likely to recognize in himself some of the faults or vices which, as a ruler, he is obligated to correct in others. When this happens his ability to feel anger may be diminished and with that his willingness to punish. Negligence, born of lack of interest, and reluctance to inflict pain, born of sympathy and understanding, are twin perils confronting the philosophical ruler.

In both *The Tempest* and *Measure for Measure*, however, Shakespeare seems to show that these perils may be successfully overcome. The philosopher may be coerced or otherwise induced to shoulder the burden of rulership, at least for a portion of his life. Seeing that failure to punish law breaking causes greater suffering for the populace than does rigorous enforcement, he will punish where punishment is necessary. But his punitive action will be tempered by mercy and understanding.

Prospero differs from the duke in that he possesses magic powers enabling him to create all manner of illusions, including the tempest itself. By means of these powers he obtains control over the imaginations of his small band of "citizens" and thus, without the use of force, is able to lead some of them, at least, from evil-doing, through repentance, to a state of grace. But Vincentio is an actual ruler in a large city, and he has no such powers available to him. His surrogate for magic is the employment of deception, disguise, and intrigue. Political skills replace supernatural agencies. "Craft against vice I must apply," Vincentio tells us (3.2.270). This very important statement leads us to one of the play's central problems. Is it legitimate for virtuous persons to employ seemingly disreputable means in the war against wickedness? Do the ordinary moral rules apply in such cases? Are there any rules that ought to be obeyed under all circumstances whatsoever?

In the play, the duke's behavior suggests a negative answer to the last two questions. Many critics have accused the duke of immoral conduct. He frequently lies, he employs every sort of deceit and trickery, he suborns officers of the law, he eavesdrops on private conversations, falsely pretends to be a member of a holy order, and in so doing violates the sanctity of the confessional. Most shocking of all to many readers is his contrivance of the bed-trick in which Mariana, instead of Isabella, is employed to satisfy Angelo's lust so that a pardon may be procured for Claudio. The duke's deliberate instigation of this plainly illegal and seemingly immoral act certainly appears to contradict his stated desire to see the law forbidding fornication more strictly enforced.

From the standpoint that regards precepts such as the Ten Commandments as exceptionless and unchangeable rules, there can be no excuse for the duke's conduct. His morality, if such it be, is of a different order. His end is the attainment of the good, but he deliberately casts off ordinary moral restraints in the process of achieving it. His is a dangerous morality, not to be widely imitated, fit only for those few possessing in the highest degree both benevolence and wisdom. Yet, despite the fact that many readers find his means distasteful in the extreme, it is an undeniable fact of the play that the duke not only aims at the good, but that he actually achieves it. Certainly the final act of the play reveals him to be a benefactor to all of his subjects.

The corrupt young rake, Lucio, slanders the duke, claiming he is a womanizer, a glutton, and a drunkard. He is the "fantastical Duke of dark corners." Lucio lies, of course. The duke is none of these things. As Escalus says, he is "a gentleman of all temperance" (3.2.231). The duke tells us his "complete bosom" cannot be pierced by "the dribbling dart of love" (1.3.29–31). Yet Lucio is not entirely without insight. He perceives that the duke does not consider himself bound by the law or by specific moral commandments. Lucio, himself a lawbreaker and an immoralist, recognizes that he and the duke are in some sense akin. But he fails to realize how utterly different their motivations are. If the duke disregards the law, he does so for reasons that are entirely unselfish. Lucio, on the other hand, breaks the law in order to gratify unrestrainedly his animal appetites. The name "Lucio" appropriately suggests a pun on "light" and "loose." But it may also lead us to think of Lucifer, the fallen angel. Lucio is an instance of the most dangerous sort of human being, a highly intelligent person who is nevertheless devoid of morality. It is not inappropriate to think of him as a comic equivalent to Iago. *Othello* is a tragedy because it is ruled by intelligent malevolence. *Measure for Measure* is a comedy because it is ruled by intelligent benevolence. Lucio is a greater threat to the duke and to the city as a whole than any other character in the play. This is why he receives the harshest treatment. We should not forget that it is Lucio who, at the end of the play, pulls off the friar's hood from the duke's head. In other words, he rips from the duke his religious disguise, but fortunately at a time when the duke, having accomplished his purposes, no longer needs that disguise.

As in the case of *The Tempest, Measure for Measure* contains one great philosophical speech delivered by the leading character. In *Measure for Measure* that speech occurs in act 3, scene 1, the ninth, and hence the central scene of the seventeen scenes that compose the play. If Lucio unmasks the duke in the final scene of the play, we may say that in this scene it is Vincentio who unmasks himself. The purpose of this speech is to woo Claudio from his attachment to the vanities of this life and to reconcile him to death. We may recall Montaigne's famous words that philosophy is a preparation for death. Since the duke is wearing the costume of a friar, we might well expect a traditional statement of Christian doctrine to the effect that this world, a vale of tears, is merely a passageway to the glories of the next. But this is most emphatically not what we get. As J. W. Lever remarks, "The Duke's description of the human condition eliminates its spiritual aspect and is essentially materialist and pagan."[4] More shocking still, his speech contains not a single reference to a deity or to the afterlife.

The immortality of the soul is tacitly rejected. Death is not a gateway to a better existence. The reason it should be welcomed rather than feared lies in the misery of *this* life. Death is nothingness. It is identified with sleep: "Thy best of rest is sleep; / And that thou oft provok'st, yet grossly fear'st / Thy death, which is no more" (3.1.17–19). We are reminded of Socrates' statement in the *Apology* that death consists either of a happy existence with the great men of the past or else it is a state of sleep. Socrates points out that most persons think themselves better off when asleep than they are in the waking life. Consequently, death should not be feared. Ironically, there is also a pointed similarity between the duke's conception of death and that attributed to Barnardine, the lowest and most animal-like character in the play. Pompey says of him:

> A man that apprehends death no more dreadfully but as
> a drunken sleep; careless, reckless, and fearless of
> what's past, present, or to come: insensible of
> mortality, and desperately mortal. (4.2.140–43)

In act 5 the duke rebukes Barnardine with these words:

> Sirrah, thou art said to have a stubborn soul
> That apprehends no further than this world,
> And squar'st thy life according. (5.1.478–80)

But the duke might well have addressed the same reproach to himself. Judged by conventional standards, the duke's philosophical and theological opinions are as disreputable as his behavior. Yet Claudio, the one person exposed to his teaching, is in no way harmed by it. On the contrary, he is enabled to face what he believes to be the approach of death with serenity. It is rather when he forgets the duke's instruction and returns to a belief in a life after death that he undergoes severe moral deterioration. Turned into a coward by the torments he imagines waiting for him in the next world, he begs Isabella to yield up her virginity in order that his life may be spared. We shall shortly see that belief in an afterlife is also a source of psychological torment and moral weakness for his sister.

It is interesting to note that the duke's speech in *Measure for Measure* bears a spiritual affinity to the famous speech by Prospero in act 4 of *The Tempest*. Prospero's speech is less offensive to a Christian audience than the duke's, but Prospero also suggests that death is no more than sleep.

> We are such stuff
> As dreams are made on; and our little life
> Is rounded with a sleep. (4.1.156–58)

However, Prospero expands the duke's teaching concerning the mortality of the soul into a metaphysical doctrine concerning the entire realm of becoming. Prospero echoes the teaching of Plato. Like the "insubstantial pageant" of Prospero's masque, the world of things that are generated and come to be is merely an image of reality. Everything in it, including the earth itself, is doomed to fade away.

Like Prospero, the duke is a philosopher-king in the Platonic sense. His rule, wholly beneficent in purpose, is the rule of wisdom unfettered by law. From his point of view no moral rules are absolute. All have exceptions. Thus it is justifiable to violate the rule against lying if so doing will result in the greatest good. Furthermore, the duke's behavior indicates clearly his belief that in the best regime each individual, insofar as possible, should be dealt with in accordance with his particular needs and deficiencies. The ultimate purpose of the law is not vengeance, but rather to bring each person to the highest degree of perfection of which he or she is capable. The duke's attitude is perfectly expressed by Prospero.

> Though with their high wrongs I am struck to th' quick,
> Yet with my nobler reason 'gainst my fury
> Do I take part. The rarer action is
> In virtue than in vengeance. They being penitent,
> The sole drift of my purpose doth extend
> Not a frown further. (5.1.25–30)

To the duke's conception of law and rulership is opposed that of Angelo. He believes the law should be applied uniformly to all those falling within its scope. Lever correctly says "Angelo would limit all judicial procedure to the determination and punishment of guilt. Claudio, having infringed the law, must die 'tomorrow.' No extenuating circumstances need be considered."[5] In other words, all violators of the law are equally deserving of punishment and to the same degree. There are no legitimate exceptions to legal and moral rules.

What is Isabella's stance on this issue? Commentators on the play have developed conflicting answers. Because she pleads with Angelo to suspend the law in her brother's case, Harry Jaffa refers to her position as "antinomianism." He maintains that the logical result of antinomianism is that "justice—and the rule of law—have no basis in nature or reason."[6] It would seem to follow that it is not obligatory to obey either manmade or natural law. Darryl Gless, on the other hand, says of Isabella:

> The essence of her nature lies in her allegiance to a system of man-made laws that are fundamentally at odds with other, transcendent laws to which the play's language persistently alludes.[7]

Thus he claims:

> . . . her impending view of chastity, defined as strict physical virginity, seems to assume for her a stature reserved in Protestant theology for much loftier, less physical laws.[8]

Her religiosity, he says, has a "legalistic character."[9]

How does it happen that two very able commentators come to such different conclusions concerning Isabella's view of the law? Is either of them correct? Can either position be ascribed to the duke? Let us turn to a consideration of these questions.

Isabella presents to Angelo a number of arguments designed to persuade him to pardon her brother. Several of them seem to support Jaffa's contention that she holds the position of antinomianism. We shall consider first the argument from mercy. This is put forward in the following speeches.

> No ceremony that to great ones longs,
> Not the king's crown, nor the deputed sword,
> The marshal's truncheon, nor the judge's robe,
> Become them with one half so good a grace
> As mercy does. (2.2.59–63)

> Why, all the souls that were, were forfeit once,
> And He that might the vantage best have took
> Found out the remedy. (2.2.73–75)

Here, it is clear, Isabella is conceiving of mercy as something entirely distinct from justice. Mercy consists of a free pardon that is in no way conditioned upon the merit or deserts of the recipient. The supreme example of mercy, of course, is that shown by Christ to a sinful and wholly undeserving humankind. Isabella urges Angelo to imitate that example. Angelo makes no reply to this appeal, but had he desired, he could have done so. The answer is that if every judge shows mercy to every criminal, no one will ever be punished and the system of justice will collapse. Thus the appeal to mercy can be considered an antinomian argument.

The second argument is based upon the command: "Judge not, that ye be not judged." Escalus had already presented this argument to Angelo in an attempt to secure Claudio's pardon.

> Let but your honour know—
> Whom I believe to be most strait in virtue—
> That in the working of your own affections,
> Had time coher'd with place, or place with wishing,
> Or that the resolute acting of your blood
> Could have attain'd the effect of your own purpose,
> Whether you had not sometime in your life
> Err'd in this point, which now you censure him,
> And pull'd the law upon you. (2.1.8–16)

Isabella repeats the argument frequently (2.2.64–66, 75–79, and 137–42). Angelo's answer to both of them is essentially this: If I am found guilty of a fault for which I condemn another man, the proper remedy is not to revoke my condemnation of him, but to punish me as I punished him (2.1.17–31). This argument of Isabella's may also be thought of as antinomian, since, according to Christian doctrine, every man is sinful and deserves to be "judged." Hence no man is qualified to judge another.

A third antinomian argument, never explicitly spelled out, is put forward by Isabella in an extraordinarily eloquent speech (2.2.111–24). Here she suggests that all human political authority, all human judgment, is a travesty of divine justice. Hence, presumably, the wise man would cease to judge and cease to wield authority.

But does Isabella really accept these antinomian arguments? Jaffa himself emphasizes that she does not. She prefaces her case for Claudio's pardon with the following speech.

> There is a vice that most I do abhor,
> And most desire should meet the blow of justice;

For which I would not plead, but that I must;
For which I must not plead, but that I am
At war 'twixt will and will not. (2.2.29–33)

So she *does* judge the vice of lechery and she does desire to see it punished. The law prescribing the death penalty for fornication she calls "just but severe" (2.2.41). At the conclusion of her appeal to Angelo she admits:

To have what we have, we speak not what we mean.
I something do excuse the thing I hate
For his advantage that I dearly love. (2.4.118–20)

Her arguments have been mere rhetorical devices designed to sway Angelo. In the next act we shall see her judging both Claudio and Angelo with the utmost severity and calling for their deaths (3.1.135–46, 232–33).

All the arguments Isabella presents are based upon principles that, if consistently carried through, would make any system of legal justice impossible. It does not follow, however, that there are not other, more persuasive arguments that would be immune to this criticism. Isabella's true view of law and justice is revealed more by the arguments she does not present than by those she does. Let us begin by considering yet another argument she does put forward that we have not yet examined.

Good, good my lord, bethink you:
Who is it that hath died for this offence?
There's many have committed it. (2.2.88–90)
So you must be the first that gives this sentence,
And he, that suffers. (2.2.107–8)

Jaffa (who seems inclined to believe that the condemnation of Claudio is not unjust) defends Angelo against this criticism.

The first falling of the "blow of justice" will appear to be, *and indeed will be*, arbitrary. It will be arbitrary, because there is no *reason* why that first blow should fall on one rather than another, of those "many" that have committed this offense. Yet, if there is to be a rule of law, one where crime and punishment are justly and reasonably and surely proportioned to each other, the blow must fall somewhere upon someone.[10]

Jaffa's defense is predicated upon the assumptions that all violators of the law are, in the moral sense, equally guilty and that there are no extenuating circumstances that make some offenders less deserving of punishment than others. But these assumptions are clearly false. Consider a government that, in the attempt to stem a wave of robberies, prescribes the death penalty for stealing. For its first arrest, it singles out a starving man who has stolen a piece of bread, ignoring bank robbers, highway bandits, and their ilk. This kind of arbitrariness is neither necessary nor just.

A case like this helps us to see how Isabella might have argued on Claudio's behalf. She could certainly have maintained that Claudio was guilty in a technical sense only. Claudio and Juliet were, as we would say today, mutually consenting adults. They were in love, they intended marriage, and they were faithful to each other. Furthermore, they had entered into a contract to marry that was legally binding and under the law of England was equivalent to marriage (1.2.134–38). Consequently it is doubtful that they were even technically guilty of fornication. Why, Isabella might have asked, do you not reserve the death penalty for the pimps and whores and their promiscuous customers who are spreading moral corruption and venereal disease throughout the city and inflict upon Claudio some appropriately milder punishment?

Interestingly enough, precisely such an argument on behalf of her condemned brother is made by Cassandra, the counterpart of Isabella in the source play, *The Historie of Promos and Cassandra*, by George Whetstone.

> Weigh his yong yeares, the force of love, which forced his amis;
> Weigh, Weigh, that Mariage works amends for what committed is.
> He hath defilde no nuptial bed, nor forced rape hath mov'd,
> He fel through love, who never ment but wive the wight he lov'd.
> And wantons sure to keepe in awe these statutes first were made,
> Or none but lustfull leachers should with rygrous law be payd.[11]

In the *Hecatommithi* of Giraldi Cinthio, Epitia makes a very similar plea.

> [S]he went to Juriste and prayed him to have compassion on her brother, because of his youth (he was no more than sixteen years old) which made him deserving of pardon, and because of his inexperience of life, and the violent impulse that Love had in his heart. She argued that many wise men held the opinion that adultery committed through the violence of Love, and not undertaken to do injury to a woman's husband, deserved

> a less penalty than if committed with injurious intent; that the same might be said in her brother's case, who had done the deed for which he was condemned not out of malice but spurred by ardent love; that he was ready and willing to marry the girl, and do whatever else the law might demand . . . . She believed that the law had been thus severely framed to strike terror rather than to be rigorously carried out, for it would be (she pleaded) cruel to punish with death a crime which could be honourably and religiously recompensed to the satisfaction of the injured party.[12]

Shakespeare, then, was well aware of what could effectively be said in Claudio's defense and deliberately withheld such a speech from the character of Isabella. Why? The answer is that Isabella was precluded from making a defense of this kind because she held a view of law and justice identical to Angelo's. Like him, she held that moral rules have no exceptions and that violation of the rule cannot be mitigated by extenuating circumstances. Lever correctly says: "At no point in the crucial debate of act 2, scene 2 does she set forth Claudio's special case, or urge the arguments for moderation which stem from his individual plight."[13]

This attitude of rigid subservience to the letter of the law goes to the roots of Isabella's character and intellect. When Angelo asks her if she would be willing to redeem her brother by yielding up her body to him, she refuses on the grounds that violating the commandment against fornication would cause her to "die forever," i.e., to be eternally damned (2.4.107–9). She attributes to God, that is to say, an inability or unwillingness to make a moral distinction between a person committing fornication out of lust and one who does so unselfishly in order to save the life of a beloved relative. The former case is an example of indulgence; the latter of self-sacrifice. This alleged inability or unwillingness on the part of God is comparable to Angelo's failure to distinguish, for example, between the cases of Lucio and Claudio. Gless aptly remarks:

> This implies that Angelo's iron law is God's law. As the debate proceeds, we recognize with growing conviction that Isabella's theology posits a God created in Angelo's image and similitude, an idea that conflicts with the vision of benign deity she had promoted earlier. (2.2.73–79)[14]

Isabella cannot comprehend that there may be exceptions to the commandment prohibiting fornication. Her fundamental misconception of the nature of morality is the ultimate cause of her moral collapse and her fiendish behavior to her brother.[15] Her terrible display of anger toward Claudio no doubt results from a conflict between her sisterly desire to save him and her selfish, but understandable, fear of eternal torment. Fear wins the battle. But her fear originates in an intellectual error concerning the nature of moral commandments.

The prominence of the debate between Angelo and Isabella leads us to believe that the most fundamental opposition in the play is between these two characters. In fact, the deepest antagonism is that which exists between Angelo and Isabella on the one hand and the duke on the other. Why, then, does Shakespeare make his duke choose to marry Isabella?

Let me suggest the following answer. *Measure for Measure* is concerned, at least in part, with the relation between the kind of morality that is expressed in terms of rigid obedience to absolutized commandments and the morality that regards such commandments as having no ultimate sanction except insofar as they contribute to the attainment of what is good. On the political level the play raises the profound question as to the proper relation between the rule of law and rule by the free discretion of a wise and benevolent statesman. We are, of course, given no easy answer, but the play seems to indicate that each kind of rule needs to be reinforced by the other. Rigid law enforcement without regard to the special circumstances of the case in hand results in injustice and cruelty. On the other hand, in actual states even the wise ruler cannot dispense with general laws that are impartially enforced. Prospero could rule over his few island subjects without benefit of laws because he was able to keep each of them under his constant surveillance and direction. A large city such as Vienna, however, cannot be governed in this way even by the wisest of rulers. The duke tried to rule without law, or at least without enforcing some necessary laws. The result was chaos and corruption.

Just as Angelo needed to make amends to Mariana, Claudio to Juliet, and Lucio to Kate Keepdown, so the duke needs to make amends to the city and its law. The marriage of the duke and Isabella, a marriage of opposites, allows each of them to correct the defects of the other. Isabella's overly rigid devotion to the letter of the law will henceforth be guided and inspired by the duke's wisdom and discretion. His wisdom will be supplemented by her law-abidingness. This will correct his tendency to be lax in enforcement and over forgiving. Her religiosity and his religious skepticism will temper each other. Very appropriately, the duke closes the play by saying to Isabella: "What's mine is yours, and what is yours is mine" (5.1.534). Their marriage represents what is politically the highest desideratum, the union of wisdom and the law.

Notes

1. Cited from Alfred Harbage, ed., *William Shakespeare: The Complete Works* (New York: The Viking Press, 1977).

2. All quotations of *Measure for Measure* are taken from the Arden edition, ed. J. W. Lever (London: Methuen and Co., 1965.)

3. These similarities between the two characters have been noted by Harry V. Jaffa, "Chastity as a Political Principle: An Interpretation of Shakespeare's *Measure for Measure*," in *Shakespeare as Political Thinker*, ed. John Alvis and Thomas G. West (Durham, N.C.: Carolina Academic Press, 1981), 181–213.

4. Lever, *Measure for Measure*, lxxxvi.

5. Lever, *Measure for Measure*, lxvii.

6. Jaffa, "Chastity," 207ff.

7. Darryl J. Gless, *Measure for Measure: The Law and the Convent* (Princeton: Princeton University Press, 1979), 141.

8. Gless, *Law and Convent*, 129.

9. Gless, *Law and Convent*, 131.

10. Jaffa, "Chastity," 201.

11. Geoffrey Bullough, ed., *Narrative and Dramatic Sources of Shakespeare*, vol. 2 (London: Routledge and Kegan Paul, 1962), 452.

12. Bullough, *Sources of Shakespeare*, 2:422.

13. Lever, *Measure for Measure*, lxviii.

14. Gless, *Law and Convent*, 125.

15. It may be argued that I am offering contradictory views of the act that Isabella would have performed if she had surrendered to Angelo's demand. On the one hand, I characterize it as a noble act of self-sacrifice. On the other hand, I call Claudio a coward for attempting to persuade Isabella to perform it. Thus it may seem that I am characterizing one and the same act as being simultaneously noble and ignoble. My reply is that Isabella's act of surrendering to Angelo, had she performed it, would not have been the same act as that of Claudio's attempting to persuade her to surrender. So there is no contradiction in characterizing the one act as noble, the other as ignoble. For example, it is easy to see that the act of sacrificing one's life may, under appropriate circumstances, be morally praiseworthy. Yet the act of attempting to persuade someone else to make that sacrifice may be morally wrong. For example, it might be praiseworthy on my part to donate a vital organ, let's say a kidney, to a relative or friend, but wrong to try to persuade me to make that donation. Just so, it might be noble for Isabella to surrender to Angelo and yet be ignoble of Claudio to try to persuade her to do that.

Even if one concedes that Isabella is morally justified in refusing to make this sacrifice, there is still the problem of her abusive treatment of Claudio when he gives in to his fear of death and the afterlife. For many different reasons I may be perfectly justified in refusing to donate a kidney to my relative or friend. This does not justify me in excoriating or cursing him when he asks for the sacrifice. On the contrary, it would seem that I was morally bound to treat the person whose request I was denying with the utmost sympathy.

4

The Portrait of Athens in *A Midsummer Night's Dream*

David Lowenthal

This is the only Shakespearean play named for an experience—whose we are not told.[1] It is also one of three plays set in ancient Greece, and one of two in Athens. By contrast to the Roman plays, all four of which are tragedies, only one of the three Greek plays, *Timon of Athens*, is plainly a tragedy. *Timon* is appropriately set in the decadence of late Athens, while *Midsummer*, a delightful comedy, takes place in early Athens. The third Greek play, *Troilus and Cressida*, occurs during the Trojan Wars, and, despite being named a tragedy even in the First Folio, seems at least equally if not predominantly comical. These facts suggest that Shakespeare thought Rome a grave place inherently unfit for the lightheartedness of his comedies. Is Rome therefore superior to Athens, or inferior because less complete? *Midsummer* is also the oldest of all the plays in its setting, reaching back to the time of Theseus and Hercules for its action, just before the Trojan War. Despite this, the play is made to feel utterly contemporary rather than antique.

Shakespeare draws most of his main characters—Theseus, Egeus, Hippolyta, Lysander, Demetrius—from the pages of Plutarch's *Lives*, but not without changing them radically. In Plutarch they are great commanders, in *Midsummer* lovers. To make this possible, the play presumes that human life has become entirely civilized, without the slightest remnant of barbarism, war or violence. Commanders are no longer needed. Shakespeare testifies to this transformation humorously by naming one of his fictional characters Philostrate (lover of war in the

Greek) and having him serve solely as master of revels for Theseus's impending wedding.

What will this wonderful and much-beloved play tell us about Athens, renowned for its democracy, philosophy, and drama? Much to our surprise, democracy is not mentioned, nor philosophy. There is even no reference to Theseus's historic role (as Plutarch describes it) of founding Athens *and* its democracy. For in Plutarch Theseus does two remarkable things that perhaps warrant Plutarch's awarding him opening position in the series of lives comparing Greeks and Romans. He brings the parts of the city together into a unified whole and establishes a people's government. But if all this is to be ignored by Shakespeare, why write a play in which Theseus is the commanding presence at all? We will see that much in the play does in fact relate to the origin of democracy in Athens, and to the Athenian source of philosophy and drama as well.

The action of *Midsummer* takes the form of four streams, some of which meet at different points within the play, and all of which converge at the end. Soon after Theseus announces his upcoming marriage to Hippolyta, the unhappy lovers and the unhappy father of one of them are introduced, and then the artisans rehearsing *Pyramus and Thisby* for Theseus's wedding. Only the dispute between Oberon and Titania, king and queen of the fairies, awaits act 2 to appear. After that point, the action involves the interplay of these four streams.

Reason and Nature

Under Shakespeare's Theseus, Athens is a dukedom governed by Theseus alone, but he is expected to rule in accordance with ancient law. No priesthood exists, and only a mild form of nobility: the lovers are obviously upper class, as distinguished from the artisans, but without the heavy trappings of feudalism. In fact, an atmosphere of equality suffuses Theseus's court itself, and even the artisans enjoy a certain elevation in Athens.

Early in the play, Theseus is presented with a political problem of great significance for the coming of democracy. Egeus (his name is taken from Aegeus, Theseus's father in Plutarch's *Life of Theseus*) stalks into the court demanding that Theseus apply Athens's ancient law to his daughter, Hermia. According to this law, a father has the right to determine whom his daughter marries, her refusal being punishable by death. Theseus does not deny the law's existence or relevance. Yet his initial effort to explain it to Hermia and the apparently strong support he expresses for it already contain subtle signs of his disagreement with it, until finally, in act 4, he "overbears" Egeus and frees the lovers to marry whom they please.

Why is this change momentous? Shakespeare seems to pay little attention to it, but there are many reasons for considering it the principal action of the play. To see this we must collate the indications he supplies about what, for want of a better term, may be called the "old regime" in Athens—the ancient form of society up till then. During this older period, life was based on force and hence on the superiority of men to women and parents to children. Wars, rapes, and conquests were common. A daughter was the property of her father—the very point Egeus makes about Hermia:

> I beg the ancient privilege of Athens:
> As she is mine, I may dispose of her;
> Which shall be either to this gentleman
> Or to her death . . . (1.1.41–44)[2]

In the play, Theseus himself has already completed great conquests and (just as in Plutarch) been involved in rapes as well. Even now, he is culminating a military victory over Hippolyta with a marriage to which she seems to have consented, thus supplying a suitable framing event for the general transformation of life presumed in the play.

Consistent with this picture, the very woods around Athens have been civilized by gamekeepers so that no wild animals threaten those, like the lovers and artisans, who remain there for extended lengths of time. Theseus praises his hunting dogs more for the music of their baying than for their savagery or ability to hunt (4.1.122). Similarly, the fierce rivalries of the lovers Demetrius and Lysander, Helena and Hermia are often on the point of breaking into open violence, and certainly threaten it, but never actually do. Oberon and Titania, when most hostile to each other, never come to blows. As if to prove the point, violence does appear only in the artisans' play, where Pyramus's error in thinking Thisby slain by a lion leads to his suicide and then hers.

The duke supplants the ancient regime based on the power of fathers, from which the law to which Egeus appeals is derived, with a regime based on voluntary love and individual consent. The coming of the new principle is foreshadowed by the atmosphere of equality already present in Theseus's court, his manner toward the common people, and the equality between the sexes already prevailing among the lovers. Theseus himself therefore prepares the way for democracy, but why? On what basis does he institute this revolutionary change?

To understand Theseus's thinking, we must put together things found in different parts of the play. At the very beginning, no reason is given for the decision he and Hippolyta have made to set their wedding at the next new moon. Later in the play, Theseus leaves the palace to perform some kind of observation or observance—a word with religious connotations (4.1.103). Shortly thereafter, stumbling upon four lovers asleep in the woods, he says: "No doubt they rose up early to observe, / The rite of May . . ." (4.1.131–32). This gives the impression that some kind of religious observance, out in nature in the month of May, was general in Athens at that time. Earlier Lysander had planned with Hermia to meet her in the wood ". . . Where I did meet thee once with Helena / To do observance to a morn of May . . ." (1.1.166–67).

This going out on a May morning is the only religious practice of the Athenians that we learn about. Their references to the traditional gods and goddesses, and particularly to those not connected with love, are remarkably rare. The gods seem to be supplanted by the immortal fairies, who generally seek to benefit men and are less fearful. Now May is generally associated with the flowering of nature, and morning with nature at its fresh and radiant awakening from night. But a particular morning, such as the first day in May, is not clearly called for by the indications we are given in the play, despite repeated commentary to the contrary. This day may or may not coincide with the new moon in a given year. Perhaps the duke's attending on the new moon and his observing the rite of May are parts of one outlook by which nature is taken as a standard or guide. The weddings are to take place in a temple, but nothing is said about the kind of ritual employed there.

Quite Puckishly, Shakespeare waits till the beginning of the last act to reveal crucial aspects of the duke's thinking. Hippolyta opens it by commenting on the strangeness of the stories the lovers have told about their forest adventure, to which Theseus makes this splendid and oft-cited reply:

> More strange than true. I never may believe
> These antique fables nor these fairy toys.
> Lovers and madmen have such seething brains,
> Such shaping fantasies, that apprehend
> More than cool reason ever comprehends.

The lunatic, the lover, and the poet
Are of imagination all compact.
One sees more devils than vast hell can hold:
That is the madman. The lover, all as frantic,
Sees Helen's beauty in a brow of Egypt.
The poet's eye, in a fine frenzy rolling,
Doth glance from heaven to earth, from earth to heaven;
And as imagination bodies forth
The forms of things unknown, the poet's pen
Turns them to shapes, and gives to airy nothing
A local habitation and a name. (5.1.2–17)

This is the finest speech in the play, but what are we to make of it? Is it not astonishing? Until that point, Theseus hardly seems given to philosophical thought, but consider the implications of his words. "Cool reason" is the standard for judging the truth of things, and reason rejects not only the imaginings of lunatics, lovers, and poets but also "antique fables"—the old stories, the old traditions, including the stories about the gods. We are not told that the practitioners of "cool reason" are philosophers, but what else but philosophy would distinguish between reason and the various forms of imagination, including poetry? What else would determine the truth or falsity of the antique tales about the gods?

In the first form philosophy took among the Greeks, using reason alone to understand the world, philosophers attributed the source of all things to nature rather than the gods. And this continued to be true among all their successors, with the exception of the Skeptics. Shakespeare seems to want us to realize that his Theseus, somewhere along the way, has come into contact with these early philosophers and been persuaded to follow a new and more peaceable life, a life according to nature. If he considers life according to nature to entail harmonizing with the rhythms of nature, he might very understandably set his marriage at the new moon and engage in his May morn observance as well.

It is also true that Theseus's celebration of "cool reason," with its critique of "antique fables," "fairy toys," and poetic imagination, could not have been completely true in Shakespeare's eyes. In fact, Shakespeare must surely disagree at certain points with his own Theseus. For if he agreed with this denigration of "fairy toys," why does he give fairies so prominent a part in the play—even to the point of having them bless the newly married couples in their bedchambers on their wedding night? While allowing poets a certain grandeur in glancing from heaven to earth and earth to heaven, Theseus nevertheless dismisses them as working solely in the realm of imagination, not reason—despite the fact that the play itself is poetry. He treats imagination generally almost as a faculty we can do without, but it is imagination that has helped produce him and the whole play.

Shakespeare does not indicate clearly just what philosophy Theseus has come to accept. Unlike pre-Socratic philosophy as a whole, it has not caused him to lose interest in human affairs, and it is at least compatible with the view that nature's regularities and beauties are what make it fit for adoption as the guide for human life. In its depreciation of religion and poetry, however, Theseus's philosophy goes too far. Yet Theseus himself is a lover, and in his last speech, just before the fairies (unbeknownst to him) actually take over at bedtime, he can say, "Lovers, to bed; 'tis almost fairy time" (5.1.353)—as if he realizes that concessions must be made to the imagination by reason itself. In fact, Shakespeare's plays can be understood as embodying the primacy of "cool reason" in directing the imagination to its own purposes. For it is reason, not imagination, that discerns truth from falsity and provides us with knowing guidance. Without reason, imagination would wander aimlessly, unconnected with truth. But reason itself may have to grant the necessity to human life of "antique fables" and even "fairy toys," despite their lacking a basis in reason. Reason alone provides man with seeing guidance, but reason needs the imagination to portray and influence humankind. Most of the time, it must even hide its own existence behind that of imagination; this speech of Theseus's is one time when it does not.

Reason and Consent

There must be some connection between Theseus's rule of reason, based on nature, and his turning from the ancient law, based on the rule of fathers, to the voluntary consent of lovers. Reason and nature must demand this choice, but on what grounds? The rule of fathers has obvious defects. It gives authority to fathers as such rather than to wise fathers, thus deriving it from the loins rather than the mind. Is it based on the father's role as progenitor, or on his superior strength? If it applies to the relation of fathers and daughters, can it be kept from making sons obey and causing authority to be shared with mothers? It might also end up requiring every generation of males and females to obey its living predecessor, with the consequence that only the oldest generation alive would command and all the rest obey. That it leads to something like gerontocracy, probably male gerontocracy, has contradictory consequences: the old are also weak, but it started from the idea of the superior strength of fathers. Finally, as in the play, it denies any place to a love between the sexes that is independent of paternal command, thereby laying an infirm basis for marriage.

This is the reasoning we can supply to support Theseus's decision philosophically. The play the artisans rehearse and then perform, *Pyramus and Thisby*, has some bearing on it. It is inherently a tragedy caused by the wall the parents of Pyramus and Thisby have erected to separate them. When Quince first allocates roles (1.2.52 ff.), Thisby's mother and both fathers are to have a part along with the others, but when the play is actually performed, these roles have silently and completely dropped out of the picture. This movement away from the parents, and particularly the fathers, parallels what happens in Athens under Theseus. Moreover, the way the artisans convert what is essentially a tender and tragic story into side-splitting comedy has a similar effect: it detracts from the claim of fathers, parents, or elders to be taken seriously. As if to underline this conclusion, Shakespeare arranges for Egeus to say nothing after hearing Theseus's final verdict about the lovers in act 4 and then to be completely absent from the festivities of the last act. The fathers, the rule of the strong and the old, and, with them, the ancestral must weaken and disappear.

This undermining of tradition and custom cannot be good in all respects. Shakespeare realizes that the voluntary principle allows for impulsive and immature behavior on the part of young lovers and will often lead them to make bad choices. Hermia is quite fresh in speaking up against her father to the duke, but Theseus seems not to take notice of it, perhaps attributing her rebellious tone to suppressed independence or pride. And it is true that Puck's use of the magic distillation to cause instant changes in the affections of the lovers he touches leaves the impression of fickleness and inconstancy on their part. Nevertheless, these lovers are remarkably steady in their affections. Hermia and Lysander do not cease on their own to love each other, and Helena to love Demetrius. Only Demetrius's inconstancy in deserting Helena for Hermia needs to be remedied by the fairies' intervention. Even Oberon and Titania, for all their jealousies and arguments, give the impression of being an enduringly happy couple. And we suspect that Theseus himself is now marrying for the first time because he realizes that, in the new society of individual consent, the ruler must exemplify the responsible use of this freedom.

Political Implications

Once the voluntary principle is established in marriage, along with its corollary equalities, it is but a short step to its political expression in the form of democracy. The democracy thus implied in the play is actually more complete than Athenian democracy ever was, since it would treat women as equals whose free consent is as important as that of men. Whether this democracy is consistent with nature in other respects is a fundamental question suggested by other parts of the play itself. We see that some of the artisans have severe intellectual shortcomings, and that Duke Theseus is the superior of everyone. Are these facts consistent with democracy? If, in addition, it can be shown that some other principle, like virtue or wisdom, is by nature higher than consent, then democracy may not end up being the demand of nature. The supreme political issue, then, of who should rule is not completely settled by this play. But with the reduction of force and violence in the world, men need no longer submit to a government they have not chosen. A variety of choices will now be open to them for the first time.

Shakespeare throws amusing light on the main alternatives through the Thespian mechanics who are preparing a play as entertainment at the duke's wedding. Peter Quince calls his group together and assigns their roles. He may also have written the original script, since he does some further writing at Bottom's behest. How he became director is not stated, but no one challenges his right to the position. Everyone seems perfectly aware that you cannot put on a play by democratic means: the company must be monarchically run, its prime object being to produce an excellent performance. Quince does, however, meet with a peculiar challenge from Bottom, who tells him what to do every step of the way. When Quince assigns Bottom the title role of Pyramus, Bottom asks whether Pyramus is a lover or a tyrant.

In Bottom's mind, these are the only alternatives, and he would rather act the part of a tyrant, associating it with the great hero, Hercules (1.2.24–25), and thus giving added confirmation to some of our earlier speculations. He considers a tyrant violent and lofty. He even proceeds to display something like a tyrannical element in his nature by wanting to play not only Pyramus but Thisby and the lion as well: he wants all the best roles. Quince does not yield to these demands, yet manages to stay in control without becoming harsh to Bottom. Nor does Bottom really mean his demands tyrannically: with no wish to exploit others, he is simply convinced of his own excellence. Quince is able to accept Bottom's often imaginative and (in its own way) sound advice while setting limits to which Bottom acquiesces. Because of this, they make a fine team.

Quince persuades Bottom to restrain his appetite for roles by appealing to the love of beauty and virtue that is in him and by praising the character of Pyramus as one Bottom can aptly portray. Bottom's love of excellence also shows itself in his exhortation to his fellows as they plan their next rehearsal: "We will meet, and there we may rehearse most obscenely and courageously. Take pains, be perfit . . ." (1.2.96–97). Not for him the mercenary attitudes of Snug and Flute (4.2.15–22). And his gentlemanliness continues under the magical spell of Puck and Oberon, when, wearing the head of an ass, he becomes the beloved of Titania, Oberon's queen. With several tiny sprites at his beck and call, he remains most courteous to them. Thus, despite his inclination to engross the action, Bottom's friends think the world of him. They value his intellect and character alike. Not only has he "the best wit of any handicraft man in Athens," but "the best person too" (4.2.9–11). In short, he is possessed of both intellectual and moral excellence!

Just as the company of artisans exhibits the working of monarchy or aristocracy at its best, with the common people sharing the aim of wiser and more virtuous rulers whom they admire, love, and obey, so something similar happens on a political plane in Athens. Democracy may necessarily grow out of Theseus's decision in favor of consent and love, but his own dukedom, for all of its near-democratic spirit, is not a democracy. It involves a form of popularized monarchy based on the love of the people for him combined with a kind of appreciative condescension on his part. When Bottom distinguished between lovers and tyrants, he may have associated the former with private life, the latter with political life. If one considers all Shakespeare's writings together, love and politics may be said to be his primary subjects too and in some ways the main alternatives in life. But Bottom is wrong to identify politics with tyranny and associate it with the violence of Hercules. Bottom does not allow for a regime akin to himself, Peter Quince, and Theseus. When the rule of barbarism declines, and civilized reason prevails, two forms of regime not based on force and violence arise for consideration. One is democracy, based on consent; the other, aristocracy, based on merit or virtue.

The Origin of Drama

Shakespeare gives an extraordinary amount of attention in *Midsummer* to the play within a play—the rehearsal and performance of *Pyramus and Thisby*. It far exceeds Hamlet's use of the "mousetrap" and may well exceed all the other plays in this respect. Is it only for the marvelous comic effects he is able to produce? The story of Pyramus and Thisby is a tragedy. It parallels the plot of *Midsummer* in having as its theme the plight of lovers blocked by their parents. In the play itself it is the duke's revolutionary change of the law that liberates the young and prevents the tragedy that would take place were the old Athenian law enforced. In the hands of the artisans, however, this play is transformed into a comedy, even a farce.

Shakespeare shows how to gain this effect. He gives a lesson in comic writing, using an essentially tragic tale as his material. Mispronunciations, missed cues, improper meter, wrong words, and, of course—among the funniest—a naive inability on the part of the artisans to appreciate the distinction between drama and reality make the laughter almost continuous. Of course, the men have no idea what havoc they are wreaking with the original as they proceed.

The most interesting of these sources of buffoonery is their inability to appreciate that a drama is a conscious imitation of life rather than life itself. Drama requires a unique capacity: the audience must be able to go along with the drama, become immersed in its fictitious action, while still realizing that it is only a drama. Through the artisans Shakespeare shows how difficult it is to achieve this frame of mind, how unnatural it is, in a sense, even on the part of those who are already makers by trade and know something about art. Or, to put it another way, since this is a play about Athens, he shows what Athens had to accomplish in order to originate and cultivate drama. By the coordinate subjects of the play, he suggests also that this development has some connection with the moral and political changes he examines, and with the coming of philosophy as well. The rule of force and bodily strength must recede; conscious reason, and imagination with it, must advance, preparing the minds of audiences who can appreciate drama, artists who can write it, and actors who can play it. With its emerging and enlarged individualism, Athens will be able to do what Sparta and other cities could not in philosophy and drama alike.

Older commentators have observed a discrepancy in the lapse of time in the play, but with some disagreement about the amount of this discrepancy. According to Theseus's opening remarks to Hippolyta, their wedding is planned for the beginning of the new moon, which they expect to show itself on the night of the fourth day after. The lingering old moon must disappear and then (leaving aside the technical fact that a short period of no moon intervenes), the sliver of new moon will first appear. But if the play is read carefully, the wedding actually takes place two nights after the one beginning the play. Lysander and Hermia arrange to meet in the woods the very next night, when the artisans also hold their second rehearsal. The lovers spend that night in the woods and are accidentally discovered early the next morning by Theseus. Three weddings instead of one and the performance of *Pyramus and Thisby* all take place that night.

There is no scene during daylight of the first day after the beginning. Acts 2 and 3 occupy the night of that day, with the transition to the following morning occurring in act 4, scene 1. The rest of that scene and all of the next are in the daylight of that second day, and the wedding takes place that night. So the promise of four days into the future for the wedding turns out, in fact, to be two. Why? No indication of time in Shakespeare, whether of period, year, month, or day, or of transition from one time of day to the next is to be ignored. In this case, Shakespeare may be imitating his own Puck, the mischievous fairy, by demonstrating the power of the artist to alter reality within the work he has produced.

If the Creator Himself can produce seven days, the poet can promise four and cause two of them to vanish. Quite simply, he is not bound by the real world, from which it also follows that he must be watched with great care, since he can effectively produce falsity as well as truth. He might even find it necessary to use falsity to convey truth. At one point Shakespeare has Bottom reveal his experience with Titania in terms that parallel, and confuse, a passage in First Corinthians concerning the life Christ prepares for us (4.1.208–10).[3] He follows this up by endowing Bottom with the gift of prophecy and having him report—before the duke has selected his entertainment for the evening—that their play has been chosen.

Despite these seeming miracles, it should be borne in mind that the setting Shakespeare chooses for most of the action lies beyond the legal limits of the city, out in nature. It is to nature, beyond the reach of convention, that he turns our attention with the lovers, and to nature again as the background for both the dramatic art of the artisans and the mischievous playfulness of the fairies. Nature becomes and remains the standard, but we must not forget that the nature typified by the forest around the city is not nature in the rough, nature wild, but nature calmed and beautified by the action of man.

We come to the final question: whose dream is being conveyed in this play, and when does it occur? Editors tell us that "midsummer night" refers to the night before June 24, a celebration of St. John the Baptist's festival the next day, involving games, merrymaking, witchcraft, enchantment, madness, etc. Midsummer itself seems to have some association with the summer solstice, June 21. As for dreams, within the play the lovers have dreams, and Bottom too. At the very end, Puck asks the members of the audience to think they were asleep and dreamed what they saw if they were offended by the play. To add to the confusion, the action within the play itself seems to take place at either of two different times. According to some indications, it occurs in May rather than on or about midsummer night. But Titania gives us the impression that, while the beginning of midsummer has passed, midsummer itself is still lingering on (2.1.82). Despite this confusion, it is plausible to assume that the dream mentioned in the title is the dream someone might have on a night like midsummer's night, with its various popular connotations. The most likely dreamer is Shakespeare himself, but the dream he dreams is the play, which in its rational structure is far from a mere dream.

Notes

1. This essay shares many themes with Richard H. Cox's fine chapter, "Shakespeare: Poetic Understanding and Comic Action," in *The Artist and Political Vision*, ed. Benjamin R. Barber and Michael J. G. McGrath (New Brunswick, N.J.: Transaction Books, 1982).

2. Harold F. Brooks, ed., *A Midsummer Night's Dream* (London: Routledge, 1979).

3. 1 Cor. 2.9.

Part II

Histories

5

Coming Home: The Political Settlement in Shakespeare's *King John*

Christopher Colmo

King John portrays the nearly successful invasion of England by the French. This success is made possible in part by the revolt of John's nobles, who aid the invaders. In the last scene of the play, Sir Richard, the bastard son of Richard Coeur-de-lion but knighted by King John, proclaims to the rebels, who have newly returned their allegiance to John, that England can never again be successfully invaded as long as these same lords remain loyal.

> Now these her princes are come home again,
> Come the three corners of the world in arms,
> And we shall shock them. Naught shall make us rue,
> If England to itself do rest but true.[1]

England is safe as long as her princes "welcome home again discarded faith" (5.4.12), i.e., are loyal to England's king.

There is an ambiguity in this homecoming, for it is not clear whether in coming home the nobles are to put the good of the nation above their own or, alternatively, to return to their own true interest. Does Shakespeare ask the nobility of England to return to their "discarded faith," according to which their first loyalty is to the throne, or does he propose a new basis for the loyalty of England's princes to her king?

According to Sigurd Burckhardt, *King John* shows us the break down of the old order—that "discarded faith"—without showing us anything new to put in its place.[2] In *King John*, law and divine right—whether directly from God or mediated by the church—are all found wanting as a basis for royal authority. But is it true that Shakespeare offers no alternative to "old right" (5.4.61)? When John asks Philip, the bastard son of Sir Robert Falconbridge, "What men are you?," Philip (who is shortly to become Sir Richard) answers, "Your faithful subject I, a gentleman" (1.1.49, 50). This is the bastard's first utterance, and it points to the actual problem of the play. The English lords are shown to act as if their own position does not depend upon the king. Is it possible to have a class of gentlemen, of nobles, who are also faithful subjects? The problem of royal authority is to be solved not by looking to the king alone but by creating a new nobility. The insight and character acquired by Philip in the course of the drama provide a model for the gentleman who can be a faithful subject.

In the first lines of the play, the French ambassador, addressing John, refers to the "borrowed majesty of England," implying John's usurped authority, not only over certain provinces in France, but also over England and Ireland. Shakespeare meets this challenge by generalizing it. All majesty is borrowed majesty, at least in the sense indicated by the play. A king who does not know this cannot build a solid foundation for his rule.

That John does not fully grasp this last point can be seen from his response when the papal legate, Pandulph, asks him why he has refused to acknowledge Stephen Langton as Archbishop of Canterbury. John's refusal to explain himself is itself explained (Is this not a contradiction?) in the following speech.

> What earthy name to interrogatories
> Can task the free breath of a sacred king?
> Thou canst not, cardinal, devise a name
> So slight, unworthy, and ridiculous
> To charge me to an answer, as the Pope.
> Tell him this tale, and from the mouth of England
> Add thus much more: that no Italian priest
> Shall tithe or toll in our dominions,
> But as we under God are supreme head,
> So under Him, that great supremacy
> Where we do reign, we will alone uphold
> Without th'assistance of a mortal hand.
> So tell the Pope, all reverence set apart
> To him and his usurped authority. (3.1.147–60)

John claims to need no mortal assistance in upholding alone a supremacy he receives directly from God (also 3.1.170). The play does not show God maintaining John's right, if he has any. Constance, Arthur's mother, seems closer to the mark when she says that Fortune has given John majesty (3.1.54–61); chance, not God, has brought John to the throne. To the extent that his luck runs out, John is, indeed, left alone; Richard's loyalty is his one continuing piece of good fortune. John's weakness when he is alone (not least, the noticeable loss of courage after the death of his mother [4.2.116–81]) coupled with his corresponding dependence on Richard, show that all majesty is borrowed from its relations with others. However much kings may think themselves absolute, their power is relative. Nothing is in itself alone. The rebel, Salisbury, says that Falconbridge "alone upholds the day" (5.4.4–5), but Richard knows it is not so (5.1.78–79). Richard counts on the friendship of those he has befriended, such as Hubert, and on the loyalty of princes now "come home again."

When Fortune fails John, he turns to the church and to the Pope's legate, Pandulph. At the beginning of act 5, John yields his crown to Pandulph, and receives it again from him, "as holding of the Pope, / [His] sovereign greatness and authority" (5.1.3–4). John thus fulfills the prophecy, delivered by Peter of Pomfret, according to which the king would deliver up his crown "ere the next Ascension Day at noon" (4.2.151). John tells himself that when he scoffed at the prophecy he thought the prophet meant to say that the king would deliver up his crown under constraint. "But, heav'n be thanked, it is but voluntary" (5.1.29). Given that John renders up his crown only as a desperate measure to get Pandulph to halt the invasion of his country by the French, we are amazed that John can comfort himself with such sophistry.

By the charter of May 1213, John made England and Ireland feudal fiefs of the Apostolic See. According to his biographer, "This unexpected move by John worked like a charm."[3] Perhaps it did, but Shakespeare does not show ultimate subservience by the king to religious authority in a favorable light. Instead, the church appears a weak reed on which to lean. Pandulph can break up the newly made peace between England and France by excommunicating John over the Langton affair (3.1.172–79), but he cannot turn back Lewis, the Dauphin, in the middle of an invasion that promises success (5.2.65–78). John gets nothing for his submission but humiliation and Richard's contempt. Perhaps the low point for John is when he asks Richard to have "the ordering of this present time" (5.1.77). If this is not abdication of his throne, it is certainly abdication of his authority. This outcome is the ultimate consequence of John's subordination of national independence to papal authority.

Pandulph arrives at Angiers with his demand that John recognize Stephen Langton as Archbishop of Canterbury shortly after King John has ended his conflict with King Philip of France through the arranged marriage of John's niece, Blanche, to the Dauphin. After excommunicating John, Pandulph requires that Philip break his newly made peace with England on pain of being likewise excommunicated (3.1.295, 319). Breaking the league with John will lead immediately to war between France and England; indeed, this is the result Pandulph wants. To the Dauphin, newly married though he be to the Lady Blanche, it is clear that "a heavy curse from Rome" is harder to endure than "the light loss of England for a friend" (3.1.205–7). Later, refusing to halt the invasion of England, Lewis has no trouble putting his own interests and ambitions above Pandulph's demands, but Lewis's father is simply torn apart by the conflicting claims upon him.[4] The theological-political problem as Shakespeare presents it is ultimately a question of what force will rule in the king's own mind, political reasoning or religious faith. While Philip is surely the legitimate king of France, he lacks the clarity of thought that is the most rational title to rule. It is embarrassing to hear him, in the utmost perplexity, tell the Cardinal, "make my person yours, / And tell me how you would bestow yourself" (3.1.224–25). The term "borrowed majesty" surely applies to one who cannot govern others because he cannot govern himself. The real danger in priestly power is the division it creates in the mind of the king himself. Philip's own loyalty seems to be divided between his political interests and what he thinks to be the salvation of his soul. As we shall shortly see, this seems to be a large part of John's problem in the last act of Shakespeare's play. It is worth noting that Pandulph suffers no such division in his own mind. While his advice to Lewis is certainly Machiavellian, he at no time seems to be in rebellion against himself (3.4.107–83). He is at one with himself in promoting the interests of his prince.

While Pandulph may be of one mind with himself, the same cannot be said of King John in his dealings with the problem of Arthur. Though he is steadfast in the matter of Stephen Langton, he is consumed by guilt when he thinks Hubert has carried out his order to kill Arthur. There is a decided contrast in John as ruler before and after he learns of Arthur's supposed murder at 4.2.68. Prior to this scene, John is shown as a just judge (in the dispute between Falconbridge and his brother) and an energetic ruler. Even after his excommunication, he conducts the ensuing conflict with the French so vigorously that Lewis and Philip in defeat cannot help but praise him (3.4.10–16). Later, he is afraid even to hear bad news (4.2.131–36). No doubt learning of his mother's death shortly before has shaken him, but in his interview with Hubert some seventy lines later, his concern seems to be with his own damnation (4.2.203–18). "Hostility and civil tumult reigns / Between my conscience and my cousin's death" (4.2.247–48). Hubert offers to "make a peace between your soul and you" by telling John that Arthur is alive (4.2.250–51). But even the knowledge that he did not, in fact, kill Arthur does not restore John's confidence. The next time we see him, he is offering up his crown to the Pope.

One of the princes who must "come home again" if England is to be secure is surely the king himself. Both kings, English and French, must come home not to "discarded faith" but to the concerns of this world; in this way they will come home to themselves. The political settlement to which Shakespeare points in *King John* is one that will be simply that, political and not religious. Political reasons, not conscience, must prompt the actions of kings. Division of mind must be replaced by unity of purpose. Shakespeare lets us see, however, that political integrity on the part of the king is only half of the answer. If the political settlement is to be stable, subjects too must be moved by political interests, above all, national independence, rather than by pangs of conscience.

In his private conversation with Lewis (at the end of act 4), Pandulph explains that John must kill Arthur and that this, coupled with John's pillaging of the monasteries in England, will cause John's own subjects to revolt (3.4.162–81). The play supports Pandulph's analysis of the revolt by the nobility, an analysis that traces the seeds of the revolt to religious sensibilities. When Salisbury suspects that John is being told of Arthur's murder, he gives a religious interpretation to the change of color in the king's face, as he is swayed "Between his purpose and his conscience" (4.2.77). John himself repents when he sees how the nobles react to the report of Arthur's death (4.2.103) and seems to think that the discovery that it is a false report will be enough to win them back (4.2.260–62). Hubert, who failed to carry out his commission to kill the prince, reports to John that the rumor of the boy's death is causing unrest throughout the land (4.2.185–202). When Salisbury forbids his soul obedience to John and makes "a holy vow" to avenge Arthur's death, Pembroke and Bigot answer, "Our souls religiously confirm thy words" (4.3.60–73). Though the last line of the play expresses the Bastard's hope that "England to itself do rest but true," Salisbury, in confirming his alliance with Lewis, declares his wish that the sea "Would bear thee [England] from the knowledge of thyself" into a league with France for the purpose of going on a crusade "unto a pagan shore" (5.2.33–39).

J. L. Calderwood sidesteps the conflict of religious and political considerations by treating the nobles' pious indignation at the murder of Arthur as so much rationalization and hypocrisy to cover their own hopes of gaining through their treason.[5] In this view, Lewis pulls the mask off their hypocrisy when he tells them: "Come, come; for thou shalt thrust thy hand as deep / Into the purse of rich prosperity / As Lewis himself" (5.2.60–62). Calderwood seems to assume that a conflict between patriotism and conscience should not be credited. At the bottom of such an apparent tension we will find self-interest, which, in one of the play's best known speeches, Richard dubs Commodity (2.1.561–98).

Calderwood's assumption, however, cannot account for the struggle each of the kings suffers in his own mind between the claims of nation and the claims of Christendom, at least as the latter are represented by the Church. Richard, indeed, seems not to be torn in this way, but then he is a man of dubious piety: "I will pray, / If ever I remember to be holy" (3.3.14–15). Shakespeare's gentleman is also a faithful subject because his loyalty belongs to England, not to Christendom. Richard's susceptibility to the attractions of Commodity lure him away from the concerns of the other world. "Since kings break faith upon commodity, / Gain, be my lord for I will worship thee" (2.1.597–98). This may be corruption, but it is a corruption that leads Richard away from the dark path of treason. Beaurline (note to 2.1.573) is only half right when he defines Commodity as "self-interest at the expense of honour and the general welfare."

Self-interest properly understood may contribute to the general welfare when pious indignation leads to treason. From this point of view, Salisbury and his fellow nobles would have been less inclined to treason if they had been more inclined to look after their own self-interest. One can hardly agree with Calderwood when he says of Richard that "it is plainly to his advantage to follow the departed nobles" into the French camp. Indeed, one wonders what blindness could cause the English lords to give their allegiance to a prince who "means to recompense the pains you take by cutting off your heads" (5.4.15–16). If, as Calderwood asserts, the highest form of honor, as it presents itself in the play, is "loyalty to the good of England,"

Shakespeare means to show that this is a basis for reconciling honor and self-interest.[6] Calderwood rightly says that Richard is loyal, not to John, but to England. Richard does not here sacrifice Commodity to Honor; Honor and Commodity are here united in a national interest that is also Richard's own interest. The common loyalty of king and subject to a shared national interest is the political settlement at which Shakespeare aims through the ambiguous figure of the Bastard in *King John*.

The settlement is political, not legal. Is John the legal heir to the throne, or is he an usurper? The problem with this question becomes clear from the legal dispute between Philip and his brother Robert. John's adjudication of this dispute takes up most of act 1 (at a time when one would think John would be too busy making preparation for his speedy departure into France). Philip is Robert's elder brother, so that by right of primogeniture Philip should inherit the lands of his father, Sir Robert Falconbridge. Sir Robert, however, disinherited his eldest son on the suspicion that Philip was the product of an illicit union between Lady Falconbridge and the king, Richard Coeur-de-lion. John sets aside the will and gives the land to Philip, on the grounds that a married woman's children are legally her husband's children, regardless of biological paternity. W. H. Matchett alleges that through John's ruling, Robert is being "legally cheated."[7] In his note to 1.1.109, however, Beaurline asserts that "the king rules strictly according to law." The point here seems to be that there are good arguments on both sides; there are even good arguments for and against primogeniture itself. Royal authority must impose a conventional solution that cannot help but be somewhat arbitrary. For this very reason, law cannot be the ultimate source of royal authority. In her desperation to defend Arthur's claim to the throne, Constance hits upon the truth. "Law cannot give my child his kingdom here, / For he that holds his kingdom holds the law" (3.1.187–88). Sovereignty is the source of law, not the other way around. These remarks on the limits of constitutionalism are, at any rate, not challenged by Shakespeare's silence regarding the Magna Carta.

Lineal inheritance as a title to the throne must ultimately come through a first king who did not hold his title by descent, and primogeniture, which determines which son will inherit, is not part of the natural order of things.[8] When, at the close of the play, Richard kneels before John's son, Henry, he is paying homage to political reality as much as to hereditary right. Half of Richard's own forces have been lost by accident in the tides (5.6.39–40). If Richard does not attempt to place himself on the throne, the reasons are more political and military than they are legal.[9]

Richard's situation at the end of the play parallels John's at the beginning. Each has an opportunity to seize the throne, and each faces a young boy as rival. History repeats itself. What should Richard have learned from the spectacle of John's rivalry with Arthur? To answer this question, we must ask another.

What should King John have done about Arthur? Murdering him in captivity in England is certainly no solution; it leads to the revolt of his nobility. For John's purposes it would have been better if Arthur had died in France, and best of all if Arthur had been killed in the attempt to capture him. (The poet himself lets Arthur die by chance while attempting to escape.) Once Arthur is John's prisoner, John becomes Arthur's prisoner, unable to get rid of this threat to his crown. As Pandulph rightly foresees, it is the murder or supposed murder of Arthur that causes the nobility to revolt (3.4.145–59; 4.2.69–102). Under the circumstances, should John have stepped aside in favor of Arthur? Perhaps John might have had "the ordering of the present time" while Arthur wore the "borrowed robes" of majesty.[10] Certainly this is a possibility for Richard in his relations with Henry.

But is this what the nobles of England should seek, Arthur wearing the crown? Only Constance, his mother, seems to think that "Nature and Fortune joined to make" Arthur great, so that he deserves a crown (3.1.50–53). The citizen who speaks for Angiers in the *Trouble-some Raigne* comes closer to the truth when he says that Arthur "is but young, and yet unmeete to raigne."[11] Shakespeare, more ruthless in a way, puts the damning assessment into Arthur's own mouth: "I am not worth this coil that's made for me" (2.1.165). From a strictly political point of view, the least rational speech Richard makes is the one in which, having found the boy dead, he calls Arthur "The life, the right, and truth of all this realm" (4.3.144). It is no accident that Shakespeare prefaces this speech by having Richard admit: "I am amazed, methinks, and lose my way / Among the thorns and dangers of this world" (4.3.140–41). Richard's speech about Arthur is confused. Is Arthur at any time anything other than a pawn of the French? Is it not for Arthur that so many French and English soldiers fall before Angiers (2.1.283–86)? Certainly Arthur is one of the princes who must come home again if England is to have peace.

While the unscrupulous Pandulph might have seen Arthur merely in such a light, we know that Shakespeare did not. Shakespeare does not allow us to see Arthur only from a political point of view. In one of the most moving scenes of the play, Constance explodes in violent grief over the loss of her son. Pandulph "comforts" her by telling her she is mad, but Constance denies it. Is it madness to be constant in a world where nothing lasts? Constance wishes that she were mad so that she might forget the loss of her son. "Preach some philosophy to make me mad," she tells him (3.4.51). Pandulph might preach philosophy to make a mother mad, but we can be sure that Shakespeare would not. Many of the most touching scenes of the play are those that show grief over Arthur. Even in a play as political as this one, or perhaps especially here, Shakespeare is aware of the limits of the political.

Not the least of those moved by pity for the plight of Arthur is Hubert, whose commission it is to torture the young prince to death. This he cannot do in the face of Arthur's pleading. As Burckhardt points out, there is a striking contrast between the arguments Arthur uses to dissuade Hubert in *Troublesome Raigne* and those he uses in *King John.*[12] In *Troublesome Raigne*, Arthur argues that Hubert's duty to God outweighs his duty to the king. He counsels Hubert not "to loose salvation for a Kings reward" (1.1390). "In the earlier play," writes Burckhardt, "Arthur pleads not so much with Hubert as for him." It is of note that while Shakespeare's play clearly presents the conflict between secular and religious authority, Burckhardt is right to say that Hubert's refusal to carry out John's order is presented in terms of human sympathy, not obedience to a higher law. Burckhardt sees in Shakespeare's version of the scene a rejection of the old order or, at least, a recognition of the breakdown of Tudor authority. One need not dispute this interpretation. One must question, however, whether the moral arguments of *Troublesome Raigne*, if valid, are not much stronger than the claims of pity raised by Arthur. Could not any prisoner, even one justly punished, plead in such terms as Arthur uses? The reader is left to ponder why Shakespeare deprives Arthur of arguments that carry moral authority.

Truly to "come home again," both the princes and the kings of England must take Richard as their model. But as his speech over Arthur's body shows, not even Richard has fully solved the problem of divided loyalties, the problem that runs throughout the play and is the antithesis of coming home again. Richard has priorities, but there are tensions among the objects that he seeks. He would rather follow John than Pandulph or the French. He seeks Commodity but he would not abandon a soldier's honor. He follows John but he grieves for Arthur. It is of note that John does not solicit Richard to deal with Arthur. If the play shows us anything, it shows that it is human nature to be divided. If the full solution of the political problems were to overcome these divisions, that solution would make us less human than we are and need to be. "The attempt to make man absolutely at home in this world ended in man's becoming absolutely homeless."[13]

The deepest theme of the play is nicely crystallized in the marriage of Lewis and Blanche. The citizen of Angiers says that before her marriage Blanche is a "divided excellence" (2.1.439), as is Lewis. These two, he says, will find completion in their union as husband and wife. Of course, as soon as the conflict between England and France is renewed, the Lady Blanche, at least, is again divided (3.1.326–38), this time between the claims of marriage and the claims of nation. An unmarried person can be spoken of as a divided excellence in so far as he or she is completed in marriage, but this completion itself divides both husband and wife from other attachments, other forms of belonging or being at home, which may themselves have been a kind of excellence, though divided from the whole which is marriage. In Blanche's case, Shakespeare lets us see the whole that should complete her, her marriage, become one pole of the conflict that divides her when her husband wars with her uncle. Strangely enough, a whole which completes us becomes a source of the division within us when it must compete with other "wholes" of which we are a part. Family, church, and nation, but also Commodity and Honor, are the competing "wholes" that define both the limits and the possibilities of the political settlement in *King John*.

Notes

1. All citations are to L. A. Beaurline, ed., *King John* (Cambridge: Cambridge University Press, 1990).

2. Sigurd Burckhardt, "*King John*: The Ordering of This Present Time," ELH 33 (June 1966): 133–53; reprinted in Burckhardt, *Shakespearean Meanings* (Princeton: Princeton University Press, 1968).

3. W. L. Warren, *King John* (London: Methuen, 1961), 208–10.

4. Did Lewis learn something from his intervening interview with Pandulph (3.4.107–83)?

5. James L. Calderwood, "Commodity and Honour in *King John*," 90–91, in Eugene M. Waith, ed., *Shakespeare: The Histories* (Englewood Cliffs, N.J.: Prentice-Hall, 1965), 85–101.

6. Calderwood, "Commodity and Honour," 85, 97.

7. William H. Matchett, "Richard's Divided Heritage in *King John*," 154,

in J. L. Calderwood and H. E. Toliver, eds., *Essays in Shakespearean Criticism* (Englewood Cliffs, N. J.: Prentice-Hall, 1970), 152–70.

8. Cf. *Troilus and Cressida*, 1.3.106 with Burckhardt, "*King John*," 139.

9. Cf. Calderwood, "Commodity and Honour," 100; Matchett, "Divided Heritage," 168–69.

10. The phrase is from *Macbeth*, 1.3.109. In *King John*, the notion of borrowed majesty is acted out in the form of borrowed robes by Austria's wearing of the lion's skin (3.1.128–29).

11. *The Troublesome Raigne of King John*, 1.759. This anonymous play dating from 1591, is often regarded as the source of Shakespeare's play. *Troublesome Raigne* is printed in full in Geoffrey Bullough, ed., *Narrative and Dramatic Sources of Shakespeare* (New York: Columbia University Press, 1962), IV, 72–151.

12. Burckhardt, "*King John*," 136–38.

13. Leo Strauss, *Natural Right and History* (Chicago: University of Chicago Press, 1953), 18.

6

The Education of Hal: *Henry IV, Parts One and Two*

Tim Spiekerman

Parts 1 and 2 of Shakespeare's *Henry IV* are just as concerned with Hal, the man who will be king, as they are with King Henry IV himself. While the plot follows Henry's ultimately successful attempt to preserve the throne he stole from Richard II, the dramatic intensity is generated by Hal's troubled relationship with his father, and his troubling relationship with Falstaff. These relationships are politically significant because Henry and Falstaff are the primary influences in the young prince's life and their effect upon Hal provides great insight into his later career as king.

Henry IV is often underevaluated or overlooked, but he is a rather impressive political figure; Hal could find worse models to imitate. With no claim to the throne, Henry quietly and efficiently installed himself as king, killed Richard II, and prevailed over his well-armed opponents. His career provides a case study of how to acquire and maintain political power successfully. But if Henry is able to do what is politically necessary, it does not come easily to him, and he spends a good deal of his reign questioning the justice of his deeds. Henry is an ambivalent Machiavellian, a prudent political calculator with a conscience.[1]

Falstaff, the other influence in Hal's life, is not a political man. He is a drunk, a lecher, a thief, and a liar. He is also delightfully entertaining and exceedingly wise, and may well be responsible for Hal's fantastic success as king. For after his experience with Falstaff,

Hal appears to adopt the Machiavellianism that is only half-realized in his father.

I

King Henry IV's reign is dominated by two problems, one political, the other moral: he must confront his armed opponents, and he must come to grips with what he did to gain the throne. These two problems converge in Henry's desire to lead a Crusade to the Holy Land, which he sometimes characterizes as a personal quest to absolve himself of his political sins, and other times as a political maneuver to divert his ambitious opponents. The key to Henry's character lies in discerning his true motive, for in asking why he wants to go to the Holy Land, one is really asking what kind of a man Henry is, a Machiavellian or an individual plagued by a guilty conscience.

The idea for a Crusade comes to Henry soon after King Richard II's death. Perhaps gazing at the funeral casket encasing the murdered king, Henry declares that "I'll make a voyage to the Holy Land, / To wash this blood off from my guilty hand" (*Richard II*, 5.6.49–50).[2] His contrition sounds genuine, and Shakespeare offers no evidence to the contrary. But when Henry repeats his desire a year later—"Therefore, friends, / As far as to the sepulchre of Christ" (*1 Henry IV*, 1.1.18–19)—his guilt appears to have subsided. One is struck immediately by the difference in tone in Henry's opening remarks in *1 Henry IV*. The self-doubt and urge to confess are gone, replaced by a measured, statesmanlike demeanor. Henry's conspiracy against a legitimate king and the ensuing civil war are recounted in the most abstract terms. Richard is not mentioned, blame is neither given nor accepted, justifications are not offered. Choosing the most distant and impersonal images to describe the civil conflict, Henry compares the warring parties to "the meteors of a troubled heaven" (*1 Henry IV*, 1.1.10). It is almost as if England had suffered some natural catastrophe, a flood or a plague, for which no individuals bear responsibility. And while Henry has not forgotten the Holy Land, his reasons for going have changed. What began as a desire to repent has become a clever political project. Apparently no longer in need of personal absolution, Henry now sees a Crusade as the perfect vehicle to unite his fractious kingdom.

The evidence that Henry's motive is now political is strengthened when we learn that he has no intention of going to the Holy Land at this time. When informed of heavy fighting in Wales as well as in the north, Henry postpones the trip. But he already knew about the battle up north (*1 Henry IV*, 1.1.62–75); he knew before delivering his speech about a unifying trip to the Holy Land that no Crusade would take place. The purpose of the speech must then be political: Henry wants the moral credit for his apparent piety and high-minded call for unity without the risk of actually leaving England. Simple common sense dictates that an astute politician with a tenuous grip on power would not leave the country, and Henry knows as much from experience: he waited for Richard to leave for Ireland before launching his own military campaign for the crown. Thus a picture emerges from the first scene of a complicated man whose public rhetoric is an untrustworthy reflection of his private aims, the same man who said publicly that he had no designs on Richard's kingship while furiously planning his deposition.

This initial impression, however, is misleading. As the plays progress, we learn that Henry has not in fact exorcised his guilt over Richard and that his motivation to lead a Crusade is not consistently political. In a private conversation with his son, Henry wonders whether Hal's riotous and disrespectful behavior is not God's punishment for his political deeds:

> I know not whether God will have it so
> For some displeasing service I have done,
> That in his secret doom out of my blood
> He'll breed revengement and a scourge for me;
> But thou dost in thy passages of life
> Make me believe that thou art only mark'd
> For the hot vengeance and the rod of heaven,
> To punish my mistreadings. (*1 Henry IV*, 3.2.4–11)

Henry's uneasy conscience appears to be the source of the illness which overcomes him in *2 Henry IV*. Falstaff diagnoses the king with "lethargy," caused by "much grief, from study, and perturbation of the brain" (*2 Henry IV*, 1.2.110, 114–15). Clarence attributes the "pangs" he fears will kill his father to the "incessant care and labour of his mind" (*2 Henry IV*, 4.4.117–18). The king himself complains of insomnia (*2 Henry IV*, 3.1.4–31) and a "weary spirit" (*2 Henry IV*, 4.5.3). Henry's guilt is also evident in his attempt to recast his rise to power in a more flattering light: "necessity so bow'd the state / That I and greatness were compell'd to kiss" (*2 Henry IV*, 3.1.73–74). This rationalization stands out because both earlier (*1 Henry IV*, 3.2.39–54, 93–96) and later (*2 Henry IV*, 4.5.183–85, 190–91, 218), Henry is remarkably frank about the true causes of his political success. Finally, Henry's preoccupation with Jerusalem in *2 Henry IV* appears to have more to do with easing his conscience than diverting his opponents. His calls for a Crusade are accompanied by guilty talk of Richard (*2 Henry IV*, 3.1.65–108), or worries about Hal's fitness to succeed him that call into question the justice of his deposition of Richard (*2 Henry IV*, 4.4.1–4).

But if Henry's motives for going to the Holy Land are confused, they do follow a certain logic. Everything depends on Hal. Henry's judgment about the morality of his own political career appears to rest on his judgment about the kind of king his son will prove to be. His persistent fear that Hal will be a spectacular failure as king leads Henry to wonder whether his deposition of Richard can be justified. His doubts about Hal fuel his guilt over Richard, and in such moods his thoughts turn to the Holy Land, full of repentance. But when Henry is confident that Hal will succeed as king—and this is true only at the very end of his life—his self-doubt is replaced by an honest and unapologetic appraisal of his rise to power and a direct admission that his motive for going to the Holy Land was emphatically political:

> God knows, my son,
> By what by-paths and indirect crook'd ways
> I met this crown . . .
> It seem'd in me
> But as an honour snatch'd with boist'rous hand . . .
> And all my friends, which thou must make thy friends,
> Have but their stings and teeth newly ta'en out;
> By whose fell working I was first advanc'd,
> And by whose power I well might lodge a fear
> To be again displac'd; which to avoid,
> I cut them off, and had a purpose now
> To lead out many to the Holy Land,
> Lest rest and lying still might make them look
> Too near unto my state. (*2 Henry IV*, 4.5.183–85, 190–91, 204–12)

And in addition to acknowledging the Machiavellian principles that guided his political career, Henry recommends a similar course to Hal: "Therefore, my Harry, / Be it thy course to busy giddy minds / With foreign quarrels, that action hence borne out / May waste the memory of the former days" (*2 Henry IV*, 4.5.212–15).

Henry's final confidence cannot, of course, erase the memory of his nearly debilitating guilt, and one can detect some residual moral queasiness in his parting advice to his son. The "foreign quarrels" Henry recommends to Hal are not specified. He does not advise a trip to the Holy Land, a project somehow intimately his own. Henry's choice of that particular political diversion was not accidental and is perfectly emblematic of this sometimes moral, sometimes Machiavellian figure. Shakespeare ends the scene with a poignant reminder of Henry's dividedness. After delivering his hard-boiled political speech to Hal, Henry asks to be carried to the palace's Jerusalem room to die:

> It hath been prophesied to me, many years,
> I should not die but in Jerusalem,
> Which vainly I suppos'd the Holy Land.
> But bear me to that chamber; there I'll lie;
> In that Jerusalem shall Harry die. (*2 Henry IV*, 4.5. 236–40)

II

Henry IV's deathbed reconciliation with Hal is preceded by years of disappointment and distrust. Hal is not the son Henry desires. In fact, he claims to prefer the son of his enemy:

> Yea, there thou mak'st me sad, and mak'st me sin
> In envy that my Lord Northumberland
> Should be the father to so blest a son;
> A son who is the theme of honour's tongue,
> Amongst a grove the very straightest plant,
> Who is sweet Fortune's minion and her pride;
> Whilst I by looking on the praise of him
> See riot and dishonour stain the brow
> Of my young Harry. O that it could be prov'd
> That some night-tripping fairy had exchang'd
> In cradle-clothes our children where they lay,
> And call'd mine Percy, his Plantagenet! (*1 Henry IV*, 1.1.77–88)

Henry's apparent preference for Hotspur is more than a passing thought. Again at act 3, scene 2, Henry's expression of disappointment in Hal is accompanied by envious comparisons with Hotspur, whose courage and sense of honor seem to be lacking in his own son. And as Hal's earlier satire of Hotspur's famed courage seems to indicate, the comparison is a familiar one:

> I am not yet of Percy's mind, the Hotspur of the North, he that kills me some six or seven dozen of Scots at a breakfast, washes his hands, and says to his wife, "Fie upon this quiet life, I want work". "O my sweet Harry", says she, "how many hast thou killed today?" "Give my roan horse a drench", says he, and answers, "Some fourteen", an hour after; "a trifle, a trifle". (*1 Henry IV*, 2.4.99–106)

But Henry's preference for Hotspur is more complicated than it might seem. In short, he is more impressed with Hotspur's virtues as a son than he is with his virtues as a warrior and a politician.

The qualities Henry praises in Hotspur are not particularly conspicuous in himself. While no coward, Henry does not impress one primarily as a courageous man (prudence comes first to mind); and while politically daring and extraordinarily shrewd, he is not singled out, as is Hotspur, for his physical courage. Henry is never shown fighting in *Richard II*, and in the battle scenes in *1 Henry IV* the field is filled with kingly clones (this is historically accurate). Neither is Henry an especially honorable man. We know from *Richard II*, where he tells everyone, including the king, that he does not seek the throne, that Henry's word is worthless. And in a play famous for Falstaff's critique of honor, Henry offers something similar when he confides to Hal the strategy he employed to gain Richard's throne. The key to politics, Henry explains, is the clever manipulation of public opinion through the presentation of an appealing public image:

> By being seldom seen, I could not stir
> But like a comet I was wonder'd at,
> That men would tell their children, "This is he!"
> Others would say, "Where, which is Bolingbroke?"
> And then I stole all courtesy from heaven,
> And dress'd myself in such humility
> That I did pluck allegiance from men's hearts,
> Loud shouts and salutations from their mouths,
> Even in the presence of the crowned king.
> (*1 Henry IV*, 3.2.46–54)

There are no appeals in this discussion to God or political tradition, no talk of what is just or right or honorable, only "opinion," "popularity," and "admiring eyes." Perceptions, Henry teaches Hal, are just as important as deeds, and praise can be earned whether or not it is deserved. This is not to say that Henry's deposition of Richard was unjust, and one must take care to distinguish questionable means from the ends they serve. But Henry is clearly more comfortable talking about how to acquire and retain power than he is in outlining its ultimate purpose, and his considerable political success would not be possible if honor were a primary concern.

Unlike both Henry and Hal, who might be described as thoughtful men of action, Hotspur is all action and little thought. Sensitive to the slightest insult, loyal to a fault, ready to fight and kill at the drop of a hat, brimming with righteous indignation, Hotspur is heroism incarnate. But like Shakespeare's Achilles, he is a simpleminded hero, the pawn of his wiser father and uncle, who manipulate him into acting without his being aware of it. (In *Troilus and Cressida*, Ulysses does the same to Achilles.) When Worcester tries to explain the rebel strategy for unseating King Henry, a riled Hotspur will not listen: "All studies here I solemnly defy, / Save how to gall and pinch this Bolingbroke" (*1 Henry IV*, 1.3.225–26). This calls to mind Ulysses's complaint about the Greek warriors in *Troilus and Cressida:*

> They tax our policy and call it cowardice,
> Count wisdom as no member of the war,
> Forestall prescience, and esteem no act
> But that of hand. (*Troilus and Cressida*, 1.3.197–200)

As Hudson notes, " . . . [Hotspur's] qualities unfit him, in great measure, for military leadership in regular warfare . . . He is qualified to succeed only in the hurly-burly of border wars, where success comes more by fury of onset than by wisdom of plan. . . ."[3]

But perhaps Henry's preference for a man so unlike himself is not so unusual after all. Those qualities desired by a father in his son are not necessarily the same as those qualities he seeks in himself. Hal is disobedient and irreverent, Hotspur the opposite. Hotspur's sense of family loyalty is impeccable. He is willing to die for the honor of an in-law, and is dutiful to a father who does not appear to be dutiful in return. (Northumberland's sickness on the eve of the rebellion is suspicious; his refusal to send Hotspur reinforcements absent himself is inexcusable.) Henry sees in Hotspur a loyal son, and loyal sons are ruled by their fathers. For all his impetuousness, Hotspur, like most honorable men, is rather predictable. He lives according to certain rules or traditions, for something outside himself. Hal is neither predictable nor, on his father's view, assuredly loyal. He is his own man and does no one else's bidding. Hal is far from an ideal son.

In *1 Henry IV* and in *Troilus and Cressida,* Shakespeare seems to associate traditional heroism with lack of cunning. Hotspur is without a trace of guile and this, finally, is why the king claims to prefer him to his own son. It is not only that Hal has the wrong friends and less than appropriately noble interests; more important than his moral disapproval or his fatherly disappointment, Henry *fears* Hal. In his lecture at act 3, scene 2, the king berates Hal for "thy place in council thou hast rudely lost." From what Henry's said earlier, one supposes that the loss of his position is due to Hal's neglect or incompetence or lack of interest. But according to Hume,

> The many jealousies to which Henry IV's situation naturally exposed him had so infected his temper that he had entertained unreasonable suspicions with regard to the fidelity of his eldest son; and during the latter years of his life he had excluded that prince from all share in public business, and was even displeased to see him at the head of armies, where his martial talents, though useful to the support of government, acquired a renown which, he thought, might prove dangerous to his own authority.[4]

Shakespeare's Henry confirms Hume's account later on in his lecture when he asks his son, "Why, Harry, do I tell thee of my foes, / Which art my nearest and dearest enemy?" (*1 Henry IV*, 3.2.122–23). The real purpose of the interview at act 3, scene 2 is to discover whether Henry can trust his own son. Seen in this light, his preference for Hotspur is less surprising.

The question is whether Henry's suspicions about Hal are, as Hume would have it, "unreasonable." Shakespeare's answer seems to be, probably not. Although Henry decides at the end of the interview to trust his son and although Hal's apology appears heartfelt, readers of the play will not have forgotten Hal's famous soliloquy at act 1, scene 2, where he explains his slumming as part of a calculated plan to advance his image by lowering and then exceeding expectations of himself. Hal is an admitted schemer with a plan to "falsify men's hopes." With this in mind, it is very difficult to know when he is earnest and when he is playing a role. Shakespeare is particularly interested in the ways a hereditary political system corrupts natural family feeling—one thinks immediately of *King Lear*—and Henry's fear of "premature inheritance" continues to be a concern in the second *Henry* play. In one scene Hal, thinking his father dead, lifts the crown to his head only to be discovered by a shocked and all too alive Henry, who accuses his son of wishing him dead. Henry is probably mistaken here, but his general suspicions are not without foundation. In *1 Henry IV*, after saving Henry from certain death on the battlefield, Hal tells his father

> O God, they did me too much injury
> That ever said I hearken'd for your death.
> If it were so, I might have let alone
> The insulting hand of Douglas over you,
> Which would have been as speedy in your end
> As all the poisonous potions in the world,
> And sav'd the treacherous labour of your son.
> (*1 Henry IV*, 5.4.50–56)

In a characteristic stroke of brutal clarification, Shakespeare has Hal remind his father that he allowed him to live. Hal, to say the least, is not prone to sentimentality. His softer father would appear to have good reason to puzzle over and even fear this strange young man.

In an uncharacteristically personal and confessional scene in *2 Henry IV*, Hal appears to set the record straight about his feelings toward his father. He confides to his friend Poins that "my heart bleeds inwardly that my father is so sick" (*2 Henry IV*, 2.2.45–46), telling him he is pained that he cannot express his true feelings without being labeled a hypocrite by the people. After long disregarding his father's wishes in associating with Falstaff and Poins and generally playing the profligate, Hal thinks he would appear unconvincing if he should show his father respect and affection only now that he nears death and as Hal nears the throne. Hal is so distressed by the uncaring image he presents to the world that he is compelled to tell Poins that he is not really like that. But he confides in Poins and not his father. If we readers are privy to Hal's true feelings, Henry, the object of those feelings, is not. Hal places public opinion and his own political career above his dying father's peace of mind. For Hal, *everything* is calculated for political effect; if his father must suffer because of it, so be it. Hal is not just a rebellious son but something much more difficult—a thoroughgoing politician, a man who puts politics above family and friendship.

III

Henry IV's criminal usurpation produced political faction and, eventually, civil war. It also produced Falstaff, a corrupt and iconoclastic figure who flourishes amid the social confusion. The times are perfectly suited to this master debunker. But Falstaff is more than a symbol of the chaotic political climate; he is the constant companion of the man who will be king. This unmarried, obese alcoholic was created by Shakespeare as Prince Hal's great friend and teacher.

And Falstaff is surely a teacher. He succeeds, for a time at least, in replacing Hal's father as the primary influence and guide in the young man's life. He presents no "doctrine" per se, but rather teaches by example, by what he cares about, what he does and does not take seriously, what he makes fun of. And so we see Falstaff drinking and carousing, listen to him talk about sack and sex, and note that his penetrating wit directs itself against the most respectable things, the law, religion, politics, and the family. But there is evidence that Falstaff once led a different kind of life. Early on he blames Hal for corrupting *him*, and says that "before I knew thee, Hal, I knew nothing, and now am I, if a man should speak truly, little better than one of the wicked" (*1 Henry IV*, 1.2.90–92). Falstaff was once the owner, he claims, of " . . . a true face, and good conscience . . . but their date is out" (*1 Henry IV*, 2.4.494–96). His numerous (and clever) biblical allusions suggest a traditional pious education and Falstaff defensively tells a drinking companion that "I have not forgotten what the inside of a church is made of" (*1 Henry IV*, 3.3.7–8). We have reason to surmise that the life we see Falstaff leading is the result of thinking through and rejecting the various prohibitions and conventions that restrain most men from acting as he does. As Masefield notes, "Falstaff is that deeply interesting thing, a man who is base because he is wise."[5]

We are introduced to Falstaff in the second scene of *1 Henry IV*. When Falstaff asks Hal what time it is, the prince, in an unexpectedly bellicose response, deftly sketches Falstaff's notorious character:

> Thou art so fat-witted with drinking of old sack, and unbuttoning thee after supper, and sleeping upon benches after noon, that thou hast forgotten to demand that truly which thou wouldst truly know. What a devil hast thou to do with the time of the day? Unless hours were cups of sack, and minutes capons, and clocks the tongues of bawds, and dials the signs of leaping-houses, and the blessed sun himself a fair hot wench in flame-coloured taffeta, I see no reason why thou shouldst be so superfluous to demand the time of the day. (*1 Henry IV*, 1.2.2–12)

Falstaff is not offended. The two apparently insult each other with loving regularity, and we come to see that much of their relationship consists in witty attempts to berate one another and defend themselves from attack. Falstaff responds to Hal with a preemptive and poetic defense of yet another one of his vices, thievery:

> Marry then sweet wag, when thou art king let not us that are squires of the night's body be called thieves of the day's beauty: let us be Diana's foresters, gentlemen of the shade, minions of the moon; and let men say we be men of good government, being governed as the sea is, by our noble and chaste mistress the moon, under whose countenance we steal. (*1 Henry IV*, 1.2.23–29)

Falstaff is an admitted and unrepentant thief. The plot of the Hal/Falstaff scenes—which otherwise would consist only of trading well-aimed barbs—will revolve around a robbery. In fact, the robbery plot becomes another occasion for witty repartee. Poins suggests to Hal that the two of them hold back and then, in disguise, rob their fellow robbers. "The virtue of this jest," Poins explains, "will be the incomprehensible lies that this same fat rogue will tell us when we meet at supper, how thirty at least he fought with, what wards, what blows, what extremities he endured; and in the reproof of this lives the jest" (*1 Henry IV*, 1.2.180–85). The robbery does, however, point to the political situation in England. Under King Henry, stealing is entertained casually, without qualms, as a matter of fun and games. References among the Boar's Head crowd to hanging and Hell are so frequent and so cavalier that one suspects they arise more from habit than from any real fear. One is impressed by the general notion of lawlessness that prevails, if not everywhere, at least in the Boar's Head circle, which, it must not be forgotten, includes the king's son. We are naturally led to speculate about the difficulties of reestablishing a respect for the law in light of Henry's usurpation, and more personally, how the example of a criminal father affects his son. Hal seems to have inherited from his father, along with political shrewdness and a penchant for cold calculation, a tendency to see himself as somehow above or beyond the law. But unlike his more conventional father, Hal moves comfortably in this sphere, and this has much to do with Falstaff.

But the fact that the heir to the throne spends so much time with a degenerate old man and his washed-out drinking companions at the Boar's Head Inn needs some explaining. Why does Hal bother with Falstaff? The prince offers something of an explanation in his "expectations soliloquy," where he characterizes his behavior as part of a calculated political strategy:

> I know you all, and will awhile uphold
> The unyok'd humour of your idleness.
> Yet herein will I imitate the sun,
> Who doth permit the base contagious clouds
> To smother up his beauty from the world,
> That, when he please again to be himself,
> Being wanted he may be more wonder'd at
> By breaking through the foul and ugly mists
> Of vapours that did seem to strangle him . . . .
> So when this loose behavior I throw off,
> And pay the debt I never promised,
> By how much better than my word I am,
> By so much shall I falsify men's hopes;
> And like bright metal on a sullen ground,
> My reformation, glitt'ring o'er my fault,
> Shall show more goodly, and attract more eyes
> Than that which hath no foil to set it off.
> (*1 Henry IV*, 1.2.190–98, 203–10)

It is, however, difficult to reconcile Hal's cold plan with his evident joy in the presence of Falstaff. It all sounds a bit abstract and one wonders whether Hal has not invented a grand rationale for his unorthodox preference for low company. One cannot dismiss Hal's soliloquy because it fits with his career, but it does not seem a wholly satisfying explanation—there must be more than political utility that draws Hal to Falstaff. More convincing, perhaps because more ordinary and less conspiratorial, are Hal's drunken boasts that he can drink with the commonest of the common and be accepted by them:

> I am sworn brother to a leash of drawers, and can call them all by their christen names, as Tom, Dick, and Francis . . . To conclude, I am so good a proficient in one quarter of an hour that I can drink with any tinker in his own language during my life. (*1 Henry IV*, 2.4.6–8, 17–19)

Hal's explanation here sounds a bit like the condescending private words of a populist politician. And yet it is clear that Hal is pleased with himself, that he likes the idea of royalty drinking toasts with commoners at questionable bars, that he likes being one of the boys: "they take it already upon their salvation, that though I be but Prince of Wales, yet I am the king of courtesy . . . and when I am King of England I shall command all the good lads in Eastcheap" (*1 Henry IV*, 2.4.8–10, 13–14). But while these two different explanations give us some insight into Hal's motives for slumming, they do not touch the heart of the matter; that is, they do not explain his desire to be with Falstaff in particular, and it is obviously with Falstaff that Hal most desires to be.

Hal and Falstaff spend most of their time together talking, so perhaps Hal's affection for Falstaff is best explained by sampling some of their conversation. As I have noted, a good deal of the pair's energy is spent exchanging inventive insults:

> *Prince*: Why, thou clay-brained guts, thou knotty-pated fool, thou whoreson obscene greasy tallow-catch,— . . .
> *Falstaff*: 'Sblood, you starveling, you eel-skin, you dried neat's-tongue, you bull's-pizzle, you stock-fish—O for breath to utter what is like thee!—you tailor's-yard, you sheath, you bow-case, you vile standing tuck! (*1 Henry IV*, 2.4.221–23, 240–44)

The robbery plot was designed by Poins to catch Falstaff in "incomprehensible lies" and watch him try to wriggle out of them. Pressed about a particularly blatant contradiction, Falstaff turns the tables on his inquisitor, Hal, with a moral objection to his method of inquiry:

> What, upon compulsion? 'Zounds, and I were at the strappado, or all the racks in the world, I would not tell you on compulsion. Give you a reason on compulsion? If reasons were as plentiful as blackberries, I would give no man a reason upon compulsion, I. (*1 Henry IV*, 2.4.231–36)

Accused of cowardice in running away from the disguised Hal and Poins, Falstaff defends himself as a loyal subject: "By the Lord, I knew ye as well as he that made ye . . . Was it for me to kill the heir-apparent? should I turn upon the true prince?" (*1 Henry IV*, 2.4.263, 264–65). None of Falstaff's ever-evolving defense is convincing, nor is it meant to be. What is on trial here is not Falstaff's valor or credibility, but his dexterity and inventiveness in defending himself with words. When Hal picks Falstaff's pocket and finds a list of debts detailing his excessive lifestyle—"O monstrous! but one halfpennyworth of bread to this intolerable deal of sack?"—Falstaff turns to the Bible for assistance: "Thou knowest in the state of innocency Adam fell, and what should poor Jack Falstaff do in the days of villainy? Thou seest I have more flesh than another man, and therefore more frailty" (*1 Henry IV*, 2.4.533–34; 3.3.164–68). The pair's teasing is not limited to one another. In an exchange with Hostess Quickly, Falstaff's sometimes bedpartner, the two enjoy their ribald selves at this silly woman's expense:

Falstaff: Setting thy womanhood aside, thou art a beast to say otherwise.
Hostess: Say, what beast, thou knave, thou?
Falstaff: What beast? Why, an otter.
Prince: An otter, Sir John? Why an otter?
Falstaff: Why? She's neither fish nor flesh, a man knows not where to have her.
Hostess: Thou art an unjust man in saying so, thou or any man knows where to have me, thou knave, thou.
Prince: Thou says't true, hostess, and he slanders thee most grossly. (*1 Henry IV*, 3.3.121–31)

Falstaff has a way of raising others to his own level of mirth and this must be part of what attracts Hal to him. As Falstaff says, "I am not only witty in myself, but the cause that wit is in other men" (*2 Henry IV*, 1.2.8–9). As Hal demonstrates in the tasteless drawer episode with Francis, without Falstaff he is merely crude, even cruel. Perhaps it is not so extraordinary after all that a young man, burdened with enormous responsibilities, should be attracted to the illicit and profane, packaged, as they are in Falstaff, with such robust and facile gaiety. As J. Dover Wilson remarks, "we know that that fat belly, so far from dragging him earthwards, bears him hither and thither like a balloon, at the slightest whim or desire. He is an emancipated spirit, free of all the conventions, codes, and moral ties that enwrap us . . . What we chiefly admire him for is his abounding vitality."[6]

Falstaff's attraction to Hal needs less explaining than Hal's attraction to Falstaff. Hal will be king and Falstaff hopes to benefit from his friendship—"I'll follow, as they say, for reward" (*1 Henry IV*, 5.4.161). A man like Falstaff can only flourish in socially lax and politically confusing times, which cannot be counted on to last forever. Falstaff's only hope is to transform the politicians before they attempt to transform him. Surely part of his education of Prince Hal is directed toward making England safe for Falstaffs. Not insignificantly, Hal pays for Falstaff's drink, loosening the tongue that so entertains him; he is a patron of the art of degenerate conversation. Falstaff also likes to think of himself as a young man. He screams at the just-robbed coach riders, "they hate us youth!," justifying his crime with, "young men must live" (*1 Henry IV*, 2.2.81–82, 86). Hanging around Hal and Poins must help reinforce this pleasing illusion. In addition to his loose women and his prostitutes, Falstaff evidently delights in the company of handsome young men. Complaining to himself of the shabby treatment he has just received from Poins, Falstaff almost sounds like a frustrated lover:

> I have forsworn his company hourly any time this two and twenty years, and yet I am bewitched with the rogue's company. If the rascal have not given me medicines to make me love him, I'll be hanged. It could not be else, I have drunk medicines. (*1 Henry IV*, 2.2.15–20)

As Dr. Johnson slyly points out, "medicines" refers to "the vulgar notion of love-powders."[7] Falstaff is a master corrupter and thus naturally gravitates toward youth and innocence. If nothing else, he needs people to talk to and his particularly irreverent brand of conversation would be shocking and off-putting to most. Thus he must cultivate a receptive audience; he must corrupt others in order to enjoy himself. Falstaff is a teacher with an agenda, near the top of which is his own pleasure.

But what exactly does Falstaff teach? While Shakespeare never shows him lecturing Hal or Poins, one supposes that there must have been some kind of preparation (or seduction) that would make the freewheeling and impious banter about respectable things possible. Falstaff may or may not be an atheist, but he is the only character in the play—besides Hal, who is probably imitating him—whose conversation is peppered with Biblical allusions, and his references are never respectful. We see the effects of a critique of family life in Falstaff's refusal to marry or in any way to limit his sexual appetite and, perhaps most importantly, in his utter disregard for Henry's role as father and moral educator of his son. Falstaff too is a kind of usurper: he steals sons from their fathers in a bid to make them like, and thus pleasing, to himself.

Perhaps the closest thing to a teaching Falstaff offers is his famous critique of honor. In true iconoclastic fashion, he calls his ode to self-preservation a "catechism." His argument is that living honorably, in this case on the battlefield, gets you nothing, that the costs are high and the benefits nil:

> Can honour set to a leg? No. Or an arm? No. Or take away the grief of a wound? No. Honour hath no skill in surgery then? No. What is honour? A word. What is in that word honour? What is that honour? Air. A trim reckoning! Who hath it? He that died a-Wednesday. Doth he feel it? No. Doth he hear it? No. 'Tis insensible, then? Yea, to the dead. But will it not live with the living? No. Why? Detraction will not suffer it. Therefore I'll none of it. (*1 Henry IV*, 5.1.131–40)

The question, "what does honor (or any other virtue) do for me?" is obviously subversive of all morality, which must be chosen for its own sake. The moral man acts honorably because it is honorable. But according to Falstaff's very practical critique, honor is liable to bring only death and detraction. Missing from Falstaff's analysis is any mention of the afterlife and I suppose it is not accidental that such a calculation holds no sway with him. Falstaff celebrates the bodily pleasures and these require a body. But Falstaff is no simple brute. Sex is accompanied by talk of sex. Clever conversation, the exchanges of intelligent and playful souls, is also a great pleasure. What Falstaff stands for in the end is tangible pleasure. What he stands against are all of those politically necessary constraints that tell us that we do not want or cannot have what pleases us unconditionally.

Falstaff's teaching, then, is decidedly antipolitical. His broadsides against lawfulness, family, and religion, his critique of honor and ordinary ambition, and his refusal to affect even the appearance of morality or propriety serve as a devastatingly thorough rejection of all of those things that must be respected if political order is to be possible. And his radical skepticism results in an unabashed hedonism. Falstaff's life provides a thoughtful testimony to the charms of the private pleasures. This is what Falstaff offers the man who will be king.

IV

Hal appears, in the end, to reject this teaching, choosing the political life over his friendship with Falstaff and all that he stands for. Our first intimation of Hal's preference comes in the role-playing scene, where the two take turns playing Hal's father. Falstaff plays King Henry, Hal himself, and then, reversing roles, Hal plays king to Falstaff's Hal. The issue in both cases is whether, in the father's opinion, Falstaff is a worthy companion or a corrupting influence. While Hal's negative portrait of Falstaff is truthful, Falstaff's portrait of himself is not. Falstaff tries to make himself look good to conventional eyes. He does not anticipate or answer the charges of corruption and offers no defense of his radical way of life. Like Socrates in the *Apology*, he tries to portray himself as harmless.[8] But Hal, who will be king and who is, in a sense, king at this moment, is not persuaded. He calls Falstaff "that villainous abominable misleader of youth" (*1 Henry IV*, 2.4.456), the same charge the Athenian fathers leveled against Socrates. The "play extempore" ends with a mock banishment: Falstaff is found guilty of being an undesirable and dangerous companion. Hal is prepared to act as a king must act. Lest we interpret this exchange as just another game, Hal makes clear later that he is dead serious. After his interview with Henry, Hal tells Falstaff that "I am good friends with my father and may do anything" (*1 Henry IV*, 3.3.180-81). From this point on, Hal is a warrior out to prove his political worth and Falstaff a fond reminder of his riotous past. Standing over what he mistakenly takes to be Falstaff's dead body lying on the battlefield, Hal declares that "I should have a heavy miss of thee / *If* I were much in love with vanity [foolishness]" (*1 Henry IV*, 5.4.104–5).[9] Unfortunately for Falstaff, Hal has no use for foolishness any longer.

In *2 Henry IV*, the distance between Hal and Falstaff can be measured by the small amount of time the pair spend together on the stage. They share only two scenes, 2.4 and 5.5, the latter when the new king banishes his old friend. The banishment of Falstaff, amply foreshadowed in Part I, is preceded by Hal's new alliance with his one time enemy and imprisoner, the Lord Chief Justice. The Lord Chief Justice has been Falstaff's most relentless and thoughtful critic. He is still pursuing Falstaff for the robbery at Gadshill, but this is really a pretext for the more serious charge of corrupting the man who will be king:

> You have misled the youthful Prince. . . . You follow the young Prince up and down, like his ill angel. . . . Well, God send the Prince a better companion! (*2 Henry IV*, 1.2.143, 162–63, 199)

More aware of Falstaff's peculiarly attractive subversiveness than is King Henry, who lumped the whole Boar's Head crowd together, the Lord Chief Justice accuses Falstaff of sophistry: "Sir John, Sir John, I am well acquainted with your manner of wrenching the true cause the false way" (*2 Henry IV*, 2.1.107–9). The speech in which Hal pledges his support to the Lord Chief Justice and assures him he has mended his ways is as sure a sign as any that Falstaff is out and law and order are in:

> My father is gone wild into his grave,
> For in his tomb lie my affections;
> And with his spirits sadly I survive
> To mock the expectations of the world,
> To frustrate prophecies, and to raze out
> Rotten opinion, who hath writ me down
> After my seeming. (*2 Henry IV*, 5.2.123–29)

Soon after Hal's reconciliation with the Lord Chief Justice, Mistress Quickly and Doll Tearsheet, tavern proprietress and prostitute, are arrested and carted off to prison.

Although it is expected, the actual banishment of Falstaff is shocking nevertheless. If Falstaff has any idea of what is in store for him, he shows no signs of it. On learning of King Henry IV's death, Falstaff exclaims that "the laws of England are at my commandment. Blessed are they that have been my friends, and woe to my Lord Chief Justice!" (*2 Henry IV*, 5.3.132–34). Standing in the crowd to greet the new king as he and his train pass by, Falstaff, with juvenile exuberance, tells Shallow "I will leer upon him as a comes by, and do but mark the countenance that he will give me" (*2 Henry IV*, 5.5.6–8). Falstaff's calls to Hal from the street—"God save thee, my sweet boy! . . . My King! My Jove! I speak to thee, my heart!"—are met with the famous and heartrendingly cold words of the new king: "I know thee not, old man" (*2 Henry IV*, 5.5.42, 46, 47). Only after the initial shock wears off does one realize that Hal's cruel and moralistic lecture is intended for a wider audience:

> I have long dreamt of such a kind of man,
> So surfeit-swell'd, so old, and so profane;
> But being awak'd I do despise my dream. . . .
> Presume not that I am the thing I was;
> For God doth know, so shall the world perceive,
> That I have turn'd away my former self;
> So will I those that kept me company. (*2 Henry IV*, 5.5.49–51, 56–59)

But as Allan Bloom points out, "what is interesting and sinister about Hal is the degree to which politics consumes him even though he is the beneficiary of a powerful critique of it."[10] Why does Hal opt for a conventional political life after his unconventional experience with Falstaff? The simplest answer is that Hal was born to be king: politics is his fate. But one might have expected the companion of Falstaff to pursue a more frivolous, decadent politics than he does, to use his public authority to further his private pleasures. This, after all, is what Falstaff hopes for and what Henry IV fears. Henry's nightmare vision of England under Hal is Falstaff's utopia:

> Harry the Fifth is crown'd! Up, vanity!
> Down, royal state! All you sage counsellors, hence!
> And to the English court assemble now
> From every region, apes of idleness!
> Now, neighbour confines, purge you of your scum!
> Have you a ruffian that will swear, drink, dance,
> Revel the night, rob, murder, and commit

> The oldest sins the newest kind of ways?
> Be happy, he will trouble you no more.
> England shall double gild his treble guilt,
> England shall give him office, honour, might:
> For the fifth Harry from curb'd license plucks
> The muzzle of restraint, and the wild dog
> Shall flesh his tooth on every innocent. (*2 Henry IV*, 4.5.119–32)

Henry's fears, of course, are not realized. As king, Hal seems almost a caricature of moral rectitude; he is the most vocally pious of Shakespeare's kings. And his youthful idleness gives way to a gigantic ambition, which culminates in his spectacular, against-the-odds conquest of France. Henry V's distinguishing characteristic is ambition and in this he could not be less like Falstaff—or more like his father.[11]

Still, the usual account of Hal's relation to Falstaff as an adolescent lark rejected in maturity fails to give either Hal or Falstaff his due. John Danby insists that " . . . Hal's rejection of Falstaff must not be regarded as more significant than his long association with the rogue. It need not even be regarded as a final rejection."[12] Hal might well possess an inner allegiance to Falstaff's teachings at the same time he appears to reject such radical views in public. His "expectations strategy" is based upon the Machiavellian contention that the people desire the appearance of morality in their ruler:

> [A prince] should appear all mercy, all faith, all honesty, all humanity, all religion . . . For the vulgar are taken in by the appearance and the outcome of a thing, and in the world there is no one but the vulgar . . . [13]

Hal knows that banishing Falstaff is the easiest and most symbolic way to acquire a good reputation. He may also know that while it is sufficient to appear virtuous to be reputed so, actual virtue can be politically counterproductive: "it is not necessary for a prince to have all the above-mentioned qualities in fact . . . [only] . . . to appear to have them. Nay, I dare say this, that by having them and always observing them, they are harmful; and by appearing to have them, they are useful . . ."[14]

Bloom suggests that Hal's ". . . abandonment of his old friend Falstaff, in order to improve his reputation for justice, follows from a teaching he could have learned from Falstaff."[15] Falstaff himself has no scruples about using others for his own advantage. For all of his warm humor and camaraderie, Falstaff is, at bottom, a rather cold and selfish man. What is less clear is how Falstaff could have taught Hal to be politic, to conceal unpalatable views beneath a morally upright exterior. Falstaff, after all, is not known for hiding his unorthodox views and is a careless and unconvincing liar. If the reincarnated Hal is indeed a moral imposter, how might he have learned to be so from Falstaff, a man so unconcerned with appearances?

The same unconcern Falstaff shows for conventional opinion is what allows Hal to pretend to be better than he is in order to gain an advantage: careful liars are carefree about morality. Thus beneath his new exterior, Hal may indeed remain faithful to the critique of morality that is the core of Falstaff's teaching. He surely rejects the sensual life that Falstaff chooses and opts instead for an ambitious political career. But if Hal chooses a different way, his success as king owes much to what he learns from Falstaff, for Falstaff showed Hal the possibility of freeing oneself from the moral and religious claims that govern most men, the possibility of pursuing one's selfish aims without regret. Falstaff's skepticism complements Hal's ambition. If Hal learns from his father about the mechanics of political power, he learns from Falstaff that thing Machiavelli most recommends to a prince: "to be able not to be good, and to use this and not use it according to necessity."[16] Henry IV never achieved the indifference to morality that Machiavelli thinks necessary for perfect political success. Given his experience with Falstaff, it should not be surprising that such indifference appears to characterize the reign of Henry V. At the very least, one ought to question the sincerity of Hal's "conversion" and approach his incessant professions of faith with skepticism, recalling Machiavelli's advice that "nothing is more necessary to appear to have" than religion.[17] For Henry V is just as guilty of political intrigue and treachery as his father. But unlike Henry IV, Henry V is untroubled by the pangs of conscience. Falstaff may be the ultimate source of Henry V's supreme confidence as king.

Notes

1. For a view of Bolingbroke as a thoroughgoing ". . . disciple of the Machiavellian philosophy . . .", see Irving Ribner, "Bolingbroke, A True Machiavellian," *Modern Language Quarterly* 9 (1948): 177–84. Contrary to what I will argue, Ribner thinks that "the murder of Richard is an act of extreme cruelty [that] does not dismay Bolingbroke in the least" and that the trip to the Holy Land is motivated solely by a Machiavellian desire to "appear pious in the eyes of his people" (183). My own interpretation begins from Allan Bloom's suggestion that Henry is "split": "he cannot bear to face the

possibility that the sin of Cain, as Machiavelli teaches, may play a role in the establishment of earthly justice. In deposing Richard he was halfway to the realization that he was committing a crime but that such crimes are sometimes necessary for the common good. However, so strong is his faith or his fear of hell-fire, he prefers to brand himself a guilty man and cripple his political sense and dedication rather than admit what his deed has shown." ("Richard II," in *Shakespeare as Political Thinker,* ed. John Alvis and Thomas G. West [Durham, N. C.: Carolina Academic Press, 1981], 60.) I think Bloom goes too far, however, in labeling a "cripple" a man who steals the throne, vanquishes all opponents, and dies a natural death, passing the crown onto his son. Further reflections on Henry IV's relation to the teaching of Machiavelli can be found in Dain A. Trafton, "Shakespeare's Henry IV: A New Prince in a New Principality," in *Shakespeare as Political Thinker,* and in Grant Mindle, "Shakespeare's Demonic Prince," *Interpretation* 20 (Spring 1993): 259–60. For Shakespeare's relation to Machiavelli, see Stephen Greenblatt, "Invisible Bullets," in *Shakespearean Negotiations* (Berkeley: University of California Press, 1988); Tracy Strong, "Shakespeare: Elizabethan Statecraft and Machiavellianism," in *The Artist and Political Vision,* ed. Benjamin R. Barber and Michael J. Gargas McGrath (New Brunswick, N. J.: Transaction Books, 1982), 193–220; John Alvis, *Shakespeare's Understanding of Honor,* (Durham, N.C.: Carolina Academic Press, 1990); M. M. Reese, *The Cease of Majesty* (London: Edward Arnold Ltd., 1961); E.M.W. Tillyard, *Shakespeare's History Plays* (London: Chatto and Windus, 1944); Moody Prior, *The Drama of Power* (Evanston, Ill.: Northwestern University Press, 1973).

2. All parenthetical references to Shakespearean texts follow the Arden edition of Shakespeare.

3. Henry N. Hudson, *Shakespeare: His Life, Art, and Characters* (4th edition, revised, 1882), quoted in the New Variorum edition of *Henry IV Part 1,* ed. Samuel Burdett Hemingway, 1936, 467.

4. David Hume, *The History of England* (Philadelphia: Porter and Coates), 2:211.

5. John Masefield, *William Shakespeare,* 1911, quoted in the New Variorum edition of *Henry IV Part 1,* 426.

6. John Dover Wilson, *The Essential Shakespeare,* 1932, quoted in the New Variorum edition of *Henry IV Part 1,* 439. Dr. Johnson's discussion of Falstaff's allure (405) culminates in a warning about its danger: "Yet the man thus corrupt, thus despicable, makes himself necessary to the prince that despises him, by the most pleasing of all qualities, perpetual gaiety, by an unfailing power of exciting laughter, which is the more freely indulged, as his wit is not of the splendid or ambitious kind, but consists in easy escapes and sallies of levity, which make sport but raise no envy. It must be observed that he is stained with no sanguinary crimes, so that his licentiousness is not so offensive but that it may be borne for his mirth. The moral to be drawn from this representation is, that no man is more dangerous than he that with a will

to corrupt, hath the power to please; and that neither wit nor honesty ought to think themselves safe with such a companion, when they see Henry seduced by Falstaff.''

7. Dr. Samuel Johnson, from his 1765 edition of Shakespeare's works, quoted in the New Variorum edition of *Henry IV Part 1,* 104.

8. On Falstaff's relation to Socrates, see Allan Bloom, *Love and Friendship* (New York: Simon and Schuster, 1993), 406–8. For much of what I write here about Hal and Falstaff, I am indebted to my teacher and friend, Allan Bloom.

9. Emphasis supplied.

10. Bloom, *Love and Friendship,* 409.

11. Toward the end of his reign, Henry IV took an active role in French affairs. He attempted, according to Hume, ''to foment the animosities between the families of Burgundy and Orleans, by which the government of France was, during that period, so distracted.'' Hal finished what his father began. Hume, *History of England,* 2:204–5.

12. John F. Danby, *Shakespeare's Doctrine of Nature: A Study of ''King Lear''* (London: Faber and Faber, 1949), 97.

13. Machiavelli, *The Prince,* trans. Harvey C. Mansfield, Jr. (Chicago: University of Chicago Press, 1985), 98.

14. Machiavelli, *Prince,* 70.

15. Bloom, *Love and Friendship,* 408.

16. Machiavelli, *Prince,* 61.

17. Machiavelli, *Prince,* 70–71.

7

Princes to Act: Henry V as the Machiavellian Prince of Appearance

Vickie Sullivan

So brilliant are the military feats of the English conqueror of France, that the Prologue of Shakespeare's *The Life of Henry V* deems that the dramatic presentation of them requires

> . . . a Muse of fire, that would ascend
> The brightest heaven of invention;
> A kingdom for a stage, princes to act
> And monarchs to behold the swelling scene!

In describing the requirements for the depiction of the play's subject matter in such exalted terms, the Prologue acknowledges the inability of a stage to contain the "vasty fields of France." The play magnifies the supreme worthiness of King Henry by depreciating its own powers to represent his military accomplishments: only when these seemingly impossible requirements are met will Henry "[a]ssume the port of Mars" (1 Pro. 1–12).[1]

Despite this forthright depreciation of the play's own ability to represent its subject matter, some scholars have found reason to conclude that by offering a subtle criticism of its hero, the play is far more adept at revelation than the Prologue's candid modesty would suggest.[2] I shall argue that the play's extraordinary revelatory ability is exemplified in the manner in which it calls attention to Henry's youth, when he was a prince and prodigal son of the usurper of Richard's crown.[3] Although the Henry of *Henry V* is, in important respects, different from the prince who appears in the plays that bear his father's name, these differences actually result from a thoroughgoing similarity of character between Hal as prince and Henry as king. They are, in fact, primarily the product of the son's application of the lessons he learned as prince from the father's admiration of the son's rival, Hotspur, the impetuous warrior. The son learns from this admiration how to win such admiration for himself by assuming the guise of an artless soldier.[4]

This guise of an artless soldier would appear to be inapt because Prince Hal had been anything but artless from the first. Part of Hal's guile entailed manipulating others as his instruments. The prince listed Hotspur among his panoply of instruments. He had initiated himself early into the art of instrumentality, an art that enabled him to manipulate others. His father's admiration of Hotspur constituted his final lesson in instrumentality, for from this exchange he learned to assume the character of one who is the instrument of another. He learned the higher art of manipulating others by appearing to be manipulated by them, an art which he applies throughout *Henry V.*

Without question, Shakespeare depicts Henry as a man of action, but in Shakespeare's rendition, Henry is also a man of acts. In addition, Henry stages scenes in which he ascribes his own intent to others.[5] Therein lies his peculiar strength, for he has others acting on his will, and often in the guise of a character who is not astute enough to have instruments of his own. As a result of this cunning method of proceeding, Henry so deftly avoids the derogatory epithets often applied to one who acts with such guile that he instead garners untarnished glory. Nevertheless, Shakespeare's art permits the attentive auditor of the play to recognize both the apparently unblemished character of this king's glory and the unseemly manner in which he gains this history. It is Shakespeare's presentation of Henry's perfection in the art of guile that allows Henry V to be likened to a prince in another sense: Henry is Machiavelli's guileful prince of appearance. As the play depicts princes who act, a portion of the Prologue's seemingly impossible conditions for a true revelation is in this manner actually fulfilled.

I

When the Prologue of *Henry V* offers the prospect that "warlike Harry, like himself" might assume the bearing of Mars, it actually reenacts, with different players and with a very different meaning, a scene from Shakespeare's depiction of Harry's earlier life in *1 Henry IV.* In that play, King Henry IV expresses his extreme disappointment in Prince Hal, who, in the father's estimation, does not act the proper role of the successor to his throne. In response to his father's censure, the prince pledges, "I shall hereafter, my thrice-gracious lord, / Be more myself" (*1 Henry IV,* 3.2.92–93). The king takes his son's pledge as specious, for he proceeds to assert that the son of his enemy—indeed, his own enemy, for both Percies, father and son, are in open rebellion against his rule—merits the succession. The basis for the father's judgment is that Henry Percy, the enthusiastic soldier perfectly devoid of cunning, represents an "infant warrior," and a "Mars in swathling clothes" (112–13; see also 1.1.78–83). So, then, the action of *Henry V* as described by the Prologue depicts the prince as king assuming the role that his father had ascribed to their enemy, Hotspur.

Henry IV's admiration of Hotspur is informed by the fact that the king sees a bit of himself in the youthful rebel, declaring to his son that "as I was then is Percy now" (*1 Henry IV,* 3.2.96). Because the two men must be distinguished in an important respect, Henry IV's identification of himself with Hotspur reveals a lack of self-understanding—or perhaps rather an understanding grounded in self-loathing. Whereas Henry IV is subject to the charge of being a "vile politician"(*1 Henry IV,* 1.3.240),[6] there is nothing politic about Hotspur; Bolingbroke himself concedes that he sought honor and recognition through the artful presentation of his person (*1 Henry IV,* 3.2.39–59). In contrast, Hotspur will win both without any admixture of subterfuge. In his view, honor is there for the taking, and one need neither color nor conceal the means by which one attains it: "By heaven, methinks it were an easy leap / To pluck bright honor from the pale-faced moon . . ." (*1 Henry IV,* 1.3.201–2). Bolingbroke has recourse to guile, Hotspur only to unmitigated force.

Hotspur reveals his attitude toward his own fate when later the rebels' plans are so advanced that they devise how to divide the realm of England among themselves. Hotspur, dissatisfied with the quality of his portion, like the impetuous and ferocious youth he is, will do battle with a river to increase his allotment. He will himself dam up the river that keeps him from the results he seeks:[7]

> See how this river comes me cranking in
> And cuts me from the best of all my land

A huge half-moon, a monstrous cantle out.
I'll have the current in this place dammed up,
And here the smug and silver Trent shall run
In a new channel fair and evenly. (*1 Henry IV*, 3.1.98-103)

But in seeking to pluck honor from the face of the moon, and in endeavoring to alter the course of a river to achieve the results he seeks, Hotspur does not apprehend that the moon waxes and wanes. He is a bluff lion, who cannot adapt his behavior to the times primarily because he does not apprehend that fortune changes.

In contrast, Prince Hal reveals that he understands the vicissitudes of fortune. When Falstaff boasts, for instance, that they, as thieves of the night, receive their governance from the moon, Hal retorts ominously that "the fortune of us that are the moon's men doth ebb and flow like the sea, being governed, as the sea is, by the moon" (*1 Henry IV*, 1.2.28–30). According to Hal's understanding, because fortune so ebbs, the fortune that brought a purse could also bring a fate that eventuates in the gallows. Although Hal's repartee with the ponderous prowler anticipates the possibility of such an ignominious end, in foreseeing its prospect he can undertake to avoid it. Indeed, by learning to assume a different aspect to suit the contingencies that his kingship will bring, he will build on this youthful understanding. Oblivious even to the rudiments of the lesson that Hal will master, Hotspur meets his fate: the body that contained his overweening spirit rests in but "two paces of the vilest earth" (*1 Henry IV*, 5.4.90).

Hal's victory over Hotspur exemplifies the reasons for Machiavelli's ultimate embrace of the tactic of fraud over that of force. Machiavelli had asserted the necessity of employing the character of both the wily fox and the forceful lion "because the lion does not defend itself from snares and the fox does not defend itself from wolves."[8] Although Machiavelli concludes his famous chapter on fortune in *The Prince* by appearing to favor simply the impetuous youth who will win fortune's favors by resisting "her" with force,[9] elsewhere he provides reasons that militate against what appears to be his extreme faith in the ability of such a forceful youth to conquer fortune. In *Discourses* 2.13 Machiavelli states, for example, that one cannot "attain to great empire through open force alone and ingenuously, but it is done quite well through fraud alone."[10] The fox must guide the application of force, in Machiavelli's view. Because Hal apprehends how fortune changes, he can alter the face that he presents to the world accordingly. Hal's understanding is superior to Hotspur's blind reliance on force alone.[11]

Before Hal has won this victory over Hotspur on the battlefield at Shrewsbury, King Henry wonders aloud in the presence of Hal whether the wayward prince, so removed from Hotspur in character—and, as yet, in deeds—is an instrument of God:

> I know not whether God will have it so
> For some displeasing service I have done,
> That, in his secret doom, out of my blood
> He'll breed revengement and a scourge for me;
> But thou dost in thy passages of life
> Make me believe that thou art only marked
> For the hot vengeance and the rod of heaven
> To punish my mistreadings. (*1 Henry IV,* 3.2.4–11)

In this way, the father reveals that he regards himself as a fit subject for divine retribution—he reveals his guilt.

As the interview continues, however, Hal offers an alternative view of instrument and master. Hal, not God, is the master; Percy, not Hal, is the instrument:

> For the time will come
> That I shall make this northern youth exchange
> His glorious deeds for my indignities.
> Percy is but my factor, good my lord,
> To engross up glorious deeds on my behalf. (144–48)

These two versions of the character of instrumentality that may be at play in the realm need not be mutually exclusive, of course. God could utilize Hal as His agent at the same time that Hotspur serves as Hal's. Nevertheless, Hal foresees a result that is different from the one that would arise from the scenario that his father posits. The prince intends an outcome that will magnify his own honor, whereas his father hypothesizes that God intends not only to bring dishonor to the throne of England, but also to render its reigning king miserable. Whether or not God intends to punish the black deeds of King Henry IV, Prince Hal's degradation will certainly not be the means to this particular end. Exactly as Hal here intends, he redeems himself and becomes glorious.

It is quite possible that Hal's explanation to his father that he uses Hotspur to gain for himself the fame that Hotspur has amassed is an invention of the moment. Such an interpretation would demand that as the conversation proceeds, the son considers his father's initial proposition that the son's dissipation is a vehicle for divine retribution.

At the first opportunity, the son counters his father's proposition with an alternative: having been confronted with the assertion that he is a mere instrument, Hal concocts a scenario that casts himself as the manipulator rather than as the manipulated.

Although this interpetation is quite plausible, Hal has already revealed much that corroborates the explanation he offers his father. If his explanation is not the mere invention of the moment, he would be a very devious character. Indeed, he would be a character worthy of inclusion in Machiavelli's *The Prince*.[12] In Hal's first appearance in the play, Hal reveals two important elements of his method of proceeding that are necessary to such a plan. First, he declares that his wantonness is merely a device. Second, he similarly reveals that his companions in revelry and riot will offer the means of displaying himself to the best advantage. Prince Hal possesses both the character that permits him to use others as the means to enlarge his own reputation and the mind capable of devising the details of such a plan:

> Yet herein will I imitate the sun,
> Who doth permit the base contagious clouds
> To smother up his beauty from the world,
> That, when he please again to be himself,
> Being wanted, he may be more wond'red at
> By breaking through the foul and ugly mists
> Of vapors that did seem to strangle him . . .
> So, when this loose behavior I throw off
> And pay the debt I never promisèd,
> By how much better than my word I am,
> By so much shall I falsify men's hopes;
> And, like bright metal on a sullen ground,
> My reformation, glitt'ring o'er my fault,
> Shall show more goodly and attract more eyes
> Than that which hath no foil to set it off.
> (*1 Henry IV*, 1.2.185–91 and 196–203)

If Hal has planned a conversion from the first and utilized his boon companions to orchestrate it, then the proposition that the wily prince has simultaneously allowed Hotspur's valorous deeds to eclipse his own promise in order to enhance further the spectacle of his transformation follows as a corollary.

In light of Hal's earlier speech, then, the revelations regarding the prince's character that emerge from the conference with his father do not themselves seem all that spectacular. Nevertheless, it seems quite possible that the conference was quite illuminating for Hal. Hal learns the extent to which the father who chastises him, the very man who here admits to having staged his own appearances in order to rob the then reigning king of his majesty, is captivated by the guileless Hotspur. Indeed, Hal learns of his father's guilt and desire to be that which he is not. The prince learns that the lion is admired, even by someone as foxy as his father.

This lesson is not lost on the prince when Hal assumes the throne. Just as he had done in his youth, Henry stages scenes that utilize others to further his own purposes, but as king he also becomes an actor in the scenes of his own devising. In assigning himself the role of actor, he assigns to another the authorship of his actions. This procedure allows him both to distance himself from questionable deeds, as he claims that he acts only in another's name, and to vindicate himself from his father's charge that he is God's instrument for dishonor as he claims to be God's instrument for England's redemption.[13]

The guise that he assumes as king, which is particularly suited to his depiction of himself as the instrument of another, is that of the guileless warrior. Indeed, in order to increase the honor that accrues to him, Henry V acts the part of Henry Percy, the hot-blooded Hotspur, in language strikingly reminiscent of that which Hal had employed to belittle his thoughtlessly impetuous rival. Therefore, in the play that portrays the mature Hal, Hotspur still serves as Henry's instrument, but the relation is much closer, for, in a manner of speaking, Henry V chooses to appear as Hotspur.

II

Henry applies the lesson that was to be gleaned from his father's admiration for Hotspur. The lion draws so much respect that Henry uses the aspect of the lion to disassociate himself from the fox. Because the fox is not trusted (cf. *1 Henry IV*, 5.2.9) and the lion draws homage, King Henry has learned to assume the aspect of the bluff warrior, that which Hotspur was to his very core, without succumbing to Hotspur's defect of a lack of cunning. Indeed, King Henry is all the more cunning because cunning is no part of the character he assumes. If the fox professes the views of the lion, it is still the fox who speaks, and contrivance is all.

In his rousing speech to his troops before the walls of Harfleur, Henry indicates that he believes an individual, who is not so inclined by nature, can choose to assume the character of a Hotspur. He exhorts his soldiers:

> But when the blast of war blows in our ears,
> Then imitate the action of the tiger:
> Stiffen the sinews, summon up the blood,
> Disguise fair nature with hard-favoured rage; . . .
> Now set the teeth and stretch the nostril wide,
> Hold hard the breath and bend up every spirit
> To his full height! (3.1.5–8 and 15–17)

Later in the French campaign, as the battle of Agincourt is to begin, Henry offers to his troops the same sentiment that Hotspur expounds before the rebels' defeat at Shrewsbury. Hotspur, upon learning that his father will not participate in the battle, finds that Northumberland's absence "lends a lustre and more great opinion, / A larger dare to our great enterprise" (*1 Henry IV*, 4.1.77–78). Hotspur's spirited desire for honor leads him to believe that a dire circumstance should be viewed as an opportunity. In this way, Hotspur again reveals his imprudent belief that force alone can overcome any exigency; alas, it cannot, and his soldier's alacrity leads him to his death.

At Agincourt, Henry reiterates Hotspur's thought, but Henry is no Hotspur. When Westmoreland, dejected by the far greater number of the French, voices in the presence of the men his desire for more troops, Henry repudiates this sentiment with his declaration that the "fewer men, the greater share of honor . . . I pray thee wish not one man more" (*Henry V*, 4.3.22–23). "The greater the obstacle, the greater the glory" is the credo by which Hotspur lived and died. Whereas the words express Hotspur's very being, Henry utters them for a very public purpose; he recognizes their utility in inspiriting his troops.

After revivifying "the former lions of his blood" by winning a stunning battlefield victory, Henry forces the French to accept his terms, among which he now ranks as primary the hand of Katherine in marriage. As the peers of France and England adjourn to discuss Katherine's fate, Henry remains to plead his love to the princess. With Henry's repetition of "Kate" and his prattle about his aptness for horse and armor that renders him unsuitable for the arts of love, Shakespeare seems to conjure up images of Hotspur's exchange with his wife: "Gods me, my horse! / What say'st thou, Kate? . . . / And when I am a-horseback, I will swear / I love thee infinitely" (*1 Henry*

IV, 2.3.90–91 and 97–98). If it were not for the fact that Prince Hal himself had astutely mimicked the comedy of a domestic exchange between Hotspur and his wife, it would be difficult to believe that Shakespeare would have us accept that Henry had ascertained enough of Hotspur's character to replicate so accurately a scene to which he could not have been privy:

> I am not yet of Percy's mind, the Hotspur of the North; he that kills me some six or seven dozen of Scots at a breakfast, washes his hands, and says to his wife, "Fie upon this quiet life! I want work." "O my sweet Harry," says she, "how many hast thou killed today?" "Give my roan horse a drench," says he, and answers "Some fourteen," an hour after, "a trifle, a trifle." (*1 Henry IV,* 2.4.97–104)

The similarity between Hotspur's exchange with his wife and Henry's courtship of the princess moved Samuel Johnson to complain: "I know not why Shakespeare now gives the king nearly such a character as he made him formerly ridicule in Percy. This military grossness and unskilfulness in all the softer arts, does not suit very well with . . . the general knowledge ascribed to him at his accession. . . ."[14]

The answer resides perhaps in the fact that Henry finds himself in a situation in which he is suspected of a recourse to guile, and his defensive strategy calls for a claim to utter ingenuousness. He has placed himself in the rather awkward situation in which he entreats the love of a woman that has for all practical purposes already been won on the battlefield. Katherine herself recognizes the situation for what it is. Indeed, she displays her understanding when Henry begins his suit with an earnest effort to sway her with romantic phrases by likening her to an angel, and she responds that the tongues of men are full of deceits. In response to this accusation of deceit he pleads his inability to captivate with words, and corroborates his claim by effecting an attitude that is utterly incapable of affectation; he chooses to offer another rendition of the imitation of Hotspur he perfected in *1 Henry IV.* Moreover, he is careful to conceal any hint of the mutability he has perfected. At a point later in the courtship scene he compares the loyalty he pledges to Katherine to the changeable moon: "a good heart, Kate, is the sun and the moon." Hal had indicated in his exchange with Falstaff in *1 Henry IV* that he understood that the moon, like fortune, is variable, and Henry V reveals he still possesses this understanding, for he immediately corrects himself: "or rather, the sun, and not the moon, for it shines bright and never changes, but keeps his course truly" (*Henry V*, 5.2.160–63). Perhaps he realizes that he has misspoken not only because the image of a variable moon is unfit for application to a loyal lover, but also because it reveals too much of himself, having just displayed his own mutability by assuming the character of another.

III

In assuming the character of Hotspur, Henry assumes simultaneously the role of the manipulated rather than that of the manipulator, for ingenuous Hotspur was Hal's agent. In becoming Hotspur, King Henry takes on this new role as well. He learns to portray himself as the instrument of others.

Henry V's propensity to stage scenes in which he induces others to become the authors of that which he intends from the first is most salient in the manner in which he manipulates the conspirators Scroop, Cambridge, and Grey.[15] In full knowledge that these men have conspired with France to assassinate him before the English can ship for Calais, Henry brings the traitors into his presence for the ostensible purpose of presenting them with their commissions for the war. Before the king turns his attention to this business, he considers the plight of a man in gaol for denouncing him. The king displays his mercy by ordering the release of one, whom Henry claims was not responsible for his petty crime, having acted under the influence of wine. Each of the conspirators, oblivious to the trap that is being laid, registers protest against the king's too great leniency displayed on behalf of the drunkard. Rejecting their feigned solicitousness with the thought that capital crimes cannot be properly punished if small faults are punished so severely, he distributes their commissions, which reveal to them that Henry knows their true worthiness. They immediately confess their guilt and submit themselves to Henry's mercy.

Now Henry will accept their earlier counsel that warned against clemency: "The mercy that was quick in us but late, / By your own counsel is suppressed and killed" (*Henry V*, 2.2.79–80). The traitors, Henry claims, are the authors of their fate; the king merely acts on the basis of their decrees, but, of course, Henry had intended that they execute his will when he induced them to offer advice that would demand their execution when applied to their own crimes. He claims that he only executes their will, but in actuality they have executed his. With this understanding, Henry's scene-opening inquiry of Scroop whether he believes the English army is capable of fulfilling "the execution and the act / For which we have in head assembled them?" (17–18) takes on a more ominous meaning than can be apparent at the point at which Henry utters the question. The king had assembled Scroop, Cambridge, and Grey to execute his will—a will that eventuates in an act of execution. After arranging a scene so as to appear to defer to the will of his inferiors, he ends the scene by deferring to his superior: "Let us deliver / Our puissance into the hand of God, / Putting it straight in expedition" (189–91). He again portrays himself as an instrument.

Why Henry goes to the effort to stage this scene with the conspirators is not readily apparent. These men, to whom he claims to have extended his greatest trust, had planned to murder him. He need not defer to their judgment in order to appear just in demanding their lives as punishment when they had sought to rob him of his own. Thus, in a case in which right appears to be manifestly on his side, he is at pains to appear not to render judgment in his own name. Having so manifestly manipulated the guilty to sentence themselves, Henry's method in this instance may cast light on his behavior in his first appearance in the play when right is not as evidently on his side.

The question at issue in this scene is whether King Henry can make a rightful claim to the French crown. The Archbishop of Canterbury steps forward to expound the reasons why the Salic Law, which bars females from inheriting the French crown, does not bar Henry, who derives his claims from his great-great-grandmother, from the throne. At the very least it can be said with assurance that the Bishop's obscure rendition of kings and queens, heirs and usurpers, cannot be said to render Henry's right to France "as clear as is the summer's sun" (*Henry V*, 1.2.86). Moreover, as Harold Goddard's famous indictment of the Bishop's casuistry points out, the reasons Canterbury adduces to support the claim undermine themselves: "The very thing that proves the title of a French king crooked—namely, inheritance through the female—serves, by some twist of ecclesiastical logic, to prove the title of an English king good."[16]

Whatever Shakespeare's final judgment on the status of the claim, he alters his source material in a way that accentuates Henry's role in urging it. In both the play and in Holinshed's chronicles, the leaders of the Church seek to avert passage of a bill that stands before Parliament that would expropriate from the Church the land that it had been bequeathed. In Holinshed's version, however, the leaders of the Church are responsible for the consideration of the claim to France, which they broach as a diversionary tactic: "the religious sort . . . thought best to trie if they might moove the kings mood with some sharpe invention, that he should not regard the importunate petitions of the commons." To this end, Holinshed relates that the Archbishop of Canterbury made a "pithie oration" in Parliament declaring that King Henry owned the title to the realm of France.[17]

In Shakespeare's version, the bishops still fret over the provision, and they indicate that they seek the means by which to forestall its passage. Bishop Ely asks of his superior: "But how, my lord, shall we resist it now?" To which Canterbury responds, "It must be thought on" (*Henry V*, 1.1.6–7). Nevertheless, in contrast to Holinshed's version, the Canterbury of the play cannot lay claim to the sharp invention of a war with France. A consideration of the order of events that comprise the first two scenes indicates that Henry orchestrates them, and that far from the Churchmen inducing the king to press his claims, he induces the clergy to support his own plans.[18]

As the first scene closes, Ely asks Canterbury whether Henry supports the bill for expropriation. Canterbury reports that the king seems sympathetic to the clergy's position and that in order to encourage further royal sympathy he had offered Henry a great sum of money to aid in the prosecution of the war. Like the Canterbury of the chronicles, Shakespeare's archbishop displays resourcefulness. Nevertheless, Shakespeare's character does not initiate the consideration of war with France, but merely responds to "causes now in hand" (*Henry V*, 1.1.77). In support of these existing causes, he would gladly have offered Henry additional aid by furnishing a vindication of his claims had not his converse with the king been broken off by an ambassador from France, who had desired an audience with England's king.

Having received an adequate indication of the degree to which Canterbury is willing to support the invasion, Henry breaks off the interview. Canterbury had told Ely that the reason for the termination of his discussion had been the interruption by the French ambassador, yet at the end of this scene, Canterbury indicates that he is to attend the ambassador's audience with the king at four o'clock. If, before the ambassador's appointment, Canterbury and Ely had enough time to expatiate on the miracle of the king's reformation, as well as on the ramifications of the bill urged by the Commons, then Henry did indeed have "time enough to hear" Canterbury expatiate on the validity of the English claim to "the crown and seat of France" (cf. 1.1.83–98). Only before an audience composed of the peers assembled to attend to the French embassy will Henry permit Canterbury to deliver his findings.

The details of the second scene corroborate this purpose of Henry's plan. At the beginning of this scene, presumably at four o'clock, Westmoreland, by offering to have the French ambassador brought into the chamber, indicates his belief that the time has arrived for the ambassador's audience. Henry refuses the offer, having just requested Canterbury's presence, and states that it is necessary to resolve some matters concerning France before introducing the ambassador. When the ambassador finally makes his appearance, it becomes clear that Henry had already resolved much with regard to France without the aid of Canterbury's investigations, for the ambassador brings the response from the Dauphin, regarding Henry's recent claim to "some certain dukedoms in the right / Of your great predecessor, King Edward the Third" (248–49). Henry has already seized the initiative. Even apart from the claim to the throne of France itself, Henry's demand of the dukedoms would prompt a war. Henry's use of Canterbury constitutes a show for the assembled lords.

Despite Henry's own initiative, however, he endeavors to lay the responsibility of war on Canterbury. Before allowing Canterbury to proceed, Henry admonishes him in the strongest terms not to bend his interpretation because his answer will decide the fate of innocents:

> For God doth know how many now in health
> Shall drop their blood in approbation
> Of what your reverence shall incite us to.
> Therefore take heed how you impawn our person,
> How you awake our sleeping sword of war.
> (*Henry V*, 1.2.18–22)

Despite the stern character of this warning, Henry's prior action reveals that he wants war. Henry is not taking much of a risk in choosing to appear to rest the decision for war on Canterbury's performance before the assembled lords, given that Canterbury has already acted on his motivation to evade the ramifications of the bill before the Commons by furnishing Henry both with the offer of monetary support for the war and with a strong indication of the drift of his interpretation of the Salic Law.

Canterbury fulfills admirably the role Henry has assigned him. After the Archbishop has assuaged the moral unease that would prohibit the proposed English invasion of France, Henry introduces a practical problem: with the English soldiers gone to prey upon the French, the Scots will launch their own invasion against the now vulnerable English. Canterbury first attempts to argue that the forays of the Scots are inconsequential, but Henry counters that the Scots must be taken more seriously. In expounding the reasons for his belief, Henry seems to recall the Machiavellian advice of his dying father, who urged him "to busy giddy minds / With foreign quarrels" (*2 Henry IV*, 4.5.213–14),[19] and to recognize that the King of Scotland is impelled by the same necessity as is the King of England. When the "giddy minds" of the English are occupied with a foreign war, their own "giddy neighbor" (*Henry V*, 1.2.145) will do to England what England does to France: "With ample and brim fullness of his force, / Galling the gleanèd land with hot assays, / Girding with grievous siege castles and towns" (150–52).[20] Henry's image of Scotland "galling" England with sieges is inapt—or perhaps rather more apt than he had intended—for the image renders England, vulnerable at the hands of the invading Scots, into the equivalent of a Gaul burdened with an English invasion. Canterbury attempts to meet Henry's elaborated argument for the formidable character of the envisioned Scottish invasion by asserting that, in fact, the last time England was engaged in France, England captured Scotland's king. Because Ely is not entirely attuned to his ecclesiastical superior's desire for England to deploy its resources immediately in a French invasion, he adduces an adage that testifies to the necessity of subduing Scotland first; Canterbury then recognizes that he must change his tack.

Canterbury recognizes his new approach in an embellishment of Exeter's view that England can, in fact, proceed directly to an attack on France by taking adequate precautions at home against Scotland's probable incursion. To support this argument, Canterbury borrows from Virgil's idyll concerning the harmonious relations among the honeybees in *The Georgics*. All strata of society, like the individual bees who compose a hive, engage in various pursuits that converge in one end, the flourishing of the whole. England, when so conceived, can imitate the industrious hive by similarly dividing its work, providing that some attend to the attack and others to the defense.

In making this argument to support the plans for the French expedition, Canterbury makes the hive that serves as his model more belligerent than the one that appears in his source.[21] In Virgil's poem the bees who collect the honey are "foragers," who "labour in the field."[22] In contrast, in Canterbury's version, the bucolic imagery gives way to that of military adventure:

> Others like soldiers, armèd in their stings
> Make boot upon the summer's velvet buds,
> Which pillage they with merry march bring home
> To the tent-royal of their emperor . . . .
> (1.2.193–96)

Although sentries appear in Virgil's description for the purpose of watching for the approach of rain and of driving from the hive those who shirk their duties, no such threatening warrior-pillagers appear.[23] The manner in which Canterbury renders the bees into a militaristic and opportunistic horde reveals his willingness to put a gloss on his sources so as to support an offensive war.

Canterbury concludes this speech with the injunction to Henry to "make all Gallia shake" (217). Thus, the Archbishop has not shrunk one whit before the prospect, to which Henry pointed, that an interpretation favorable to English claims will make the Churchman responsible for the war. With the responsibility so poised, Henry finally calls for the French ambassador, who bears the Dauphin's even more offensive response to Henry's offensive claim to French dukedoms. By virtue of this insulting response, Henry finds an alternative source of blame. The Dauphin's soul, the king claims

> Shall stand sore chargèd for the wasteful vengeance
> That shall fly with [the gunstones]; for many a thousand widows
> Shall this his mock mock out of their dear husbands,
> Mock mothers from their sons, mock castles down. (284–87)

Henry has orchestrated this scene in a manner that allows him to minimize his own responsibility for the invasion. First, he is the agent of the Archbishop; then, he merely reacts to the Dauphin's insult; finally, he minimizes his own responsibility by appealing to God. The dire consequences for the French of the Dauphin's response lie "within the will of God, / To whom I do appeal, and in whose name, / Tell you the Dauphin, I am coming on" (290–92). King Henry now will be the agent of God.

Henry's strategy that blames others for his own transgressions borders on the absurd when he addresses the citizens of the besieged Harfleur. He proclaims before its walls that if the town continues to resist its attackers, its defenders will themselves suffer not only the most dreadful consequences, but also the blame for the atrocities to which they are subjected. Because the citizens perpetuate civil war by resisting their rightful ruler, Henry is absolved of any wrong: "What is't to me, when you yourselves are cause, / If your pure maidens fall into the hand / Of hot and forcing violation?" (*Henry V,* 3.3.19–21). Informed by such logic, Henry offers the citizens their only salvation:

> Therefore, you men of Harfleur,
> Take pity of your town and of your people
> Whiles yet my soldiers are in my command,
> Whiles yet the cool and temperate wind of grace
> O'erblows the filthy and contagious clouds
> Of heady murder, spoil, and villainy.
> (*Henry V,* 3.3.27–32)

Henry here maintains that he is the barrier between the townspeople and the terrible crimes that his soldiers, under his command, are capable of committing. Only his temperate indulgence keeps these clouds of destruction at bay.

This formulation, "contagious clouds," unique to Henry in the Shakespearean corpus, recalls Henry's soliloquy in *1 Henry IV,* in which he offers an explanation for his association with his wanton companions. The youthful Hal uses the image to contend that his undesirable friends serve as his foil; he is like the sun, which will appear to shine all the more brilliantly when it has thrown off the "contagious clouds" that it allows to obscure its beauty. As prince he permitted such clouds to smother the radiance of his visage in order to effect later a more spectacular display.

As king, however, Henry is acutely concerned that clouds do not unnessarily mar his countenance, as he endeavors to contrive a "history [that] shall with full mouth / Speak freely of our acts" (1.2.231–32). Although the king has this different relation to the clouds that could disfigure his history, both strategies work to enhance his appearance. Surely if the citizens of Harfleur had persisted in their resistance, compelling the Engish army to gain the town through force rather than surrender, Henry would have been quick to blame any unfortunate incidents on the Harfleurians themselves. He had, in fact, used just such a procedure in asserting that the conspirators had determined their own sentence and in laying the blame for the French assault on Canterbury's interpretation of the Salic Law and on the Dauphin's insult. Nevertheless, in so distancing himself from these clouds, they are still at his command.

Henry wins for himself a glorious history by perfecting the ability to be artfully artless. If the epitome of guile is to receive its benefits while avoiding its reputation, then Henry has achieved its height.

IV

As we have seen, it is precisely when he declares that he is submitting to the will of others that Henry is most willful. In such instances, Henry is all theater; he is an actor in the scenes of which he himself is the author. Because Henry has proven himself to be such a master of artifice, one cannot help but question his sincerity in claiming to be God's agent in his military conquest of France. Perhaps when he claims to be God's instrument, he remains true to his manipulative character and is, in fact, utilizing God as his own. Indeed, when he endeavors to be the author not only of the actions of others but also of his own history, it can be said that he displays such an arrogance in asserting his own autonomy that he appears to wish to displace the role of God as author.[24] This view of Henry's purpose is perfectly commensurate with the position he takes when he defends himself against his father's accusation that the dissolute son is God's instrument for retribution. Henry endeavors to take God's place as the manipulator of an instrument.

A glance at another English king's attitude toward God and instrumentality furnishes an instructive contrast that highlights Henry's arrogance in seeking to be both author and instrument. Shakespeare's earlier tetralogy dedicated to what is actually the sequel to the events of his later tetralogy—of the consequences of Henry IV's usurpation of the throne and of Henry's conquest of France, the loss of France and the War of the Roses—presents Henry VI as a king dedicated to prayer beads to the exclusion of military exploits, and ultimately of political rule entirely. So feeble is Hal's son that he depends on an agent to regain the crown when the sons of York have wrested it from him. In expressing thanks to his liberator, he expresses his extreme piety:

> But, Warwick, after God, thou set'st me free,
> And chiefly therefore I thank God and thee;
> He was the author, thou the instrument.
> (*3 Henry VI*, 4.6.16–18)

Between father and son, between the imperial conqueror of France and the hapless loser of this spoil, there appears to be no middle ground. One endeavors to be both author and instrument, the other claims to be neither author nor instrument. The third alternative, the one who neither seeks to be entirely autonomous nor is entirely ineffectual, the leader who *acts* in the service of deeds that he understands as serving God's ends—who thereby understands himself as God's instrument for God's purposes—is here absent.

This reading of the plays, then, contravenes the view that Henry V is himself that Christian king. Aside from the statement of the Chorus, and Henry's dubious assertions and skillful submissions, there is one point in *Henry V* that would appear to justify the view that Henry is a Christian king. It occurs when, on the eve of battle, alone on the stage, he offers a prayer. Because he lacks an audience of his subjects to audit his words, he lacks also any motivation to continue his theatrical posturing. Although the prayer may offer evidence of Henry's personal piety, its content in actuality suggests that Henry V is *not* Shakespeare's Christian king. Again, Shakespeare's first tetralogy offers an instructive contrast. Further, this contrast, in fact, proffers the missing middle ground between Henry V's impious usurpation of the roles of both author and instrument on the one hand, and Henry VI's pious resignation on the other.

The Earl of Richmond, the future King Henry VII, embodies this middle element when he marshals troops in an invasion of his homeland to rid England of the tyrannical and guilefully murderous Richard III.[25] On the eve of battle, Richmond, like Henry V, implores divine succor, anxious in anticipation of the morning contest that will decide the fate of his enterprise. Richmond entreats:

> O Thou, whose captain I account myself,
> Look on my forces with a gracious eye; . . .
> Make us thy ministers of chastisement,
> That we may praise thee in the victory.
> (*Richard III*, 5.3.109–10, 114–15)

In addressing God, Richmond immediately acknowledges that he understands himself to be acting as an agent of providence, and proceeds to ask that his understanding of his actions be confirmed by the success of his troops.

The content of Henry V's prayer offers a significant contrast. Although Henry's mere offering of prayer acknowledges that he recognizes a power superior to himself, he does not declare that he believes himself to be His captain, as does Richmond. Instead, he begins with the rather pagan appeal: "O God of battles, steel my soldiers' hearts, / Possess them not with fear" (*Henry V*, 4.1.275–76). He then asks God to withhold from his soldiers the faculty of "reck'ning" if the superior numbers of the French should dispirit them. The remainder of the prayer—more than fourteen lines in a speech consisting of eighteen—amounts to a type of bargaining with God. The king implores that tomorrow's battle not be the occasion of divine recompense for his father's guilt in usurping the throne from Richard II. If that ugly day of reckoning is forestalled, Henry promises that he will augment the resources he has already employed in penitence. What Henry does not say in his prayer is more revealing still. In private converse with God, Henry does not speak of his agency in God's purposes. One possibility for Henry's omission is that he is not confident that his purposes warrant God's direction, his cause not being good.

Of course, after the French are vanquished, Henry is quick to ascribe the victory to God: "O God, thy arm was here! / And not to us, but to thy arm alone, / Ascribe we all!" (*Henry V,* 4.8.101–3). But armed with an audience on this occasion, it is more than likely that Henry has returned to his habitual theatricality that disingenuously ascribes roles to others, and that would, as a result, make God his instrument rather than himself God's.[26]

At the time that he offers his empty prayer, Henry has returned from an exchange that may very well have rendered him reluctant to proclaim the justness of his purposes. In wandering among his troops, under benefit of a costume that cloaks his royal identity, he offers the following sentiment to a group of commoners: "Methinks I could not die anywhere so contented as in the king's company, his cause being just and his quarrel honorable" (4.1.119–21). A soldier retorts: "That's more than we know." The possibility of the king's tainted motives later moves the same soldier to draw their woeful consequence:

> But if the cause be not good, the king himself hath a heavy reckoning to make when all those legs and arms and heads, chopped off in a battle, shall join together at the latter day and cry all, "We died at such a place" . . . (122, 127–31).

Without addressing the question of his cause's goodness, Henry succeeds in silencing his challenger's objections.[27] Nevertheless, if a common soldier possesses at once the consideration to be insecure in the goodness of his king's cause and imagination enough to look to Henry's day of reckoning with such grisly detail, it is no wonder that Henry on his return would entreat God to restrict his soldiers' "sense of reck'ning." After the shock of encountering a common soldier who voices such a challenge to him, and after his refusal to meet this challenge on its own grounds, it is also no wonder that Henry in prayer would neither declare the goodness of his enterprise, nor propose to God, as does Richmond, that the impending battle render judgment on the issue of whether he acts as God's own captain.

The effects of the previous night's challenge appear to linger the next morning, for the king does not broach the merits of his cause in his address to his troops before battle. It cannot be denied that Henry V's speech before Agincourt is magnificently stirring; however, in contrast to Richmond's before Bosworth, it is strikingly vacuous. Honor is the theme of Henry's oration: "But if it be a sin to covet honor, / I am the most offending soul alive" (*Henry V,* 4.3.28–29). Henry from the first has pursued this adornment in preference to all other prizes. Its pursuit had led him to perfect the art of manipulation. Now, before battle, he offers to his troops the prospect that his enterprise can reward them with the treasure he has so unswervingly sought. Its paucity of substance, of course, is not to be marvelled at given the previous night's exchange and prayer. His speech anticipates how the anniversary of the battle will be observed in England, and offers that those who will fight on the "Feast of Crispian" will have participated in an event to be remembered to "the ending of the world." In viewing the battle in these terms, he inspirits his troops by offering to establish a kinship between them and him: "We few, we happy few, we band of brothers; / For he to-day that sheds his blood with me / Shall be my brother" (40, 58, 60–62). In casting his cause in these terms, he renders those who will fight under his command into his own likeness; if Henry is the most offending soul alive, then his speech renders the English into the most offending souls alive.

In contrast, Richmond's speech before Bosworth Field dwells upon the justness of his cause. He invades England's shores to depose its king, but he emphasizes that he opposes one who is a "bloody tyrant and homicide." On this basis, he declares that his cause is just: Richard is an enemy of God and in fighting "against God's enemy, God will in justice ward you as his soldiers." He proclaims that "God and our good cause fight upon our side" (*Richard III,* 5.3.247, 254–55, 241).[28] Richmond proclaims before God and his followers what Henry V will not: that his cause is good and in pursuing it he can regard himself as a minister of God.

The being of Hal and Henry V is all seeming—all appearance. The pursuit of honor renders Shakespeare's theatrical king mute as to any purpose higher than honor. Moreover, if his unspoken purpose is to employ the Machiavellian strategy contained in his father's injunction to quell domestic strife by engaging giddy minds in foreign strife—a principle Henry V indicates he understands in his discussion of a possible Scottish invasion—his strategy is a reactive one that cannot posit an end. The principle regards friends as enemies. One employs the countrymen one fears in conquest of foreigners, but once these foreigners are subdued they become friends and hence, paradoxically, enemies to one's rule. As a result of this transformation, more conquests are required in order to domesticate one's newly enfranchised subjects. When so utilized, the bloody process is without end, and the bounties of peace cannot be claimed. Burgundy's lament for France illustrates the devastation that ensues from war:

> . . . our houses and ourselves and children
> Have lost, or do not learn for want of time,
> The sciences that should become our country;
> But grow like savages, as soldiers will,
> That nothing do but meditate on blood . . . .
> (*Henry V*, 5.2.56–60)

Henry's marriage to Katherine, the event that was hoped to issue in the benefits of peace, would not end France's ordeal, however.[29] Nor England's. Valiant Englishmen would continue to die in France, and civil war would engulf England. England's bloodbath would not cease until Henry VI's prophecy is fulfilled. As he foresaw, Richmond would be England's true redeemer. The long nightmare that issued from the Lancastrian usurpation would cease only after Richmond matures, and invades his homeland to announce his intention to pursue a path different from that of Henry V:

> Enrich the time to come with smooth–faced peace,
> With smiling plenty, and fair prosperous days!
> Abate the edge of traitors, gracious Lord,
> That would reduce these bloody days again
> And make poor England weep in streams of blood! (*Richard III*, 5.5.33–37)

In attempting to employ Machiavelli's endless and self-destructive strategy in the manner in which he does, Henry V can be deemed a Machiavellian prince. The king, whose martial striving renders him a prince, does indeed play out a tragedy on French soil (cf. *Henry V*, 1.2.103–10).

V

What are we to make of Shakespeare's play, which presents so unattractive a portrait of a monarch whose surface is so undeniably beguiling? An answer appears to emerge from a recognition of the tension between an unthinking acceptance of the claims that the Prologue and Chorus make on behalf of the worthiness of Henry and his cause on the one hand, and their demands that the members of the audience "[w]ork, work [their] thoughts" on the other (*Henry V*, Cho. 3.25).

In bellicose tones the Chorus lends its unswerving support to the English cause. For instance, it describes the preparation for the French invasion in noble phrases that inspire admiration of the sacrifices that Henry's enterprise demands:

> Now all the youth of England are on fire,
> And silken dalliance in the wardrobe lies.
> Now thrive the armorers, and honor's thought
> Reigns solely in the breast of every man.
> They sell the pasture now to buy the horse,
> Following the mirror of all Christian kings
> With wingèd heels, as English Mercuries.
> (*Henry V*, Cho. 2.1–7)

Nevertheless, the play itself shows us much more regarding the character of the English preparations. In the act that follows the Chorus, the audience witnesses in Pistol's behavior an eagerness for the invasion that is much at variance with the exalted images of the Chorus. Not a yeoman who must sacrifice his freehold for a steed, Pistol is instead a parasitic horsefly: "Let us to France, like horse-leeches, my boys, / To suck, to suck, the very blood to suck!" (2.3.50–51). Similarly, there exist additional disjunctions between the action of the play and the assertions of the Chorus. For example, even after Henry has boldly declared that he covets honor to the exclusion of all other goods (4.3), the Chorus asserts that the king is "free from vainness and self-glorious pride" (Cho. 5.20). Thus, the action of the play is often at odds with the Chorus's proclamations.

The problem that this recognition raises may be explained by the Prologue's apology for the difficulty of depicting the play's exalted subject matter.[30] It asks indulgence; it asks that the audience members aid it by seeing more than appears immediately on the stage:

> O, pardon! since a crooked figure may
> Attest in little place a million;
> And let us, ciphers to this great accompt,
> On your imaginary forces work. . . .
> Piece out our imperfections with your thoughts:
> Into a thousand parts divide one man
> And make imaginary puissance. (Pro. 15–18, 23–25)

The obvious meaning is that the stage is inadequate to present battles in which thousands contend; indeed, the Chorus reemphasizes this theme of the necessity of the employment of the audience's imagination to the presentation of the play's subject matter. But more generally, the Prologue wishes the audience to learn to see more than what appears most immediately. One could also say that the audience learns to see beyond appearance when it pursues the implications of Henry's method and purpose. If these implications are pursued, then it could be truly said that the audience's "thoughts . . . now . . . deck our kings" (Pro. 28).

It is the opposite feat that Henry wishes his subjects to employ. He wishes his troops to see less than what is apparent. After hearing from a subject an account of his own day of reckoning, Henry prays that the reckoning power of his subjects be curtailed. It is not surprising that Henry, the master of staging scenes—the master of appearance—desires that his subjects recognize less than what might otherwise be visible. Nevertheless, Shakespeare's play, which depicts the king of appearance, instructs us to see beyond mere appearance. Therefore, on the level of drama, at least, Shakespeare offers the possibility of a challenge to Machiavelli's dictum: "Everyone sees how you appear, few touch what you are . . . So let a prince win and maintain his state: the means will always be judged honorable, and will be praised by everyone."[31]

Notes

I am grateful to Joseph Alulis, Michael Davis, Tim Spiekerman, and Michael Zuckert for their helpful comments on earlier drafts of this essay.

1. Citations from the plays are from Alfred Harbage, ed., *William Shakespeare: The Complete Works* (New York: The Viking Press, 1979).

2. For interpretations of the play as an encomium to Henry, see J. Dover Wilson's introduction to the Cambridge edition of the play (*King Henry V* [Cambridge: Cambridge University Press, 1947]) and J. H. Walter's introduc-

tion to the Arden edition (*King Henry V*, The Arden Shakespeare, ed. Richard Proudfoot and Ann Thompson [London: Routledge, 1990]). Some of the more sophisticated of his detractors show how the scenes depicting Pistol and his cohorts serve to comment on the actions of Henry V. See particularly Harold C. Goddard, *The Meaning of Shakespeare* (Chicago: University of Chicago Press, 1951), 226–28, 232–37, 259–61; Roy Battenhouse, "*Henry V* as Heroic Comedy," in *Essays on Shakespeare and Elizabethan Drama in Honor of Hardin Craig*, ed. Richard Hosley (Columbia: University of Missouri Press, 1962), 176–77. Gordon Ross Smith, "Shakespeare's *Henry V*: Another Part of the Critical Forest," *Journal of the History of Ideas* 37 (March–January 1976): 3–26, has gone so far as to maintain that Pistol serves as an abstract of the king. After Norman Rabkin argued that both views were inextricable parts of the whole, neither of which could vanquish the other ("Either/Or: Responding to *Henry V*" in *Shakespeare and the Problem of Meaning* [Chicago: University of Chicago Press, 1981]), the cultural materialists shifted the ground of debate by examining the role of ideological forces in shaping the meaning of the play. See, for example, Jonathan Dollimore and Alan Sinfield, "History and Ideology: The Instance of *Henry V*" in *Alternative Shakespeares*, ed. John Drakakis (London: Methuen, 1985) and Stephen Greenblatt, "Invisible Bullets: Renaissance Authority and Its Subversion, Henry IV and Henry V," in *Political Shakespeare: New Essays in Cultural Materialism*, ed. Jonathan Dollimore and Alan Sinfield (Ithaca: Cornell University Press, 1985). By arguing that Shakespeare intended both to arouse hostile feelings in the audience toward the character of Henry V and to transfer these feelings to the Irish, England's foreign enemy of the time, Joel B. Altman posited an ambitious model of interpretation that utilized the insights that emerged from the textual readings of the formalists, as well as from the examination of the cultural materialists of the ideological forces abroad in Elizabethan England ("Vile Participation': The Amplification of Violence in the Theater of *Henry V*," *Shakespeare Criticism* 19 [1991]: 133–50). Altman makes a convincing case that the play's patriotic scenes infused a sense of shame in an audience largely ambivalent, if not resistant, to the mustering of troops. From this evidence Altman concludes that Shakespeare is "a time-server in the best sense—as one who, unable to transcend his time, perceived its liberties and its restraints as mutually entangling filiations and played out their possibilities on his stage" (146). Yet, the theme of the conflict between the good of the individual and that of his or her community, which Altman identifies as the driving force of the play, is one that transcends any given time period, and as Altman has admirably shown, the details of the particular conflict that impinged on Shakespeare's first audiences are recoverable and can be made intelligible to the play's contemporary readers.

3. Moody Prior objects to such a comparison on the grounds that the "directness and straightforward simplicity of *Henry V* begin to disappear in complexities" when considered in light of the earlier plays (*The Drama of*

Power: Studies in Shakespeare's History Plays [Evanston, Ill.: Northwestern University Press, 1973], 264). Although his point is well taken that the play must be able to stand alone as a performable work, it is also conceivable that the other plays in the tetralogy can supplement an understanding of Henry's character. Indeed, John Alvis provides an abundance of evidence for a thoroughgoing similarity of character between the prince and the king based on the degree of self-calculation displayed by Henry Monmouth in the tetralogy (John Alvis, "A Little Touch of the Night in Harry: The Career of Henry of Monmouth" in *Shakespeare as Political Thinker*, ed. John Alvis and Thomas G. West [Durham, N.C.: Carolina Academic Press, 1981]). See also John C. Bromley, *The Shakespearean Kings* (Boulder: University of Colorado Associated University Press, 1971), 77; Robert Ornstein, *A Kingdom for a Stage: The Achievement of Shakespeare's History Plays* (Cambridge, Mass.: Harvard University Press, 1972), 182–83.

4. Peter Erickson ("Fathers, Sons, and Brothers in *Henry V*," in *William Shakespeare's Henry V*, Modern Critical Interpretations Series, ed. Harold Bloom [New York: Chelsea House Publishers, 1988], 111–33) takes a psychological approach in examining the influence of Henry IV on his son to find that the mature Hal is defined by his father's guilt and lacks an independent voice. Although I too find a Henry V who is profoundly influenced by his father, I identify a son who is more self-conscious in a cunning attempt to surpass his father's example and understanding.

5. Mera J. Flaumenhaft points to Henry's theatricality and attributes his success to his ability to manipulate others through a "combination of carefully staged seeming 'miracles' and extraordinary speaking abilities" (*The Civic Spectacle: Essays on Drama and Community* [Lanham, Md.: Rowman & Littlefield 1994], 130). Flaumenhaft's work on the play came to my attention after I had completed this essay.

6. It is Hotspur who speaks. Cf. the Host's questions in *The Merry Wives of Windsor*: "Am I politic? am I subtle? am I a Machiavel?" (3.1.91–92). For interpretations of Henry IV as a Machiavellian prince see, Dain A. Trafton, "Shakespeare's Henry IV: A New Prince in a New Principality," in *Shakespeare as Political Thinker*, and Irving Ribner, "Bolingbroke, A True Machiavellian," *Modern Language Quarterly* 9 (1948): 177–84.

7. The warrior's struggle with a river exemplifies his fierce spiritedness. See Achilles' struggle with Skamandros, the furious river-god (Homer *Iliad* 21.228–327). Cf. Machiavelli's comparison of fortune "to one of these violent rivers which, when they become enraged, flood the plains, ruin the trees and the buildings, lift earth from this part, drop in another" in chapter 25 of *The Prince*, trans. Harvey C. Mansfield, Jr. (Chicago: University of Chicago Press, 1985), 98.

8. *Prince*, 69. Cf. Cicero's comment: "While wrong may be done, then, in either of two ways, that is, by force or by fraud, both are bestial: fraud seems to belong to the cunning fox, force to the lion; both are wholly unworthy of

man, but fraud is the more contemptible'' (*de Officis*, 1.13, trans. Walter Miller [New York: Loeb Classical Library, 1928], 45). Bromley utilizes Machiavelli's imagery in commenting on *1* and *2 Henry IV* and *Henry V*, arguing that Henry V overcomes Hal's defects as lion by successfully combining the fox and the lion (*Shakespearean Kings*, 76–79). Although at points Bromley claims that Henry V has perfected the combination, he concludes that in conquering France Henry turns into the ''lion run riot.'' In Bromley's view, Henry is ultimately devoid of self-understanding (Ibid., 85–86).

9. *Prince*, 101. Cf. Francis Bacon, Essay 12, ''Of Boldness'': ''boldness is ever blind, for it seeth not dangers and inconveniences. Therefore it is ill in counsel, good in execution; so that the right use of bold persons is that they never command in chief, but be seconds and under the direction of others'' in *Francis Bacon: A Selection of His Works*, ed. Sidney Warhaft (New York: Macmillan, 1982), 75.

10. *Discourses on Livy*, trans. Harvey Mansfield and Nathan Tarcov, forthcoming University of Chicago Press, 1996.

11. In this manner, Hal appears to offer the possibility that a person can successfully vary his method of procedure with the times—a possibility that Machiavelli at points denies: a man cannot be found who is ''so prudent as to know how to accommodate himself to this, whether because he cannot deviate from what nature inclines him to or also because, when one has always flourished by walking on one path, he cannot be persuaded to depart from it'' (*Prince*, 100).

12. Machiavelli explicitly praises the use of others as one's instruments when he recounts approvingly how Cesare Borgia made use of Messer Remirro de Orco as his minister in reducing the Romagna ''to peace and obedience'' (*Prince*, 29–30). Borgia's ultimate failure is linked to the fact that, although he successfully manipulated Remirro, he was not a master manipulator. Machiavelli reveals later in *The Prince* that Cesare was the instrument of his father, who was in turn the instrument of the Church (46–47).

13. Whereas I argue that Hal as king far surpasses his father's cunning, Alvin B. Kernan maintains that he returns to his father ''in spirit and person'' (''The Henriad: Shakespeare's Major History Plays,'' in *Modern Shakespearean Criticism: Essays on Style, Dramaturgy, and the Major Plays*, ed. Alvin B. Kernan [New York: Harcourt Brace Jovanovich, 1970], 275).

14. Cited in J. Dover Wilson's introduction, xlii. Wilson, an admirer of Henry V, does not accept Johnson's judgment, '' . . . nor does Hotspur's offhand treatment of his married Kate bear any real resemblance to Henry's forthright conversation with his unmarried one.'' Cf. Ornstein's judgment that ''[i]f Harry's wooing lacks the tender humor and intimacy of Hotspur's moments with Kate, it is because the conqueror of Agincourt cannot, even in his 'passion,' forget his royal self; and he will not allow the others to forget that Kate is one of the prizes of war . . .'' (*Kingdom*, 198).

15. For a helpful examination of the historical issues surrounding the

conspiracy, see Karl P. Wentersdorf, "The Conspiracy of Silence in *Henry V*," *Shakespeare Quarterly* 27 (Summer 1976): 264–87.

16. Goddard, *Meaning of Shakespeare*, 221.

17. Geoffrey Bullough, ed., *Narrative and Dramatic Sources of Shakespeare*, vol. 4 (London: Routledge & Kegan Paul, 1962), 377–78.

18. See also John Palmer, *Political Characters of Shakespeare* (London: Macmillan, 1961), 221–24.

19. Machiavelli asserts that war is necessary in a republic to overcome domestic problems: "if Heaven were so kind that [a republic] did not have to make war, from that would arise the leisure to make it either effeminate or divided; these two things together, or each by itself, would be the cause of its ruin" (*Discourses*, 1.6).

20. Reese, who maintains that Shakespeare fully approved of Henry, notes that "Henry's detractors say that he had not forgotten his father's advice to busy giddy minds with foreign quarrels, and that he was base enough to seek the clergy's blessing for a war for which he had no better excuse than this need for diversionary activity, coupled with personal anger at the resulting message sent by the Dauphin." "If this is a just interpretation, Henry is beyond our pardon. The idea of the godly ruler fails at once, and all the later heroism and fair words and gallant comradeship in battle cannot gild the fault. Henry's reformation would be mere expediency, and Shakespeare's picture of him as the mirror of all Christian kings would be a shocking irony," he continues. This alternative must be rejected in Reese's view because "[i]t is improbable that Shakespeare would have deliberately wrecked his play in the first ten minutes" (*Majesty*, 322–23). On the contrary, Henry's failure as a godly king may reveal Shakespeare's extreme artistry. Cf. Prior, *Drama of Power*, 266.

21. In his notes to the Arden edition, Walter states that Shakespeare's source was Virgil rather than Pliny (22).

22. Virgil, *The Georgics*, trans. L. P. Wilkinson (New York: Penguin Books, 1982), 129.

23. Cf. T. W. Baldwin, *William Shakspere's Small Latine and Lesse Greeke* (Urbana: University of Illinois Press, 1944), 2:473–81. Although Baldwin argues that Shakespeare used Iodocus Willichius's commentary on Virgil for the Archbishop's speech, he notes that he was unable to find in any source the Archbishop's comparison of the bees to merchants and soldiers (475).

24. The impious implications of the attempt at authorship are more clearly defined in the sequel to Machiavelli's account of Cesare's use of Remirro as instrument. Machiavelli relates that Remirro's cruelty quickly produced the results that Cesare sought. Nevertheless, Cesare feared that the harshness of his "minister" might cause him to be hated. As a result of his fear, Cesare "placed [Remirro] one morning in the piazza at Cesena in two pieces, with a piece of wood and a bloody knife beside him" (*The Prince* 7, pp. 29–30). Cesare's ploy was successful in deflecting attention from the fact that he

himself was the author of his minister's deeds. Because Remirro's death bears an uncomfortable likeness to Christ's crucifixion, Cesare appears to make himself the equivalent of God in this scenario.

25. Interestingly, Richmond makes his first appearance in Shakespeare's corpus in the very scene that contains Henry VI's acknowledgement of his debt to Warwick and God—the very scene that suggests the absence of a middle element between the two extremes of father and son. When Henry VI turns his attention to the youthful Richmond in this scene, the king foretells that Richmond "will prove our country's bliss" (*3 Henry VI,* 4.6.70).

26. Alvis argues that Henry's magnanimous gesture to God actually serves to magnify his own glory, in the same way that Hal's similar gesture to Falstaff after Shrewsbury redounds to the prince's credit. Alvis attributes the boldness that places God in the position of Falstaff not to a conscious plan on Henry's part, but rather to "Shakespeare's own audacious playfulness" ("Career of Henry Monmouth," 119; for Alvis's discussion of Hal's treatment of Falstaff after battle, see 101–2; cf. Prior, *Drama of Power*, 81–82). Battenhouse sees an ironic connection between Henry's "murdering of the prisoners and his pious eagerness to give God's 'arm' the whole credit for the victory" ("*Henry V*," 178).

27. Alvis, "Career of Henry Monmouth," 120.

28. Richmond, however, does not fail to promise his troops rewards in victory. See Grant Mindle, "Shakespeare's Demonic Prince," *Interpretation* 20 (Spring 1993): 270.

29. Queen Isabel expresses the fervent hope that the marriage will bring peace to the two realms. Henry V reveals his view of the necessity of war when he expresses the hope that the marriage that would make friends of the French would produce a son who would undertake greater conquests: "Shall not thou and I, between Saint Denis and Saint George, compound a boy, half French, half English, that shall go to Constantinople and take the Turk by the beard?" (*Henry V,* 5.2.200–3).

30. Goddard challenges the notion that the "windy chauvinism" of the Prologue and Chorus are simple represention of Shakespeare's own views (*Meaning of Shakespeare,* 216–18). Given the manner in which the action of the play is in tension with these proclamations, this appears to be a valid conclusion. I suggest below, however, that on a deeper level the Prologue and Chorus may actually give voice to Shakespeare's injunction to the audience.

31. *Prince,* 71.

Part III

Tragedies

8

"This is Venice": Politics in Shakespeare's *Othello*

Pamela K. Jensen

It is a widely held view that *Othello, The Moor of Venice*[1] is the play in which Shakespeare comes closest to writing a purely domestic tragedy. Not only is the focus on private rather than public life, our attention is especially directed to the most private or hidden aspects of the characters themselves. The political dimension of *Othello* seems at most, then, to be a foil to the real action, allowing the psychological factors dominating the play to emerge more clearly by contrast. Arguing for the distinctiveness of *Othello*, for instance, G. R. Hibbard notes its departure from the close interconnection between the public and the private characterizing the other tragedies.[2] Even in the first act of the play, where political issues of great moment to Venice are clearly in evidence, what strikes Hibbard most is the haste with which they are dispatched.[3] In act 2, Shakespeare's speedy disposal of the enemy Turks by a storm at sea rather than by war attests further to his interest in the protagonist's purely private preoccupations. Thereafter, to the end, Othello's surrender to "the green-ey'd monster" is the only theme.

It is insufficient, I think, to account for the presence of politics in the play by reference to the need for a counterpoint to the contraction in Othello's vision. On the contrary, to understand the action, we need to consider the political foundation Shakespeare lays for it. In this essay I will try to elaborate the features of *Othello* that make it decidedly a Venetian story.

That the establishment of a political basis for *Othello* enters into

Shakespeare's design is evident from the relation between the play and Cinthio's novella, the source for the plot.[4] Leaving aside for the moment the metamorphosis Cinthio's characters undergo in Shakespeare's hands, the most notable of Shakespeare's additions are the political facts. The original story is about domestic intrigue and private vengeance, culminating in the assassination of the Moor by Disdemona's relatives "as he merited."[5] By following out, as well as by altering, Cinthio's brief allusions to Venetian political life, Shakespeare demonstrates that he thought about the political setting for his story far more seriously and systematically than Cinthio did. In so doing, he accommodates a purely fictional account to history.[6]

Shakespeare's politicization of Cinthio's story is achieved by the deliberate political enhancement of the characters, by intertwining throughout the play political and private events—showing parallels as well as contrasts between them—and, above all, by showing the influence of commercial and Christian Venetian society on the aspirations and chief concerns of the characters. It is only under certain political conditions that domestic issues as such could be elevated to the importance they have in *Othello*; conditions not to be found, for instance, in ancient Rome or medieval England. We are consequently led to consider the events that take place on the island of Cyprus in light of his depiction of Venetian life in the first act.

The Republic of Venice

The juxtaposition of public and private events in the play acquires its special character because of the kind of regime Venice is. I have in mind the relations between political and military authority; the need to harmonize private and public orders; the intimate connection between honor and private life; the limitations on the rule of law to render one's possessions secure; and, as a consequence, possessiveness, and the possibility of private tyranny.

The principles of civic humanism infusing the Renaissance, which had produced an enthusiastic surge of interest in ancient republicanism, especially the Roman Republic, produced as well a search for a modern example of republicanism that might escape the perceived disadvantages of Rome—its perpetual turbulence and contentiousness, which made it vulnerable to mob democracy, and its ultimate vulnerability to tyranny. To numerous writers throughout the sixteenth and seventeenth centuries, Venice appeared to supply just such a model.[7]

The tendency to view Venice in explicit contrast to Rome was a familiar one. The chief difference between the two republics presents itself as the orientation of Venice toward the activities of peace and the orientation of Rome toward war. Roman military aims required the city to keep the plebeians armed and in turn to grant them a share in political power with the patricians. As a result, Rome was forced throughout its history to contend with the clash of ambitions between its two classes. By contrast, since Venice lacked a large armed populace, the city seemed able to maintain its political exclusivity in perfect tranquility. Venice called itself *Serinissima*, the most serene republic.[8]

The second outstanding feature of Venice distinguishing it from Rome, pertinent to its reputation for repelling tyranny, is the strict separation of the political and military functions and the subordination of the latter to the former. As a commercial rather than a martial republic, Venice sought to avoid war. Nevertheless, as an imperial power seeking to expand both on *terra firma* and in the Mediterranean, Venice could not exactly dispense with an army. In consideration of the causes of the fall of the Roman Republic as Venice interpreted them, however, it seemed necessary to arm the city in such a way that it could avoid the civil disturbances and the threat of tyranny that ambitious military heroes among the aristocrats might pose.[9] Venice found the solution, at the beginning of its greatest period of imperial expansion, in the disarming of its own nobility and the reliance on mercenaries, i.e., professional soldiers or *condottieri*, to pursue its war aims. In the interests of domestic unity, Venice divided political and military power, making the military force it built a mere adjunct to the city—as it were, for it, but not of it.[10]

This central feature of Venetian society figures prominently, both in its obvious form and in the effects it produces, in *Othello*. In fact, Shakespeare's depiction in act 1, scene 3, of the division of political and military responsibility provides the basis for concluding that Venice is a city to whom martial virtue is as such alien and strange, as far outside of the purview and normal preoccupations of the modern commercial republic as it is of the essence of the ancient Roman Republic. As Shakespeare himself depicts the Roman Republic in *Coriolanus*, for instance, the city virtually alleges that it needs no other virtue.[11] There is no place for martial virtue strictly speaking in Venice.

At first glance the calm and orderly reflections of the Signiory seem to be perfectly congruent with the judgment of the strongest proponents of the Venetian arrangements. Although Shakespeare makes the Signiory's deliberations rest of necessity upon mere surmise about Turkish stratagem and upon conflicting estimates of Turkish strength, they conclude in a response that is neither rash nor cowardly. In short, the Signiory's deliberations reflect the solidly conservative and cautious collective judgment of men who have the full responsibility to initiate and none of the responsibility to wage war. By so arranging matters that their surmises are proven to us to be correct, Shakespeare compliments the senators' prudence. In a play in which things are typically not what they seem, the senators' resolve to look beyond appearance is the hallmark of political wisdom. Thus, they refuse to countenance Brabantio's accusations against Othello without "proof" (1.3.106–9). Nor are they duped by Turkish stratagem: "'tis a pageant / To keep us in false gaze" (18–19). Like their estimate of Turkish strength, their decision to install Othello in place of Montano as governor of Cyprus shows that they prefer rather to err on the side of excess than deficiency (223–26). Although they respond admirably in their circumstances, however, Shakespeare indicates that the Signiory's caution is itself occasioned by the immediacy of the threat of war and by no means expressive of a general martial vigilance.

The Venetian Signiory has in the first place no direct experience either of the field of action or of the enemy. Since the senators have never witnessed Othello's military prowess either, they must defer to "opinion, a sovereign mistress of effects" in choosing him to lead their expedition. They have made no preparation in advance for war with the Turks, and their most trusted advisors are either out of town or out of the way and must be recalled to Venice "post-post-haste." We learn from the conversation between the duke and a senator that in terms of defending itself, Cyprus "altogether lacks th' abilities / That Rhodes is dress'd in" (25–26). The senator readily acknowledges the greater "importancy" of Cyprus than Rhodes to the Turks and also the greater inclination the Turks would have to invade Cyprus than Rhodes, especially if it is not well-fortified. If, as the senator urges, "[w]e must not think the Turk is so unskillful / To leave that latest which concerns him first," we must wonder why the Venetians, who are in full possession of these facts and to whom Cyprus was no less important, were so unskillful as to leave Cyprus poorly defended (19–30). By not fortifying Cyprus, they actually provoke attack and thereby increase, if inadvertently, the likelihood of war. By inventing a cause for war in the renewal of Turkish attacks on Cyprus and drawing our attention to the situation there in a detailed way, Shakespeare points to Venetian negligence with respect to matters of defense.

In this instance, rather than prudence, the separation of political and military responsibilities depicted in the first act of *Othello* seems to have produced an untoward passivity in the political authority that soundly jeopardizes the very tranquillity the whole arrangement was designed to achieve. Less than respite from war, peace supplies a condition in which the Venetians disdain to consider their defense. Even when war is imminent, the Signiory appears to regard it as more the business of its commanders than an affair of the city. As he dispatches Othello to the Cyprus wars, the duke is altogether silent on matters pertaining to the conduct of war—men, armaments, strategy, etc. Once he has dismissed Othello, he has effectually dismissed the war.

In Cinthio's story, the Moor's marriage and his subsequent appointment as governor of Cyprus are unrelated events—separated by an indefinite span of time—neither of which is affected by war.[12] In the play, Othello's marriage and the imminent Turkish attack on the Venetian held island of Cyprus are simultaneous events that come simultaneously to light. Iago, whose uncanny nose for news enables him to be apprised of both the marriage and the Cyprus war before anyone else, understands as well the relationship their coincidence establishes between them (1.1.147–53). Shakespeare heightens the political interest in Othello's marriage, and yet makes Venice helpless to resist it. His depiction of Venice intimates as well that the city has a share in responsibility for the ensuing tragedy.

Venice's remoteness from war seems to have engendered a lax complacency, both in the city and its inhabitants, toward what belongs to them. Mercenaries will defend the empire on which their material security depends; law will deter crime; a high and urbane civilization will repel barbarism. As a consequence of these beliefs, Venice and Brabantio alike leave their possessions ill-protected from foreign invasion. Brabantio's position with respect to Desdemona is, as he bitterly points out, parallel to Venice's position with respect to Cyprus. When the duke tells the "robb'd" father to foil the thief of Desdemona by acting as if the loss doesn't matter, the anguished Brabantio responds, "So let the Turk of Cyprus us beguile, / We lose it not, so long as we can smile" (1.3.208–11). In an ironic twist that could hardly be lost on anyone, Othello, the expedient against the one theft, executes the other.

Because of the deeply rooted conviction among Venetians in their imperturbability, both the war and Othello's marriage to Desdemona intrude upon the city unexpectedly to catch them unawares, "as when, by night and negligence, the fire / Is spied in populous cities'' (1.1.76–77). The serenity that figures so prominently in such appeal as Venice may have had for Shakespeare's contemporaries as a testament to their political prudence, appears in the play as a kind of sleepiness that is actually derivative of disregard for the conditions of quiet. Night is doubly evocative of negligence and, therefore, the appropriate setting for the action that occurs in Venice in the first act. Not only does night evoke the soporific effect of Venetian prejudices, it also shelters secret conspiracies: the innocent sleep; the guilty are awake. The events of act 1 comprise a single movement in which two nocturnal conspiracies, one political and one private, rouse the citizens from slumber, are ''disputed on'' and ostensibly resolved without unduly ruffling the city's equipoise.[13]

Following his transfer of the Cyprus command to Othello, the duke sends the Venetians back to bed. No one sees the hatching of a third conspiracy. Unlike the audience, the characters are left in the grip of an optical illusion or charm; a pageant of order keeping them ''in false gaze.'' Iago remains alone on the stage at the end of the first act, vigilant and wide-awake: ''Hell and night / must bring this monstrous birth to the world's light'' (1.3.403–4).

Soldiers and Civilians

If the Venetian arrangements are unreliable in preventing war, they are also inadequate to maintain the strict subordination of the military force to the political authority. Not only does the city establish that authority as essentially independent in its own sphere, its arrangements deepen the city's reliance upon the mercenaries it employs, thereby courting their ambitions. Both of Shakespeare's Venetian plays depict the insufficiency of the city to the attainment of its own purposes as the cause of the great power granted to foreigners in its midst. In *The Merchant of Venice*, we see that Shylock thrives in the city because of the uncertainty that accompanies the pursuit of gain through trade and the need for ready capital.[14] Othello thrives in Venice because the city must protect its commercial empire and has no wish to occupy itself with that end. In both plays the city is forced into unwitting compliance with the private will of a foreigner.

In ancient Rome, the city's assiduous attention to its soldiers in the form of civic honors was intended to moderate or train their ambitions. Cinthio sees the same principles operating in Venice: to advance ''the interests of the state," he says, Venice rewards deeds of valor.[15] But there are essential differences between Roman and Venetian practices. No amount of valor entitles Othello or any soldier to political power in Venice. However high Othello rises in the military ranks, there is a ceiling to his political ambitions. In Rome, as *Coriolanus* suggests, evidence of military prowess of itself entitles a soldier to lay claim to the highest civil offices.[16]

Rather than heaping accolades and rewards on its soldiers, Venice seeks to moderate them by making the city's exploitation of them palpable. The governorship of Cyprus, which passes in the play from Montano to Othello to Cassio, is treated as the highest political honor a soldier can attain. Not only is it a temporary one, it is one that can only be enjoyed outside of Venice. In Rome civic honors are conferred conditionally and after the fact, so that no soldier can miss the political gratitude that is implied by them. They are the wages for services rendered. In Venice, the city only lends honors and offices to its soldiers and grants them in advance of their achievements, like a bribe or fee.

The political regulation of the ambitions of martial men moderates both their ends and their means. By making them an integral part of the community and keeping them eager for a share in it, a city like Rome ties their interests to the public interest. Like Iago, they may keep their hearts attending on themselves, but to do so is not harmful to the city: Rome's soldiers can thrive only if Rome does.[17] In Venice, by contrast, martial virtue is deprived of its political character. To achieve the desired harmony of public and private ends, the city is dependent, therefore, on the personal moderation of its soldiers, on their characters. Venice is for this reason especially vulnerable to the arts by which men can disguise their characters; arts that thrive precisely in luxurious, highly civilized, and very "populous" cities. As is revealed in the play, Venice cannot in fact extinguish ambition by refusing to take responsibility for managing it. Rather, by abjuring the public means for regulating ambition, Venice merely drives it underground; creating thereby a subterranean political realm—parallel to the underground economy of Shylock's Venice—where the aspirations of men are set beyond the city's control, limited only by the personal dispositions of ambitious men themselves.

Evidence of the depoliticization of martial virtue in Venice is found in the composition of the army in the play. Like the city itself, the army consists of a motley of men, who are drawn into the service of Venice from various places and for a variety of private reasons: natives and foreigners, strangers and friends, professional soldiers after gain and gentlemen like Cassio, who embark on a military career as a part of their own education for private life. So easygoing are the practices, that Roderigo can put on a beard and head out to Cyprus on a whim (1.3.340–41). For Shakespeare to portray these soldiers in war would have meant seeing them with their private interests at least ostensibly submerged in the common cause. By not doing so, he emphasizes the purely instrumental character of a military career, its absorption into the private lives of men. To be sure, we see the spirited side of the soldiers, but only when it comes to the defense of what is their own as something apart from what belongs to the city.

In a significant sense, Venice acknowledges the importance of character to its well-being by fostering certain kinds of human qualities. Venice fortifies itself against untoward ambition or anger not only by staying remote from war, but also by the positive cultivation of qualities conducive to gentleness in its own inhabitants, giving Venice a charm and appeal that is unavailable in ancient Rome. We might characterize the ruling principle of Venice as gentility or civility. By inculcating the skills and graces of civilized peace, Venice suppresses political ambition, tames the animosities that may arise among its inhabitants, and renders human beings agreeable to one another. The Venetians' civility is reflected both in their moderating habituation to the rule of law and in their attachment to an urbane and punctilious social intercourse. Accordingly, Venice shows a greater tolerance for lapses stemming from an over-gentle condition than from anger or incivility, as the case of Cassio, who fully embodies the Venetian standards of civility, demonstrates.[18] Whatever boldness he exhibits, whatever excesses he is capable of, derive from his preoccupation with civility. He falls prey to drinking because it is the entertainment devised by "courtesy." And as he kisses Iago's wife upon greeting her on the island, he excuses himself by saying, "Let it not gall your patience, good Iago, / That I extend my manners; 'tis my breeding / That gives me this bold show of courtesy" (2.1.97–99).

The rule of civility in Venice establishes a pronounced distinction between a martial way of life, suited to honest or true men, and a civilian way of life, which, because it renders men especially agreeable to women, makes them susceptible to the accusation of effeminacy. From Iago's point of view, the attractive and eager ladies' man Cassio is "bookish" and like "a spinster." Returning the favor, from Cassio's point of view, Iago's misogynistic and cynical refusal to enter fully into gallant badinage with the ladies makes him, as he proudly says, a "soldier," but not "a scholar" (1.1.23–24; 2.1.165–66).

The lives of both Iago and Othello are shaped by the fact that in Venice the military life has been turned into a profession, the "service," exploited by the city, and extraneous to it. Without ever obscuring the difference between the transcendent nobility of Othello and the enterprising baseness of Iago, Shakespeare draws them as parallel characters, whose lives intertwine and are in a way eventually exchanged for one another (1.1.57; 5.2.284). Their differences become visible in their respective responses to the situation of a professional soldier in Venice, which is for both of them the source of discontent.

Iago

On the surface, Iago seems to fit the customary picture of the itinerant soldier of fortune well. He is carefree and crass, a hard drinker who knows all the bars in Europe, crude in his speech, lewd about women, a fomenter of the back-alley brawl, and a seeker in war and peace after only those trophies that redound to his "sport and profit." However, in the very soliloquy in which he points gaily to his custom of making his fool—in this case, Roderigo—his purse, he is bent on clarifying his relationship to his fool, lest someone believe that their association places him in subservience to a fool's ends. "For I my own gain'd knowledge should profane / If I would time expend with such [a] snipe / But for my sport and profit" (1.3.384–86). Iago's pride in his "own gain'd knowledge" and in his independence, appearances to the contrary notwithstanding, indicates that he is not and could not be contented with an essentially mercantile life, supported by the wages of service and conducive to the satisfaction of the pleasures of the senses. Iago's choice to become a soldier reflects his disdain for a life like Roderigo's. Moreover, in contrast both to Roderigo and Cassio, whose sexual appetites are evident in their relationships with women and in the fact that they are bachelors, Iago is married. Like Othello, he repudiates "those soft parts of conversation / That chamberers have" in the name of manly sternness (3.3.264–65). Not lust, at least not "absolute lust," but vengeance is the sin he prefers to admit to (2.1.291–96).

When the play opens we gather that Iago has just been accused of double dealing by Roderigo, urging *him* on to woo Desdemona, all the while knowing she was about to marry Othello. In the ensuing exchange, Iago must reestablish his credibility with Roderigo by proving that he hates Othello. His demonstration is peculiarly qualified—on the one side, by an outburst of contempt for the effeminacy of Cassio and, on the other, by an outburst of contempt for the service. His speeches add up to an impassioned defense of his manliness, which is assailed first and foremost by the service. If it is clear that Iago could not actually be placated by winning the lieutenancy that has been given to Cassio, it is also clear that he is determined to win full recognition for his manliness and that being in the service has not solved, but rather exacerbated that problem. In Venice, men's valiant deeds are insufficient to produce a reputation for manliness.

Lionizing valiant men and showering soldiers with public accolades, as is the practice in regimes employing citizen armies, makes men willing to be esteemed for service by obscuring their subordination. Venice, however, as indicated above, chooses not to assume full responsibility for honoring its soldiers or managing the competition among them. Instead, the city turns the army into something akin to a private sinecure; establishing in lieu of open dependence on the city for honor and advancement, a great personal dependence on the general. Cassio and Iago see themselves to be utterly subject to Othello and not Venice for their advancement. Othello sees himself and not Venice as the ultimate arbiter of their careers. Since advancement is subject to the whims of the commanders, influence becomes at least as important as valor to promotion, and perhaps more so. Iago claims to have provided Othello with the notorious "ocular proof" of his honest martial merit in abundance. Yet, he complains: "Preferment goes by letter and affection, / And not by old gradation, where each second / Stood heir to th' first" (1.1.36–38).

Although Iago's own attempt to win Othello's notice by influence demonstrates that he does not disdain such practices, his complaint against them highlights a peculiar problem of the professional military service as presented in the play. Iago is decidedly a man's man. The "arithmetician" Cassio's appointment suggests, however, that civility is as important to advancement in the military as in civilian life. In a more austere political setting, or in a citizen army, Iago's vanity would not have incurred the same wound; even if it did, however, he would not have had the same latitude for his course of revenge.

Shakespeare invents the dispute over the lieutenancy and the rumors about Othello and Iago's wife, Emilia, that kindle Iago's ire. We do not see the service as it culminates in valiant deeds, but rather as the realm of petty wrangling and rumor-mongering in the scurry for place.[19] Iago is obviously susceptible to these things, but Cassio is no less sensitive to the rank he has won than Iago is (2.3.109–10), and no less willing than Iago is to use outside influence to regain it. The importance of private influence makes it impossible to keep the manly preserve of the service insulated from the civilian realm, in which women can more easily rule. Commanders are subject to the persuasions of their wives and are reachable through them, or so Cassio hopes, and, in the ranks, ambitious men may be persuaded to make way for others by disseminating innuendoes about their wives, as Iago knows from his own experience. Emilia inadvertently hits the mark about her husband when she confirms this general view of the service (4.2.130–47). Othello's susceptibility to the influence of civility, evident in his choice of Cassio, and, of course, in his marriage to Desdemona, can only corroborate in Iago's mind the rumor circulating "abroad."

The "curse of service" prevents Iago from achieving the public effect he desires by means that are most in accord with his self-image. Ambition for a public attestation to his manliness prevents him from leaving the service, and, therefore, keeps him bound in an "obsequious bondage" to Othello. Even the dim Roderigo grasps the imputation of unmanly servility that service under these conditions entails. If he were spurned by Othello, Roderigo insists, "I would not follow him then" (1.1.40). Roderigo's remark touches off Iago's most impassioned tirade in the first scene, although it is altogether irrelevant to the establishment of Iago's credibility with his cohort. It is not even clear whether Iago's speech interests Roderigo particularly; he makes no response to it. What is clear is that Iago is at greater pains to justify his association with Othello and to "this snipe" than his hatred of him. And we note as well that Iago takes exquisite care throughout the play to hide from Roderigo the assault on his manliness that in fact gnaws at his "inwards," the suspicion that he has been cuckolded.

The keystone to Iago's defense is that his servility is merely apparent or outward, in brief, that he is a dissembler.

> Others there are
> Who, trimm'd in forms and visages of duty,
> Keep yet their hearts attending on themselves,
> And throwing but shows of service on their lords,
> Do well thrive by them; and when they have lin'd their coats,
> Do themselves homage. These fellows have some soul;
> And such a one do I profess myself. (1.1.49–55)

Iago implies that a true man in the service has no choice but to dissemble—to hide his heart—to show what he is made of. As a dishonest "knave," Iago is a true or honest man.

The very fact that Iago takes such care to clarify to Roderigo the deceptive nature of appearances, suggests that he will not be content until he has brought outward appearances into accord with the inner reality. Since Iago has become famous for his ability to confound appearance and reality, it is useful to keep in mind his own honest concern for their harmony. To show the world that he is a man—to get his "good name"—Iago will wreak havoc.

For all his flashy devotion to his private or "peculiar" end, Iago's depredations on the other characters soon lose all contact with anything that could be called his own interest.[20] Iago sets himself to dispossess others of what is rightfully their own, not so that he can enjoy it, but so that they cannot. His very first "turn" on Othello, for instance, is to "poison his delight" (1.1.68). In general, Iago exhibits a satanic preference to blacken innocence and cause chaos and destruction for its own sake. Despite the ingenuity that his hasty improvisations in the play are meant to suggest, in his madness, Iago would not actually be content until he had serially depopulated the planet and uprooted all concord and order.[21]

Upon Desdemona's safe arrival on the island of Cyprus, Cassio muses that her beauty caused the malevolent forces of nature to exempt her from harm. "Traitors ensteep'd to enclog the guiltless keel, / As having sense of beauty, do omit / Their mortal natures, letting go safely by / The divine Desdemona" (2.1.70–73). Iago's viciousness suggests the truth of the opposite case. There may be men who understand order, beauty, and innocence without having the power to possess or to attract them. For that very reason, they can become traitors against them and *put on* their mortal natures. As a man long gone from the garden, Iago's inveterate hatred of innocence, in particular, may be connected to the fact that it is the one thing he can never regain or possess.[22]

Iago possesses the wisdom of the serpent. His intelligence is striking. He understands Othello better than any other character in the play—his naiveté (1.3.399), his constancy (2.1.289), and the completeness of his subjection to Desdemona (2.3.345, 3.2.90–92). Even beyond any immediate utility, he seems to take almost a clinical or professional interest in Cassio's psychology (2.3.294–95). Seeming always to be in the know himself, Iago seduces his victims with the appearance of wisdom, tantalizing them with what look to be fruits of the tree of knowledge (3.3.258–60). He is a vendor of false sophistication. Thus, exactly when Othello seems to know the most, he is shown up to be, as Emilia calls him, a "gull," a "dolt," and "ignorant as dirt" (5.2.163–64).

Iago's own sophistication makes him well-suited to take advantage of the disharmony between appearance and reality that is a characteristic of highly civilized societies. In his famous complaint against modern civilization, Rousseau points to the replacement of morals by "manners," that is, uniform rules of politeness that make duplicity possible, or rather, that make insincerity ubiquitous.[23] To paraphrase Iago, in modern cities, no one is who he is. Rousseau's citified men and women have "the semblance of all the virtues without the possession of any."[24] Iago, who represents this disparity in its most refined form, also plays on it as an instrument to rule the other characters. Venetian men and women are, he contends, "super-subtle." Cassio, he tells Roderigo, dons "the mere form of civil and humane seeming" the better to hide "his salt and most hidden loose affection" (2.1.239–41). And, as for Venetian women, he tells Othello "their best conscience / Is not to leave't undone, but keep't unknown" (3.3.203-4). In Rousseau's picture of polite society, real virtue is ridiculous, and everyone knows he or she is playing a part. Because Venice, by contrast, still takes virtue seriously, Iago's deftness with smoke and mirrors is a game in which real damage can be done.

Iago sees himself as the perfect alchemist, who can transmute everything (including himself) into its opposite at will. As the master of how things look, he can change white to black and vice versa. As his own "blackest sins" can be hidden by "heavenly shows," so Desdemona's pure white virtue can be turned into "pitch." Despite the horrifying damage he causes, however, Iago's alchemy does not and cannot succeed. In the end, he must confront the fact that the impediments standing in the way of his receiving proper recognition are not merely external or public, but also internal or private. Finally, for instance, he has to admit that the Cassio he had vigorously lampooned, "hath a daily beauty in his life / That makes me ugly . . . No, he must die" (5.1.19–22). It proves, above all, to be impossible for Iago to bring Othello down to his level, for Othello is "great of heart" (5.2.370). Iago lives to see the man who became his agent in injustice recover himself sufficiently to become the arm of justice again (5.2.352–56). Finally, then, Iago is forced to realize that he could not dispossess or rob his victims of what is most intimately or most genuinely their own—their characters, their good names (3.3.156–61).

Iago's "birth" or creation is negation—the negation or destruction of the order that man, with nature's assistance, seeks to impose on the world. The "tragic loading of this bed" at the end of the play, is his "work." His desire to be recognized as a man for the magnitude of the destruction he has wrought is a goal foiled by the means: manliness, abstracted from all considerations of justice or injustice, is not its own reward. Iago promised to come out of the shadows once he brought his work to light. So soon as the worker is revealed, however, his handiwork is hastily concealed from view: it is an "object [that] poisons sight, / Let it be hid" (5.2.363–64).

Othello

By contrast to Iago, Othello does not see the service as a form of bondage in any respect, because he believes he is free of the city. By means of his character Othello has been able to support a politically homeless condition, transforming a life that most men would find odious, if not altogether unendurable, into an arena for the display of manly virtue. Iago's outward contentedness masks an inner restlessness; Othello's outward restlessness and wandering life seem to bespeak an inner calm. His soul appears to be perfectly accommodated to his way of life.

Othello has actually lived the life only imagined by Shakespeare's Coriolanus, his exemplar of the ancient Roman republic; a life devoted to noble, heroic activities performed outside of political society. Because Coriolanus thinks he can be a Roman wherever he goes, he convinces himself at the moment of his exile that he does not actually need the city. On the contrary, "each chance" that throws itself in his way will provide new opportunities for the display of his virtues. His equanimity is exceptionally short-lived, however, as is the time he spends in the interstices of political orders, which he calls living "[u]nder the canopy . . . [i'] th' city of kites and crows."[25] He is drawn almost immediately back to some sort of civic life—at the head, as it happens, of the Volscian forces bent on Rome's destruction.

For his part, Othello has flourished "under the canopy." Not any city but "the tyrant custom" has forged Othello's character, giving him the power to withstand, by the fixedness of his own disposition, the most severe fluctuations of fortune, including being sold into slavery, without debasing himself. What the feckless Coriolanus calls the "slippery turns" of the world have neither broken Othello's spirit, nor depleted his resources for noble action, nor rendered him bitter or angry at his destiny. He exhibits the patience of Job. Calling him "all in all sufficient," the Venetians ascribe to Othello a nature "whose solid virtue / The shot of accident nor dart of chance / Could neither graze nor pierce" (4.1.266–68).

Othello and Iago alike express the resolve to conquer fortune. Unlike Iago's Machiavellian preoccupation with effects attained by the strategic manipulations of others, Othello's mastery of fate is rooted in his ironclad mastery of himself and in his manly brand of Christian resignation. His Christianity imparts dignity and lends solace to his way of life, pressing the anger that might otherwise be aimed outward in the service of self-government. "For he that is slow to anger is better than the mighty; and he that ruleth his spirit than he that taketh the city."[26]

Not only has Othello been left essentially unscarred by his surrender to every wild caprice of the world, he claims to love his "unhoused free condition"(1.2.25–28). As a man without attachments to hearth, home or country, he is superior to political men, whose lives are limited in one way or another by love. Othello does not fully acknowledge his own inner restlessness—the longing in his soul to which Desdemona answers—until he loses her. Since his virtues are eminently portable, he believes without question, until the moment he realizes his dead wife's innocence, that there is always "a world elsewhere"[27] for him.

> Here is my journey's end, here is my butt
> And very sea-mark of my utmost sail.
> Do you go back dismay'd? 'Tis a lost fear;
> Man but a rush against Othello's breast
> And he retires. Where should Othello go? (5.2.267–71)

Othello seeks to command the respect of Venice and Desdemona for his strength of character and noble self-containment, rather than for military prowess per se, which, of course, his character supports. When he talks about himself, he says nothing about victories he has won, except for his personal victory, which, unlike military skill, is even more evident as equipoise and resiliency in the face of defeat than in triumph over one's enemies. Even *on* the battlefield Othello's self-government is his most prominent feature (3.4.134–37). Throughout, it is his "portance" in his traveler's history—his personal carriage or bearing—that he, like others, dwells on. Shakespeare's emphasis on Othello's self-possession is, of course, a necessary preparation for the startling inversion he, of all people, is about to undergo. Until the undeniable facts intrude, however, Iago's disingenuous query might well be on everyone's lips: "Can he be angry?" (134).

Othello harbors no ambition to usurp political power in Venice, either directly or by catapulting himself to a position of influence through Desdemona. Unlike the *condottieri* in its employ whom Venice had actually to fear more than its enemies—men like Carmagnola and Francesco Sforza[28]—Othello submits himself willingly to the political ends of Venice. He appears to be a perfect adjunct to the city. His graceful subordination to the city's authority in this regard, however, is less a reflection of eager subservience than of his sense of self-sufficiency. He shows restraint in the matter of political ambition because he is not indebted to any political authority for his honor. In other words, the potential for conflict between Othello and Venice that is realized at the end of the play exists from the beginning.

Othello confers his highest honor upon himself, appropriating his own rewards in accordance with his deserts. He acts here as he does throughout the play, as a law unto himself. From the outset, Othello needs no "prompter" and countenances "no other suitor but his likings" (1.2.84–85, 3.1.148). His marriage to Desdemona demonstrates that he acknowledges no restraints external to himself while it belies the ostensible self-sufficiency on which such action is based. And in both respects, his marriage foreshadows his murder of his wife. By his own admission, Othello took the "gentle Desdemona" without regard to anything but that he loved her. He also believes he has earned her, both by what he has done and what he is (1.2.19–24). Othello's cool reply to Iago about the resistance Brabantio will show to the marriage, suggests that Othello claims Desdemona as his recompense from the city for his military services. "Let him do his spite; / My services which I have done the signiory / Shall out-tongue his complaints" (1.2.17–19).

Though confronted by Brabantio in the second scene of the play, Othello refrains from any attempt in private to allay or confirm the father's horrified fears, whether by presenting Desdemona to him or recounting how he won her. Throughout this scene Othello speaks both as a man who is conscious of his deserts and with a very telling self-possession; he shows his new father-in-law a combination of gentleness and condescension (1.2.84–91).

Both the search parties looking for Othello are left partially in the dark until the confusion in the streets can be transferred to the more dignified arena of the Senate chambers. Othello may be reluctant to produce Desdemona in private, but he is downright eager to produce her as his star witness in front of the assembled duke and senators.

> Send for the lady to the Sagittary,
> And let her speak of me before her father.
> If you do find me foul in her report,
> The trust, the office I do hold of you,
> Not only take away, but let your sentence
> Even fall upon my life. (1.3.115–20)

Othello's sublime equanimity in the first act, especially in the face of Brabantio's brutal insults, expresses conviction in his political importance: he can disregard the domestic authority without having to sacrifice public approval. When Desdemona speaks "before her father," repudiating her father's authority, she will confirm his rightful public, as well as his rightful private place. Above all, though, Othello's self-confidence is owing to his trust in his own rectitude. If Iago's security lies in the opaqueness of his character, Othello's lies in the transparency of his. His own innocence is the best defense he has and the only one he needs: "My parts, my title, and my perfect soul / Will manifest me rightly" (1.2.31–32).

Marrying Desdemona does honor to Othello because of her place and importance in Venetian society, to which he is sensitive (1.3.236–39), but, more than these things, he is moved by her sympathy for the man he really is. Othello frames his responsiveness to Desdemona entirely in terms of her responsiveness to him: "She lov'd me for the dangers I had pass'd / And I lov'd her that she did pity them" (167–68). In contrast to Iago's proclaimed immunity from the soft charms of civility, moreover, Othello's customary hardness, his austere and rude life, has not inured, but rather attracted him to them. Thus, he appreciates fully Desdemona's beauty and her proficiency in the genteel arts of civilization (3.3.184–86, 4.1.178–206). She appears, then, to supply the lack of his former life, enabling him to possess or get hold of what he is missing in himself and, combined with his choice of Cassio as his lieutenant, to surround himself with civility.

Offering a final consolatory sop to the anguished Brabantio at the end of act 1, the duke tells him, "If virtue no delighted beauty lack, / Your son-in-law is far more fair than black" (1.3.289–90). Othello's marriage to Desdemona is, in fact, an admission that his virtue is actually insufficient to supply its own "delighted beauty," while inevitably longing for it. Desdemona is Othello's other half. Her particular fairness completes Othello's own fairness and so graces a life that has been full of virtue, but barren of beauty. Not only does her beauty set off his virtue, it also seals him off forever from his Moorish heritage, which, with his "baptism, / All seals and symbols of redeemed sin," he has renounced (4.2.52–60).

While Othello may see Desdemona's love as supplying the ornament of beauty to an otherwise perfectly self-subsistent virtue, however, such an interpretation cannot account for the ensuing tragedy. Othello is completely dependent, as Iago knows, on Desdemona's love. Othello himself later confesses to Desdemona that he could have "found in some place of my soul / A drop of patience" to endure any sort of humiliation, including even the name of "cuckold," but that he could not bear being rejected by her.

> But there, where I have garner'd up my heart,
> Where either I must live or bear no life;
> The fountain from the which my current runs
> Or else dries up: to be discarded thence! (4.2.52–60)

To understand the depth of Othello's dependence on Desdemona, we might say that, until he marries her he has no durable horizon, such as that provided by political or social life, within which to view his own virtues. His marriage is essentially a surrogate for the political existence he never had. In both domestic and political society men become accustomed to seeing themselves through the eyes of others and, thus, through the honor bestowed on them by others. Rather than the merely beautiful addition to Othello's virtue, Desdemona's honor of it is or proves to be the necessary complement of it, without which it does not exist. To be loved and honored for that which one loves in oneself—"for she had eyes, and chose me"—is the most thoroughly satisfying kind of love, but to enjoy it one must stake one's whole life on the opinion of another human being. Because Othello allows himself to be seen only through Desdemona's eyes, he is utterly dependent on her judgment and on her love. Losing her is therefore unendurable; losing her, he loses not only love, but also virtue, as indicated in the connection Othello makes between the loss of his love and the loss of his valiant "occupation" (3.3.347–57). Othello would not have been driven to kill Desdemona for discarding him if she did not mean everything to him. We might ask, though, whether Othello's loving, "not wisely but too well," is an excess connected to the fact that he has been forced to abjure a fully political life. However that may be, in the first act, Othello's vulnerabilities, which will be masterfully exploited by Iago, already show themselves: his pride in his own righteousness, his sense of self-sufficiency, his concern for his public status, and his overall lack of self-knowledge.

In light of the depth of Othello's attachment to Desdemona, his remarks about the marriage in the Senate chambers in the first act seem to be disingenuous. They are, while not deliberately untruthful, calculated to create a certain effect, an effect similar to that created by Iago's speeches in the first scene. Although Othello does not and would not defend the fact of his marriage, he does defend—openly and staunchly—his own manliness. As much as Iago, Othello wants to show his immunity to the influences of Venetian civility that threaten to emasculate men. Together, Othello's and Iago's speeches confirm that the martial virtues are put on the defensive in Venice and are vulnerable to attack in a way that is peculiar to such a city. They are viewed against the background of the soft preoccupations of peace, with which they are not, therefore, in harmony, and to which they are nevertheless subordinated. Venice's soldiers must not appear too martial or stern, for fear of being thought arrogant or refractory. For this very reason, however, their insulation from the vices of civility is not taken for granted. This means as well that the issue of masculine honor can, in fact, be detached altogether from achievement in war, to have as much to do with one's condition in private life.

Shakespeare's Coriolanus also goes to excessive lengths to demonstrate that he is a full soldier, untainted by the soft pursuits of peace. The particular softness from which he wishes to dissociate himself is not love, however, but flattery—that is, a political softness or irresoluteness born of too great a love of public praise.[29] In *Othello* the soldiers all seek to dissociate themselves from the appearance of falling prey to the charms of women and therewith to the enervating dissoluteness that can accompany the desire to please them. When Cassio expects to run into Othello, for instance, he shoos Bianca away, regarding it as "no addition, nor my wish, / To have him see me woman'd" (3.4.194–95). In both *Coriolanus* and *Othello*, the appearance of austerity is as important to maintain as the reality. Indeed, Coriolanus is no more impervious to popular praise than Othello is to attachments of the heart; both men nevertheless strive to appear more austere and unassailable than they are. The desire to be honored for a manly fortitude produces in them a moderating sense of shame, which, as it infuses their public actions, hides from view their actual aspirations and dependencies.

When the duke tells Othello that he will not be permitted to celebrate his marriage in Venice, as if to sober Othello to his responsibilities, Othello responds as if he would rather do nothing else in the world on his honeymoon than go to war, and fairly jumps at the chance to do so.

> The tyrant custom, most grave Senators,
> Hath made the flinty and steel [couch] of war
> My thrice-driven bed of down. I do agnize
> A natural and prompt alacrity
> I find in hardness; and do undertake
> These present wars against the Ottomites. (1.3.229–34)

The same sense of shame leads Othello at first to "crave fit disposition" for Desdemona in Venice (though not with her father), leaving her behind while he travels off to war. When Desdemona pleads to be permitted to accompany Othello because he means everything to her, Othello seconds her request as if she meant almost nothing to him. While he does not reduce love, as Iago does, to "a species of lust," he still tosses such matters off as the "light-wing'd toys of feather'd Cupid." Insofar as he is willing to admit he loves the beautiful Desdemona, he abstracts from love anything to do with the body or sensuality. Underlining his judiciousness and maturity, he means to be "free and bounteous to her mind." It is only under the duress he feels in losing her that Othello discloses the full range of his feelings. Only then, pointing to "her body and her beauty," does he characterize Desdemona in terms of her sexuality, but then he casts her natural gifts as the lures of an unnatural and wanton temptress: "O Thou weed! / Who art so lovely fair and smell'st so sweet / That the sense aches at thee, would thou hadst never been born!" (4.2.67–69).

Othello's blunt—indeed, vehement—repudiation of a susceptibility to softness at the end of the first act is deliberately intended to counter an imputation that might well be made, that he is a man not merely susceptible to a woman's charms, but in fact ruled by a woman. His accession to the spirited request Desdemona made, over his own head, as it were, to the duke, is, after all, clearly a subordination of his will to hers. In any case, without having to ask or even to appear to do so, Othello surely gets what he really wants; piling on top of the barely credible marvel of Desdemona's existence, the equal marvel that they will actually be together. Following the storm at sea, in another "hair-breadth scape" in his life story, Othello greets Desdemona as if he were a pilgrim just arrived at the Holy Land; a wandering soul come safe to harbor (2.1.183–98). She is the miracle in his life.[30]

Desdemona

The Venetian relegation of martial virtue to an ancillary body of men who are not citizens, which affects both Iago and Othello, also alienates Desdemona. In order to satisfy her love of valor, albeit in a manner appropriate to a woman, Desdemona must marry an outsider. That Desdemona gladly forsakes "so many noble matches, / Her father and her country and her friends" (4.2.125–27) to marry Othello reflects her discontent as a lover of all virtue, with the city. Desdemona possesses in herself the virtues associated with civility in a perfect form, but she does not possess in herself all of civilized virtue. She sees in Othello the necessary complement to her virtues and without any mixture of the Venetian vices, as they are found, for instance, in Cassio. As Othello loves Desdemona for possessing what he lacks in himself, so Desdemona loves Othello for what she lacks in herself. Their marriage completes them both, making them one whole person and, therefore, self-sufficient.

Although it may seem overly abstract to put the marriage of Desdemona and Othello in terms of a union of valor and virtuous civility, there is something distinctly abstract and disembodied in Desdemona's own description of her love of Othello that in fact enables her to skip so lightly over the formidable barriers dividing them.[31] "I saw Othello's visage in his mind, / And to his honors and his valiant parts / Did I my soul and fortunes consecrate" (1.3.252–54). That Desdemona's profoundest desire is to possess the virtues of Othello by sharing in his life and not the man himself is reflected in her complete imperviousness to the fact that she is "the great captain's captain" (2.1.74, 2.3.315), and in her contentment to be of secondary importance in his life. Othello compares her to a woman like Cleopatra (4.1.184–85).[32] She herself would never do so. Indeed, as her impact on Othello becomes ever more obvious to the audience, she seems to become ever more innocent of it (3.4.144–55).

The love between Othello and Desdemona is the most unconventional union in the tragedies. While their marriage is presented as more problematic for Venice than Cinthio portrays it, it is also more rare and beautiful than the one in the source.[33] Cinthio's judgment is indicated by the moral Desdemona draws from her life on his behalf: "I fear that I shall prove a warning to young girls not to marry against the wishes of their parents, and that the Italian ladies may learn from me not to wed a man whom nature and habitude of life estrange from us."[34] Shakespeare renders his more sympathetic judgment of the match by making Desdemona his mouthpiece as well. Not only does she corroborate Othello's self-portrait, she also transfers her confidence about him to us (1.3.180–90). Nevertheless, despite the capacity for fidelity and devotion that both Desdemona and Othello have, in the play Shakespeare conveys his own sense of the fragility of the marriage. The couple are put in the position of uniting in their marriage what the city wants to keep permanently apart.

Their difficulties are compounded because, once they are "housed" or married, Desdemona and Othello acquire a new vulnerability. Their hopes to be self-sufficient as a couple are thwarted by their mutual dependence as individuals. Their marriage heightens rather than coalesces their respective differences as man and woman, that is, differences in the virtues they must make manifest in their lives, while making them dependent for their very lives upon the distinctive virtue of the other. Othello's honor and, by his own admission, his life depend as much upon the virtuous conduct of his wife in erotic matters as they do on himself. Desdemona's very life depends upon the imperturbable predominance of virtuous ambition in Othello (3.4.134–57, 4.2.44–47). Iago takes it on himself to tempt Othello into believing that the miracle he has witnessed in his life did not really happen. What borders on the supernatural in Desdemona is made to seem simply aberrant or unnatural. Othello forgets or is blind to what is extraordinary in his wife, and she remains innocent of what is ordinary or all-too-human in him (3.4.26–30, 144–45).[35]

The Family and the Political Order

Desdemona's remarkable penetration of Othello's formidable, or, as it is portrayed, even repellent, exterior to get to the real man makes their courtship a variation on "Beauty and the Beast." No one else in the play is likely to see only what she sees, least of all her father. Brabantio's situation in the first act of *Othello* points to another problem characteristic of a commercial aristocracy like Venice. The city must strive to maintain its political exclusivity and the familial integrity on which it is based while promoting cultural heterogeneity. In the interest of trade, Venice openly promotes a cosmopolitan spirit in the city, for instance, by according civil rights to foreign residents and by encouraging its citizens to travel abroad.

By ascribing paramount importance to "forms" and reducing, "the art of pleasing to set rules,"[36] modern and luxurious cities like Venice are able to set themselves apart from the less than savory aspects of the mercantile life on which they depend. Refined manners and rigorous standards of taste help the Venetians to hold at bay any unsettling foreign influences they may have inadvertently imported along with foreign goods and foreign men. At the same time, however, Venetian politeness tends to confound the distinction between citizens and foreigners, making assimilation into the city easier than it otherwise would be.[37] Insofar as outsiders seek entry into Venice by embracing the uniform code of conduct, that same code gives rise to another distinction, which in turn acquires greater power than the political one—namely, the difference between the civilized and the barbaric. Although that distinction comes to sight in the play through its association with luxury and secular pursuits, its ultimate basis is the difference between Christian and pagan. The urbane civility of Venice serves then both to leaven the commercial spirit at the foundation of the city and to adorn Christian virtue.

Judging from Brabantio, we can say that Venice stimulates an appetite for the exotic and novel, at the same time as it leads citizens to trust implicitly in the power of custom to keep the barbarians at the gate. Clearly, it is Othello's difference that intrigued Brabantio in the first place and resulted in the meeting of Othello and Desdemona. Othello tells the Signiory that Brabantio "lov'd me; oft invited me; / Still questioned me the story of my life / From year to year—the [battles], sieges, [fortunes], / That I have pass'd" (1.3.129–31). We may wonder, however, whether this is an instance in which Othello's "free and open nature" misleads him; that he takes as love what eventually comes to light as Brabantio's lurid curiosity, consequently missing the contempt concealed in Brabantio's invitation. In a way, Brabantio's relations with Othello constitute a private exploitation of a foreigner that parallels the official one. Othello's military position in Venice insures that inviting him over offends no social propriety.

From Brabantio's perspective, Othello—the "extravagant and wheeling stranger of here and every where"—is the quintessential outsider or Other (1.1.136–37). As a kind of living relic of the primitive world in its untrammeled state, Othello offers Brabantio an extraordinary traveler's tale. Unlike the men who know only settled and "populous cities," Othello has wandered the empty and barren parts of the earth, and he is, as it were, on speaking terms with monsters, *viz.*, "[t]he Anthropopophagi; and men whose heads / [Do grow] beneath their shoulders" (1.3.140–45).

Desdemona's father, unlike her, never penetrates much beyond

Othello's exterior. Since, for his part, Brabantio could never "fall in love with what [he] fear'd to look on," and is, therefore, as much repelled as attracted by Othello (1.3.98), it would have been hard to persuade him in advance that his own appetites could harm his daughter. His foray into alien realms merely relieves a potentially deadening tedium that can accompany a life governed by the uniform rules of civility. Through Othello he can give himself over for a while to the psychic commingling of titillation and revulsion that we associate with the exotic. Unconsciously, this sort of appetite rules Brabantio, as indicated by his admission that he has dreamed about the "accident" Roderigo reports (1.1.142). His dream does not portend that incident so much as it forces his mind to witness shamelessly what is for him the most repulsive horror conceivable. Once he has been awakened, so to speak, he may indeed come to regard his dream as prophecy. It certainly supports the revulsion and dread that now dominate his perception of Othello completely. As if he had forgotten the appeal of Othello's tales on himself, he now insists to Othello that nothing but "spells and medicines" could have drawn Desdemona to "the sooty bosom / Of such a thing as thou—to fear, not to delight!" (1.2.70–71). It is the duke who underlines the charm these stories might exert on the daughters of Venice, indicating in the process that he and other senators are indeed capable of feeling Brabantio's case as their own (1.3.171).

When Brabantio is forced to confront his daughter's "treason of the blood," he does not initially take any of the blame for it. He has after all directed her "life and education" in accord with the customs of Venice and has been a discriminating supervisor of her love life. He has passed over the rich but silly Roderigo and presented Desdemona with the opportunity to choose her husband from among a suitable pool of "wealthy curl'd [darlings]" from Venice. That he has otherwise allowed Desdemona complete sway in matters of the heart cannot, he might insist, be adduced against him. To be loved a father must be civil as well as wise, and Brabantio has shunned the sort of temptation to which Portia's father entirely succumbs: we witness his effort to curb "the will of a living daughter" even from beyond the grave.[38] If Desdemona has rejected *in toto* the array of suitors placed before her, let this not be taken as willful disdain of her father's authority. Brabantio interprets it as the response of one who is content with life under his aegis and simply "opposite to marriage" (1.2.67).

Although Brabantio's first and final reaction to Desdemona's elopement is to rail against her for deceiving him (1.1.164–71, 1.3.292–93), to admit as much would mean confessing his own negligence and hence deal a mortal blow to his pride. Almost immediately, then, Brabantio latches on to an explanation—wonderful in its sheer plausibility—that at once exonerates both Desdemona and himself from blame.

> Is there not charms
> By which the property of youth and maidhood
> May be abus'd? Have you not read, Roderigo,
> Of some such thing? (1.1.171–74)

Once this theory has dawned on Brabantio, it proves to be so satisfactory to his desperate hopes for Desdemona's obedience that, by the time he discovers Othello, it has become his unshakable conviction. Surely Desdemona could only have acted as the Venetian she is, and Othello as the "[d]amn'd" barbarian he is. And what, indeed, is more "palpable to the thinking" than that, as in the case of Roderigo, for a Venetian to deviate from "the sense of all civility," some foreign "spirits" must be introduced (1.1.99, 130–31). Very little effort is therefore required for him to make the leap from the practice of black magic to the "practiser" (1.2.72–79).

In Brabantio's turn to the law to redress his grievance against Othello, we can see more clearly the political foundation for the preoccupation with private possession in the play.[39] The modern commercial republic is explicitly fashioned to facilitate private pursuits. Its laws form a network of guarantees to the security of what its citizens choose to call their own. Precisely by promoting private advantage, the city also intends to benefit itself. In the first place, domestic pursuits depend upon a stable and pacific political order for their enjoyment. In addition, economic and familial concerns work against the emergence of potentially disruptive political ambitions. In the ancient republic the city's need to promote civic virtue is met in part by the minute regulation of private life; it is necessary to insure against any rival centers of authority.[40] In the liberal republic, however, the political authority is meant to be secured precisely by the constitutional priority of private orders; they inspire the calculations by which citizens will accustom themselves to living within the law.

Shakespeare's characterization of Brabantio shows how such a system works successfully. Brabantio believes that law exists solely to protect the interests of men like himself and, thus, that it may be called upon to quell any interruption, however small, of their "quiet" (1.1.102–4). That Brabantio vents such anger at Roderigo's bad manners in the first scene reflects his conviction that Venice, and therefore, he himself, is in every serious respect imperturbable. He may reluctantly admit that drunken men can become raucous and uncivil, but he altogether rejects the possibility of theft. From his concealed position, Iago shouts at him to "[l]ook to your house, your daughter, and your bags," but Brabantio is serene. "What tell'st thou me of robbing? This is Venice; / My house is not a grange" (1.1.80–81, 104–5).

Although Brabantio may have been put in mind first of his ducats rather than his daughter,[41] he demonstrates thereafter that he regards the law as no less interested or efficient an instrument of redress when daughters and not ducats are stolen. In the Senate chambers, the duke himself stresses the congruence of the law and Brabantio's private will, no matter what the cost: "the bloody book of law / You shall yourself read in the bitter letter / After your own sense; yea, though our proper son / Stood in your action" (1.3.67–70). To elicit this response, Brabantio must, to be sure, literally force himself into the duke's eye, which had settled as intently as Brabantio's own on Othello, though for different reasons (49). Without knowing exactly why the Signiory is in session, Brabantio tells the duke he is so consumed by the private grief he suffers as a father as to be insensible of whatever "general care" he must address as a senator: "for my particular grief / Is of so flood-gate and o'erbearing nature / That it engluts and swallows other sorrows, / And it is still itself" (54–58).

If the ancient republic is characteristically threatened by the effects of too rigid an identification of what is one's own and what belongs to the city, the characteristic threat for the modern liberal republic lies rather, as this situation in the play suggests, in the divergence of private and public ends. The freedom Venice grants to the domestic orders gives them power to rival the political order, as an independent center of authority.[42] Thus, in principle, Iago's remark that Brabantio "hath in his effect a voice potential / As double as the duke's" is an apt one (1.2.13–14). Moreover, by setting on Roderigo to "incense" Brabantio's kinsmen, Iago means himself to draw upon the power that influential families have in Venice. Brabantio's own initial response to the discovery of Desdemona's absence is to gather his relations around him. "Call up all my people! . . . Raise all my kindred" (1.1.141, 167).

Brabantio extends his kin relationships, however, to include his "brothers of the state," the aristocrats with whom he shares political power. Thus, rather than two competing centers of authority, in the play Shakespeare presents grounds for the intimate cooperation of the domestic and the political orders. Brabantio enters the Senate chambers armed with the conviction that an identity of interests exists between him and the other senators. As if the connection were all too obvious, Brabantio does not spell out to the senators what he made explicit to Othello: his is no "idle cause," but a profound concern that

> [t]he Duke himself,
> Or any of my brothers of the state,
> Cannot but feel . . . as 'twere their own;
> For if such actions may have passage free,
> Bond-slaves and pagans shall our statesmen be. (1.2.95–99)

Leaving aside the way in which Shakespeare treats the bond between Othello and Desdemona, the imitation of their marriage by others would in fact pose a more serious threat to the established political order than a direct political attack could do; even were miscegenation not an issue. The political exclusivity of Venice rests on a hierarchical distinction among families that is protected by intermarriage among them. In turn, intermarriage promotes the homogenous cultural and social matrix within which Brabantio's perception of an identity of interests among aristocrats becomes widespread, and so acquires its full force. It is only in the expectation of a coincidence of interests that Brabantio is so avidly and wholeheartedly devoted to the law; not only eager to avail himself of its severity, but also willing to confine himself within its limits.

Although muted by the war, the duke's solicitude to Brabantio in this scene shows the public protection guaranteed to private orders and the Venetian desire to maintain harmony between them. At the same time, Shakespeare's characterization of Brabantio shows the moderation invariably imposed on men who embrace political means to guarantee the security of their own.

By means of "the bloody book of law" Venice gives a certain latitude to the vengeful impulses of aggrieved citizens. As a publicly wielded instrument of private vengeance, however, the law regulates the acrimonious passions that attract aggrieved citizens to it in the first place. Citizens are, after all, not entirely free to interpret the book of law "after [their] own sense," if they are not permitted to deviate from "its bitter letter." Brabantio may use the law "with all his might to enforce it on" to seek vengeance on Othello, but he is helpless to pursue "a capable and wide revenge" outside it (1.2.16, 3.3.459). Nor does he attempt to push the law beyond its own limits. Since the law itself supports Desdemona's freedom of choice, Brabantio must limit the scope of Othello's legal culpability. Not that Othello took her, but how he won her, is the only issue of which the Signiory can take notice. For Brabantio, however, the real tragedy does not lie in the conditions of the contract, but in the very fact of it. Nevertheless, once learning that Othello has only beguiled Desdemona of him and not her of herself, Brabantio retreats. While he will never recover his sensibilities as a senator, Brabantio is yet sufficiently mindful of his political position to refrain from interfering further in the duke's dispatch of Othello to Cyprus. Deliberately removing himself from the duke's vision as he had earlier intruded upon it, he urges the duke twice to proceed with the "state affairs."

Brabantio is defeated not as Shylock was—by the letter of the law—but by the escape of Desdemona. He is compelled to recognize that his accusation of Othello is useless against the shattering of his parental authority, and thus that law is insufficient to afford the protection he seeks. The duke counsels him to take away from "the mangled matter" whatever remains—the "broken weapons"—of his authority rather than to proceed any further without it (1.3.173–74). If a spurned father who is no longer in a position to resist the untoward marriage of his daughter wishes yet to act like a father, the only thing left him is to sanction it. Thus, in the end, Brabantio gives Desdemona to Othello (193–95).

Because the sanctity of private orders is of utmost concern to Venice, they acquire a public status there they would not necessarily have elsewhere. Men's honor is consequently bound up with the prudent management of what is their own, over which the law grants them dominion and then graciously recedes. With no one else to blame but oneself, however, the ignominy attaching to failures in private rule; that is, control over one's own people or property, is, therefore, that much greater. Brabantio will spend what remains of his "despised time" reeling from the stunning extent of Desdemona's rejection of the "life and education" he gave her and suffer mightily from the dishonor and "general mock" he will incur from her revolt: the influential "magnifico" who "may command at most" houses in Venice, but who could not govern his own (1.1.181).

The insufficiency of law and custom to protect Brabantio's possession imparts a bitter lesson he claims to have learned too late: "For your sake, jewel, / I am glad at soul I have no other child, / For thy escape would teach me tyranny, / To hang clogs on them" (1.3.195–98). Brabantio's despair draws our attention to the issue with which the rest of the play is concerned: private dominion over Desdemona, that is, management of the possessions that resist possession.

Shakespeare makes the situation of Brabantio in act 1 an adumbration of Othello's in act 4, even portending what is to come in Brabantio's final words: "Look to her, Moor, if thou hast eyes to see. / She has deceiv'd her father, and may thee" (1.3.292–93). The two men reveal their differences in the respective manners in which they seek to avenge themselves for their loss. By putting them in parallel positions, Shakespeare prepares us to feel the contrast between Brabantio's proceedings regarding Desdemona and those we are to witness later with Othello—the difference between Othello's "trial" and Desdemona's. Although Desdemona will place her trust, exactly as Othello does, in the manifest "authority of her merit" to vouch for her innocence, Othello will deny to his wife the opportunity to correct appearances by reality on which he depends in the first act (1.3.106–9, 2.1.144–46, 5.2.66–83). Desdemona's innocence is the only defense she has and the only one that is perfectly useless under the circumstances (5.2.39).[43]

In one important respect, Othello's outlook is identical to Brabantio's. In act 1, both men seek official confirmation of the legitimacy of their private desires, and both believe their private interests are perfectly compatible with the public good. Othello believes his past services to Venice will lead the Senate gladly to sanction his private victory. Brabantio believes the common interests of Venetians will allow his private loss to be avenged as a political one. Because of the particular nature of the state affairs, however, whether wanting to or not, Venice is deprived of all power to resist the marriage. Othello temporarily succeeds in driving a wedge between the domestic and the political orders. Although both men show the possibility of a tension in Venice between private and political rule, only in the case of Othello is that tension dangerous to the regime. Othello is sent beyond the reach of the city, a law unto himself, and Desdemona is effectually exiled from the protection both of the law and of her family and friends.[44]

Othello begins and ends with a conflict between a private or "particular grief" and "state-matters," both of which involve possession of the "jewel" or "pearl," Desdemona. Brabantio loses Desdemona through a negligence that is exacerbated by public policy and rooted in a self-satisfied faith in the potency of public curbs to render his possessions secure. Othello loses Desdemona by the pressing force of the belief that his hold over her is merely illusory, a belief that, although accelerated by Iago, derives from his own deeply rooted insecurity. Othello's tragic readiness to believe he has been "robb'd" is a perfect inversion of Brabantio's blithe insistence that he cannot be (3.3.268–69, 342–43). If the father did not think he could lose Desdemona, the husband does not think he can keep her. Believing that Desdemona fulfills her father's prophecy, Othello applies her father's remedy.

The movement of the play's action from Venice to Cyprus appropriately echoes the transfer of dominion over Desdemona from the lenient tutelage of Brabantio to the potentially tyrannic tutelage of Othello. It represents a departure from a pacific and orderly political setting that encourages a lax and complacent ownership, both political and private, to a volatile political setting, the potential chaos of which requires a concerted and stern vigilance, both political and private, toward one's own.[45] In both settings, confusion reigns beneath a merely surface calm.

Notes

1. All citations to Shakespeare's plays are to *The Riverside Shakespeare* (Boston: Houghton Mifflin, 1974). An earlier version of this essay was delivered at the 1981 Midwest Political Science Association meetings in Cincinnati, Ohio. I would like to thank Joseph Alulis and Vickie Sullivan for their generous editorial assistance.

2. G. R. Hibbard, " 'Othello' and the Pattern of Shakespeare's Tragedy," *Shakespeare Survey* 21 (1968): 40.

3. Hibbard, " 'Othello,' " 40–41; 2n, 45. Cf., Dieter Mehl, *Shakespeare's Tragedies: An Introduction* (Cambridge: Cambridge University Press, 1986), 65.

4. Giraldi Cinthio, *The Hecatomminthi*, Novella 7, trans. John Edward Taylor, in *A New Variorum Edition of Shakespeare*, ed. Horace Howard Furness (New York, Dover Publications, 1963), 377–89. Cinthio's stories were first published in 1565.

5. Cinthio, *Hecatomminthi*, 388.

6. On Shakespeare's knowledge of Venice, see Horatio F. Brown, "Shakespeare's Venice," in *Studies in the History of Venice* (London: J. Murry, 1907; reprint New York: Burt Franklin, 1973) 159–80; Zera S. Fink, *The Classical Republicans*, 2d ed. (Evanston, Ill.: Northwestern University Press, 1962), 35, 42–43; Violet M. Jeffrey, "Shakespeare's Venice," *Modern Language Review* 27 (1932): 24–35; A. D. Nuttall, *A New Mimesis: Shakespeare and the Representation of Reality* (New York and London: Methuen, 1983), 120–43;

Richard H. Perkinson, " 'Volpone' and the Reputation of Venetian Justice," *Modern Language Review* 35 (1940): 11–18.

7. See William J. Bouwsma, *Venice and the Defense of Republican Liberty* (Berkeley and Los Angeles: University of California Press, 1968), 108, 151–52, 239ff; Fink, *Republicans*, 19, 28, 34–39, 41ff; Felix Gilbert, "The Venetian Constitution in Florentine Political Thought," in *Florentine Studies*, ed. Nicolai Rubinstein (London: Faber & Faber, 1968), 463–500; Frederic C. Lane, "At the Roots of Republicanism," *The American Historical Review* 71 (1966): 403–20, esp. 414–19; William H. McNeill, *Venice: The Hinge of Europe, 1081–1797* (Chicago: University of Chicago Press, 1974), 148, 288–89; J.G.A. Pocock, *The Machiavellian Moment: Florentine Political Thought and the Atlantic Republican Tradition* (Princeton: Princeton University Press, 1975), 99–100, 103, 185–86, 199–201, 306, 320–28. Gasparo Contarini's *De magistratibus et republica Venetorum*, published in Paris in 1543, is perhaps the most influential pro-Venetian account of the republic; it was available in an English translation by Lewis Lawkenor in 1599. On Shakespeare's possible familiarity with Contarini's history, see Furness, *Variorum*, 40–41, 92n. and 47, 61n. See Gaspar Contareno, *The Commonwealth and Government of Venice*, trans. Lewis Lawkenor, London, 1599 (facsimile reprint published in Amsterdam and New York: De Capo Press/Theatrum Orbis Terrarum Ltd., 1969), 5, 15, 89, 138–39.

8. On the Roman republic and its contrast with the Venetian, see William Roscoe Thayer, *A Short History of Venice* (Boston: Houghton Mifflin, 1908); Machiavelli, *Discourses* 1.1–6, 34–36, 49–50, 2.19, 30; 3.31; Harvey C. Mansfield, Jr., *Machiavelli's New Modes and Orders: A Study of the Discourses on Livy* (Ithaca and London: Cornell University Press, 1979), 45–62, 134, 386–88.

9. See Lawkenor, *Commonwealth*, 70–71, 77ff., 130–32; Machiavelli, *Discourses* 3.31; *The Prince,* ch. 12; *Florentine Histories* 1.6,7. See also McNeill, *Venice*, 69–70, 138–141; Thayer, *History of Venice*, 180–81, 195–96, 257–58. Debate about Venetian practices tends to organize itself around the different views of Contarini and Machiavelli. See Elizabeth G. Gleason, *Gasparo Contarini: Venice, Rome, and Reform* (Berkeley and Los Angeles: University of California Press, 1993), 110–26; Bouwsma, *Venice*, 68, 103ff., 135, 149–53; Pocock, *Moment*, 100, 328, 492.

10. As if in response to the segregation of political and military affairs, Iago complains that "the toged counsels" know war about as well as the "bookish" and inexperienced Cassio does (1.1.23–26). In the introduction to his translation of Contarini, Lawkenor also speaks of "long robed citizens," the "unweapon'd men in gownes" who preside over Venetian affairs. See Lawkenor, *Commonwealth,* 3.

11. See *Coriolanus,* 2.2.83–85; Paul Cantor, *Shakespeare's Rome: Republic and Empire* (Ithaca and London: Cornell University Press, 1976), *passim.*

12. Cinthio, *Hecatomminthi*, 377.

13. The disturbances created by the two conspiracies converge literally at 1.2.28–56.

14. See *The Merchant of Venice*, 1.3.
15. Cinthio, *Hecatomminthi*, 377.
16. See *Coriolanus*, 1.9.228–30; 2.2.
17. Cantor, *Rome*, 55–77.
18. Cassio is "a Florentine" (1.1.20).
19. See Iago's speech to Montano, 2.3.129–35.
20. See also *Macbeth*, 4.1.144–54.
21. See also *Macbeth*, 4.3.97–100.
22. For a modern parallel to Iago, see the discussion of Claggart in Thomas J. Scorza, *In the Time Before Steamships: "Billy Budd," The Limits of Politics, and Modernity* (De Kalb: Northern Illinois University Press, 1979), 65–84.
23. Jean-Jacques Rousseau, "Discourse on the Arts and Sciences," in *The First and Second Discourses*, ed. Roger D. Masters, trans. Roger D. and Judith R. Masters (New York: St. Martin's Press, 1964), 37–38.
24. Rousseau, "Discourse," 36.
25. See *Coriolanus*, 3.3.133–35; 4.1.51–33; 4.5.39–42.
26. Prov., 16.32. See also Allan Bloom, with Harry V. Jaffa, *Shakespeare's Politics* (New York: Basic Books, 1964), 35–74.
27. *Coriolanus*, 3.3.135.
28. Machiavelli, *The Prince*, chs. 11–12.
29. See, for example, *Coriolanus*, 1.9.37–53; 2.3.112–24; 3.1.65–74, 254–55; 3.2.110–23.
30. The "wonder" and "absolute" contentment Othello experiences before his actual wedding night takes place is, contrary to appearances, a premonition of the anxiety he will experience thereafter; possessing Desdemona of itself ushers in his fear of losing her (2.1.183–98) Cf. *Romeo and Juliet*, 3.2.26–32.
31. Cf. Portia in *The Merchant of Venice*, 1.2.128–30; 2.7.8–9.
32. See *Antony and Cleopatra*, 3.1.21–24.
33. Note the contrast between Disdemona's view of Moors (Cinthio, *Hecatomminthi*, 380), and Desdemona's (3.4.26–29); and between the Moor's efforts to conceal his murder (Cinthio, *Hecatomminthi*, 386–87) and Othello's determination to make his "sacrifice" public (5.2.203, 210–17). Othello may also be contrasted with the Moroccan prince in *The Merchant of Venice*, 2.1.1–11.
34. Cinthio, *Hecatomminthi*, 384; see also 2.1.346–56; 3.3.228–38.
35. Desdemona's and Othello's mutual misunderstanding is set against the background of the age-old battle of the sexes. There are notable blind spots in the other characters as well. For instance, the prostitute Bianca, who belongs to anyone and thus to no one, and who therefore cannot be the object of jealousy, is nevertheless "jealious" of Cassio (4.1.96-97). Iago's and Emilia's own mutual misunderstanding echoes that of their superiors. In the play, the difficulties in communication lead men and women alike to fall back on general formulas to cover a more complex reality. See Brabantio on daughters (1.1.170–71); Othello on wives (3.3.268–70); Emilia on husbands (4.3.93–103).

36. Rousseau, "Discourse," 37.

37. As the Englishman Sir Politic Would-be exclaims in Ben Jonson's *Volpone*, "Within the first weeke, of my landing there, / All took me for a citizen of *Venice*: I knew the forms, so well;" cited in Perkinson, " 'Volpone,' " 14.

38. *The Merchant of Venice*, 1.1.24; see also *Romeo and Juliet*, 3.4.12–18; 3.5.126–200.

39. On the political significance of the attachment to children in the play, see Mera J. Flaumenhaft, "Begetting and Belonging in Shakespeare's *Othello*," *Interpretation* 4/3 (Spring 1975): 197–216.

40. See *Coriolanus*, 2.8.15–24; 3.1.

41. See *The Merchant of Venice*, 1.3; 2.1; 5.3.

42. To indicate how far this authority can go, see Cinthio, *Hecatomminthi*, 387–89.

43. See also *Macbeth*, 4.2.73–79.

44. Venice travels officially, as it were, to Cyprus in act 4. Desdemona's relatives, who carry the news of Brabantio's death, have also been deputed to appoint Cassio to the Cyprus command in Othello's place, and to recall Othello to Venice. Venice may intend by these actions to check Othello (see 4.1.235–37, 275–76; 4.2.64–67), or, alternatively, simply to depute Othello in Brabantio's place. However that may be, like Brabantio in act 1, Othello is utterly insensible of any general care, being completely absorbed in his particular grief.

45. See 2.1.55–61, 213–17; 3.1.44–50; 3.3.11–13.

9

King Lear: The Tragic Disjunction of Wisdom and Power

Paul A. Cantor

> What is the price of Experience do men buy it for a song
> Or wisdom for a dance in the street? No it is bought with the price
> Of all that a man hath his house his wife his children.
>
> —William Blake, *The Four Zoas*

I

Many critics regard *King Lear* as the greatest of Shakespeare's plays and also as his most tragic. Indeed, many would claim that it is the most tragic play ever written. And yet, curiously, in most critical accounts of the play, it is difficult to see why we should even regard it as tragic at all, whether we are using an Aristotelian or a Hegelian definition of tragedy. In the view of most critics, Lear is basically a pathetic old man, vain and foolish, rash in his judgment and incapable of controlling his emotions—and he is all these things from the very beginning of the play.[1] This characterization seems to preclude viewing Lear on the Aristotelian model of a tragic hero, as someone raised above the ordinary level of humanity, except in the most conventional sense of his social status. Moreover, in the view of the majority of critics, the play charts the growth of Lear's wisdom, as he learns the emptiness of worldly glory and comes to embrace the love of his daughter Cordelia as the one true value in his life.[2] As consoling as this vision of Lear's education through suffering may be, it leaves us with a sense that the dramatic issues of the play can in the end be fully resolved. But if that is the case, then Lear cannot be in a tragic situation as Hegel defines it, that is, he is not caught in the clash of two legitimate principles, a situation from which there is no simple escape, no matter how much he learns. In concrete terms, critics generally do not view Lear as caught between genuinely conflicting loyalties, his political and his personal obligations; on the contrary, in their reading of the play, Lear would simply be right to abdicate the throne and retire into private life.

In short, in the view of most critics, at the beginning of the play Lear is simply mistaken in both his attitudes and his actions, and the course of the drama should in effect teach him the error of his ways.[3] This reading of *King Lear* makes it an edifying play, but it drains it of its tragic power by oversimplifying Shakespeare's understanding of the complexities of political life. Ultimately, this kind of reading threatens to reduce *King Lear* to a form of melodrama, a story of the straightforward conflict of clearly identifiable and separable forces of good and evil, in which the outcome is tragic only in the sense of being disastrous for the main characters. Above all, many critics end up undermining the stature of King Lear as a tragic figure by suggesting that with a little more wisdom he could have avoided the catastrophes in his life. Critics may go on speaking of the grandeur of Shakespeare's achievement and of Lear as a character, but if the standard readings of the play were correct, a more honest reaction would resemble that of Groucho Marx, when, in a meeting almost as improbable as Lear's encounter with Tom o' Bedlam, he was attempting to explain the play to T. S. Eliot:

> I said the king was an incredibly foolish old man, which God knows he *was*; and that if he'd been *my* father I would have run away from home at the age of eight—instead of waiting until I was ten. . . . I pointed out that King Lear's opening speech was the height of idiocy. Imagine (I said) a father asking his three children: Which of you kids loves me the most?[4]

I am sure that most critics would, as Eliot evidently did, reject this characterization of *King Lear*, but the question remains: is there anything in their readings of the play that would allow them to counter this view of its hero? As convinced as critics are of the greatness of *King Lear* as a work of art, they evidently have a hard time giving an account of the play that explains that greatness. In the delightfully insouciant way in which Groucho projects himself into the world of *King Lear*, he unwittingly reveals the problem with many interpretations of the play. In our eagerness to identify with Shakespeare's characters, we run the risk of bringing them down to our own level. The Lear described in many critical essays sounds less like Shakespeare's monarch than the middle-class recreations of Lear in the nineteenth-century fiction of writers like Balzac and Turgenev.[5]

From this perspective, the turning point in the criticism of *King Lear* was Harry Jaffa's brilliant analysis of the opening scene of the play, in which he shows that Lear has a sophisticated scheme in mind for dividing up his kingdom, one in which he hopes to secure the bulk of his land for Cordelia, together with an alliance with the House of Burgundy.[6] As Jaffa shows, Lear's plan, far from being the product of senility, is, if anything, too clever for his own good. I will not go over the details of Jaffa's subtle analysis; suffice it to say here that he points the way to understanding Lear as a tragic figure. The king is not behaving like a doddering old fool in the opening scene, but attempting a remarkable political feat: to pass on his royal inheritance in a way that will avoid the defects of following the conventional rules of primogeniture. Lear fails in his plan, but in Jaffa's view, he fails nobly and hence tragically. Jaffa's reading is true to the text of the play and also to the impression Lear in fact makes on stage in the opening scene. Far from coming across as a pathetic old man, Lear projects a commanding presence in his first appearance, dominating the action and, for all his errors, towering over the other figures on the stage.

In another essay on *King Lear*, I have tried to extend Jaffa's analysis, analyzing the process of education the king undergoes when he loses power.[7] Like Jaffa, I try to show that Lear's errors are not, so to speak, *vulgar* errors; they do not simply proceed from stupidity or lack of thought. I argue that, in tragic fashion, Lear's failings are bound up inextricably with his greatness. Precisely what makes him powerful as a king incapacitates him for seeing the truth about himself and his kingdom. In part this outcome results from his being surrounded by hypocrites and flatterers, who reinforce his self-image and his confidence in the justice of his rule. But as Shakespeare presents it, the problem runs deeper. Lear's errors are a kind of occupational hazard of his kingship. In order to exercise command, he must project an aura of authority, and this need in turn dictates that he have a high opinion of himself, thus fatally tempting him to overestimate his capabilities in such tasks as disposing of his kingdom.

The powerfully tragic vision of *King Lear* is rooted in Shakespeare's understanding of political life, its limitations and its demands. The play turns on what I will call the disjunction of wisdom and power. When Lear is in command as king, he is tragically cut off from the wisdom he needs to rule justly. He gains access to this wisdom only when he loses power, but that process in turn incapacitates him for further rule. In this essay, I will examine largely the second half of *King Lear*, and trace what happens to Lear when he learns the truths to which his position as king initially blinded him. Acts 4 and 5 are crucial to a full understanding of Lear as a tragic figure, but most critics fail to follow the subtle turns Shakespeare portrays in the king's attitudes, because they do not think through the implications of Lear's radically changed view of the world. In many accounts of the play, Lear's education is presented as an unequivocal good, as if there were nothing problematic about his experience. These accounts in effect present private life as simply superior to public life, suggesting that Lear has everything to gain and nothing to lose when he is thrust out of power. Without questioning Lear's legitimate gains in wisdom in the course of the play—indeed I have discussed them at length elsewhere—I want to explore here the possibility that *King Lear* is tragic precisely because of the complexity of the process Shakespeare is portraying in the king's development. Lear's gains in wisdom come at the expense of his initial grandeur and hence his ability to rule. In the unsettling logic of the world of *Lear*, the characters pay a terrible price for the wisdom they gain, and none more so than Lear himself.

II

Lear's process of education reaches its crisis in act 3, especially with his encounter with Edgar disguised as Tom o' Bedlam, and the insights he gains and even articulates as a result are indeed remarkable. It is tempting but far too simplistic to treat Lear's shattering experience in act 3 as a kind of civics lesson or a seminar at a school of public administration. However much Lear grows in wisdom in act 3, he could not simply translate that wisdom back into a form of rule. For one thing, the wisdom Lear gains in act 3 has a questionable character. In trying to articulate what Lear learns, it is easy to distort the nature of his experience, presenting in an organized and coherent form insights that in fact come to Lear in fits and starts. Lear gains many insights in act 3, but we cannot grasp what he is going through if we do not see how deeply unsettling and disorienting these truths are for him, shattering his self-image and his whole view of humanity. However disturbing it may be to admit, the Lear of act 3 is in no condition to walk back into the court and resume command of his kingdom. What is precisely characteristic of Lear in act 3 is that he cannot hold together the two images of human nature he observes in Edgar as first Tom o' Bedlam and then as the "noble philosopher" (3.4.172), and that is the deepest reason why his experience on the heath at least momentarily unfits him for rule. Lear is agonizingly wrenched back and forth between images of the lowest degradation of the human body and images of the highest development of the human soul. Obsessed with his insights into the extremes of humanity, Lear understandably loses sight of the middle range, but that is precisely the realm where politics ordinarily takes place.[8]

Shakespeare repeats this pattern in Lear's appearances in act 4. The juxtaposition of scenes 6 and 7 shows Lear recapitulating his encounter with the lower and higher sides of human nature, and once again he is unable to integrate his widely diverging images of humanity. Encountering the blind Gloucester in act 4, scene 6, Lear dwells obsessively on the animal side of man and above all woman:

> Behold yond simp'ring dame,
> Whose face between her forks presages snow;
> That minces virtue, and does shake the head
> To hear of pleasure's name—
> The fitchew nor the soiled horse goes to't
> With a more riotous appetite.
> Down from the waist they are Centaurs,
> Though women all above;
> But to the girdle do the gods inherit,
> Beneath is all the fiends'. (4.6.118–27)[9]

This vision is the equivalent of Lear's earlier view of the "bare, fork'd animal" in Tom o' Bedlam (3.4.107–8), as he effaces the distinction between human being and beast. Because Lear is convinced that all human beings are consumed by sexual appetites, he refuses to see anyone punished anymore for violating the conventional rules of sexual conduct:

> I pardon that man's life. What was thy cause?
> Adultery?
> Thou shalt not die. Die for adultery? No,
> The wren goes to't, and the small gilded fly
> Does lecher in my sight. (4.6.109–13)

In Lear's refusal to support conventional marriage contracts, we see what the political consequences would be of the new doctrine of natural justice he learns during the storm on the heath. As ruler he would no longer have any legitimate basis for punishing any of his subjects or enforcing any law. Once Lear views all human beings as alike in their animal urges, for him the difference between legally constituted authorities and criminals dissolves: "see how yond justice rails upon yond simple thief. Hark in thine ear: change places, and handy-dandy, which is the justice, which is the thief?" (4.6.151–54). Though Lear once embodied the majesty of the law in his own person, he loses faith in all authority once he concludes that conventional appearances hide an inner corruption:

> Thorough tatter'd clothes small vices do appear;
> Robes and furr'd gowns hide all. Plate sin with gold,
> And the strong lance of justice hurtless breaks;
> Arm it in rags, a pigmy's straw does pierce it.
> None does offend, none, I say none. (4.6.164–68)

Speeches such as this continue Lear's impulse in act 3 to reject a conventional view of political reality in the name of what is natural to human beings. In particular he displays the same hostility to clothing because it hides the truth about humanity.[10]

Lear's speeches in act 4, scene 6 are very powerful and express some fundamental truths about politics; Edgar is moved to comment on the king's words: "O, matter and impertinency mix'd, / Reason in madness" (4.6.174–75).[11] But before we are tempted simply to equate Lear's viewpoint here with Shakespeare's, we need to look more critically at what the king says. Shakespeare deliberately builds an error into Lear's reflections in this scene: "Let copulation thrive; for Gloucester's bastard son / Was kinder to his father than my daughters / Got 'tween the lawful sheets" (4.6.114–16). These lines should give us pause; Lear's preference for the natural over the conventional child is clearly as mistaken as his earlier tendency to accept conventional professions of love over his true daughter's natural feelings. Like Lear's two auditors at this moment, Edgar and Gloucester, we know how misguided the king's praise of Edmund is. Modern interpreters seem disposed to follow Lear in his thoroughgoing disillusionment with politics and human nature in this scene,[12] but Shakespeare took pains to prevent us from wholly identifying with Lear's one-sided view of man as beast. Even Lear momentarily recognizes the diseased character of his imagination in this scene (4.6.130–31).

Indeed, Lear's jaundiced view of women as all "centaurs" is immediately contradicted by Cordelia's appearance in the next scene. Lear's reunion and reconciliation with his true daughter is one of the most beautiful and moving scenes Shakespeare ever wrote. Act 4, scene 7 provides the dreamlike answer to Lear's nightmare vision of humanity in act 4, scene 6. From his obsession with human carnality in act 4, scene 6, Lear moves to a vision of human spirituality. He is barely aware of his own body in this scene ("I will not swear these are my hands," [4.7.54]) and in his eyes Cordelia has transcended the physical level: "You are a spirit, I know" (4.7.48). By trying to kneel to Cordelia, Lear is finally willing to reverse their relative positions of power. In act 1, scene 1, Cordelia could not express her true love for her father because his power over her stood in the way, threatening to obliterate the distinction between a sincere profession of devotion and the hypocritical and self-serving flattery of her two sisters. Now that Lear has lost his power and admits to being nothing but "a very foolish fond old man" (4.7.59), Cordelia can no longer be accused of any base motives in her love for her father. In rallying to his cause, she, like Kent and the Fool, has nothing to gain and everything to lose. Free of the conventional political roles that complicated and distorted their relationship earlier, Lear and Cordelia are finally able to be simply father and daughter.

Indeed in view of the reversal of their customary positions in this scene—the fact that Lear is willing to kneel to Cordelia—it is arguable that they are liberated even from the conventional roles of parent and child, and face each other as human being to human being in a condition of equality.[13] Lear and Cordelia move beyond any kind of conventional moral accounting, as she rejects his seemingly justified assumption of guilt for their breach:

> *Lear*: I know you do not love me, for your sisters
> Have (as I do remember) done me wrong:
> You have some cause, they have not.
> *Cordelia*: No cause, no cause. (4.7.72–74)

In act 4, scene 6, Lear rejected conventional morality out of contempt for human nature and on the basis of the lowest possible view of human beings as indistinguishable from beasts. In act 4, scene 7, Lear and Cordelia rise above conventional moral considerations just as they appear to rise above the level of their bodies.

Shakespeare's juxtaposition of act 4, scene 6 and act 4, scene 7 conveys a deeper wisdom than Lear is able to encompass in either scene alone: the two scenes embody alternative and complementary visions of what is natural to humanity. It is a sad commentary on our times that we are all too eager to acknowledge that Lear is talking about what is natural to the human condition in act 4, scene 6. But on reflection, we can appreciate that in some sense of the term the behavior of Lear and Cordelia in act 4, scene 7 is also a paradigm of nature, now thought of in terms of human perfection, rather than some kind of lowest common denominator of humanity. The simplicity of their dialogue in this scene, the fact that they speak in brief, declarative sentences, above all, the fact that they are finally speaking *to* each other, no longer *at* each other, lends what can be called a natural quality to their interaction here. Neither act 4, scene 6 nor act 4, scene 7 tells the whole truth about the human condition, and to accept one at the expense of the other is to risk falling prey to an overly cynical or an overly idealistic understanding of human nature. Shakespeare was guilty of neither.

However contradictory the images of humanity presented in act 4, scene 6 and act 4, scene 7 may be, the two scenes have one thing in common: in both Lear effectively rejects political life. In act 4, scene 6 his cynical view of humanity undermines all claims to legitimate authority by political figures. In act 4, scene 7 his idealistic view of the human condition leaves all ordinary political considerations far below. The juxtaposition of these two scenes thus points to an important truth about politics. In act 4, scene 6 Lear talks about human beings as if they were all body and no spirit; the result of this view of human nature as purely animal is to eliminate every possible justification for political action. In act 4, scene 7 Lear talks about himself and Cordelia as if they were all spirit and no body; the result of this contrary view of human nature as purely spiritual is to eliminate every need for political action; Lear and Cordelia pass beyond the world of good and evil. The conjunction of these two scenes suggests that either of these views is one-sided and hence incomplete. As the bifurcation of vision throughout acts 3 and 4 of *King Lear* suggests, man is a composite being, a perplexing mixture of body and spirit. It is precisely for this reason that human beings require political life: to deal with the problems created by the tension between body and spirit. Neither animals nor angels require politics.

We can now see more fully why Lear's gains in wisdom in acts 4 and 5 come at the expense of his ability to rule. At the beginning of the play Lear is the captive of many illusions about himself and his world, but his very overestimation of his own powers is what gives him the aura of authority he needs to command his subjects. The Lear of act 4, scene 6 has learned a great deal about his own limitations, but the result is that he has developed a universal contempt for political authority. He has lost all faith in the ability of political action to improve the human condition, or even to control its worst excesses of passion. The Lear of act 4, scene 7 is simply indifferent to politics; having achieved a spiritual communion with Cordelia in an intensely private moment, he no longer has any interest in public life. Failing to integrate his antithetical visions of humanity in act 4, scene 6 and act 4, scene 7, Lear is unable to grasp the fundamental truth that the political authority he despises and rejects in act 4, scene 6 would be necessary to protect the fragile spirituality he comes to cherish in act 4, scene 7.

III

Lear's loss of his ability to rule is not simply to be traced to the change in his opinions about politics in acts 3 and 4. Shakespeare also focuses on the matter of Lear's temperament. The Lear of act 1, scene 1 is headstrong and rash; those are not the virtues of a philosopher, but they are the qualities of the kind of man who often succeeds in getting other men to obey his will. When we say that Lear has a kingly temperament, we mean in part that he is a spirited man, capable of what he himself calls "noble anger" (2.4.276). His capacity for indignation is one of the forces that attaches him to political life and fuels his ability to get things done. Lear's tendency to identify his personal cause with justice pure and simple is unphilosophic and leads to many of his errors in judgment. Nevertheless, his pride and titanic overestimation of himself are also what makes an admirable man like Kent say that he can see authority written on Lear's face (1.4.26–30).

Thus the more Lear comes to think of himself as an ordinary man, sharing the weaknesses of his fellows, the less capable he becomes of inspiring their awe and hence their obedience. To be sure, Kent, the Fool, and Cordelia come to love Lear more in his defeat and humiliation, but that is precisely a private reaction on their parts and not the same as political loyalty. The Lear we see in the second half of the play has become temperamentally unfit to rule England. We must realize that Lear's learning in the play is not a purely intellectual process; it is not a matter of Lear picking up a textbook in political science and calmly reading about what went wrong with his administration. Lear's education in self-knowledge is a soul-wrenching experience. It rips asunder the deepest fibers of his being. For Lear's titanic ego to be shaken, he must be painfully humiliated, and that is the terrifying process we witness in acts 1 and 2, as his wolfish daughters strip away every shred of dignity he has left. With all his pride, Lear resists this process:

> You see me here, you gods, a poor old man,
> As full of grief as age, wretched in both.
> If it be you that stirs these daughters' hearts
> Against their father, fool me not so much
> To bear it tamely; touch me with noble anger,
> And let not women's weapons, water-drops,
> Stain my man's cheeks! (2.4.272–78)

Lear realizes that nothing less than his manhood is at stake in this scene, and he futilely wishes that he had the power to act like a manly king and take vengeance on all those who have slighted his dignity. When Lear is confronted by the cruelty of his daughters, he is torn between the contradictory emotions of anger and grief. His anger is rooted in his pride as a king, and makes him ashamed of the grief he feels as an ordinary human being. As Lear himself recognizes, the tension he experiences between wanting to express his grief as a wronged father and the need he feels as a king to suppress any such public display of weakness eventually causes his mind to snap: "O Fool, I shall go mad" (2.4.286).

As much as we are moved by seeing what Lear gains in the process of his education, we should not blind ourselves to what he loses. The Lear of act 4, scene 7 is a broken man, his pride in himself and in his regime shattered. He is a wiser man in this scene, more capable of love, and in many important respects this Lear is preferable to the one we saw in the opening scene of the play. But not in all respects. Unlike the Lear we saw in act 1, scene 1, the Lear of act 4, scene 7 could not walk into any room and just by his regal bearing command the instant respect of any human being in range of his voice. A king who expects to be obeyed cannot go around proclaiming: "I am old and foolish" (4.7.84). We may admire Lear for this frank admission of his weakness, but we must also recognize its consequences for his ability to rule in the future as anything other than a figurehead. The Lear of act 4, scene 7 is completely without anger; as the Doctor says: "the great rage, /

You see, is kill'd in him'' (4.7.77–78). It may be a relief for us as audience to see this calm descend upon Lear, but we must recognize that with his rage, something else is for the moment killed in Lear: his pride. And, bound up as it is with his spiritedness, Lear's pride was the source of his greatness as well as of his failures as a king. Up to this point in the play, even in his madness, Lear has displayed an acute awareness of everything going on around him. If anything, he has been too ready to see affronts to his dignity in his subjects' actions, but that hypersensitivity has been profoundly linked to Lear's concern for justice. In act 4, scene 7, he ceases to be aware of his surroundings; he even has to be reminded that he is in Britain (4.7.75). With Lear's ''great rage'' goes his ''noble anger,'' and with that, his ability and even his desire to govern his kingdom.

In short, we must realize that Lear cannot absorb the kind of unnerving truths he learns about himself and remain the same man. The Lear we see in act 4, scene 7 is profoundly changed from what he was in act 1, scene 1. His newfound wisdom and self-awareness are purchased at the price of his original grandeur.[14] We may ultimately judge the result worth the exchange, but we should not deny that Shakespeare is confronting us with a kind of choice. Shakespeare's tragic world is profoundly disturbing to us. We do not like to think about the tragic disjunctions he presents. We would like to think that it is possible to be a powerful ruler and a wise man at the same time. Perhaps it is possible, and in the case of Henry V Shakespeare offers an example of a man who seems to unite wisdom and power (Prospero is another such case).[15] But even if it is possible, the conjunction of wisdom and power is surely not easy to achieve, and in *King Lear* Shakespeare most fully explores the problems of bringing the two together. When Lear is in power, he is blind to his own limitations, not just out of stupidity, senility, or simple error, but because, as Shakespeare shows, there is something in the very nature of kingship that blinds even and perhaps especially a successful ruler to fundamental truths about his situation. When Lear finally gains access to those truths, it is only through a process that disillusions him about politics in general and shatters the very spirit that made him a commanding figure. That is why *King Lear* is such a tragic play, perhaps the most profound of all tragedies. It offers no easy way out of Lear's dilemma. Shakespeare uncovers a deep and abiding tension between the preconditions of power and the preconditions of wisdom.

IV

The Lear we see in act 5 has recovered his sanity, but he is still a far cry from the regal figure we first saw in act 1. He has become totally absorbed in his private bond with Cordelia:

> Come, let's away to prison:
> We two alone will sing like birds i' th' cage;
> When thou dost ask me blessing, I'll kneel down
> And ask of thee forgiveness. So we'll live,
> And pray, and sing, and tell old tales, and laugh
> At gilded butterflies, and hear poor rogues
> Talk of court news; and we'll talk with them too—
> Who loses and who wins; who's in, who's out—
> And take upon's the mystery of things
> As if we were God's spies; and we'll wear out
> In a wall'd prison, packs and sects of great ones,
> That ebb and flow by th' moon. (5.3.8–19)

This is a beautiful speech, and we want to rejoice in Lear's newfound happiness with his daughter. But Lear here betrays his complete indifference to conventional politics; what once was his greatest concern has been reduced to the level of gossip, a mere matter of "who loses and who wins; who's in, who's out." Lear now looks down upon politics as a realm of merely transitory triumphs. He seems to have achieved a kind of philosophic detachment from life, which allows him to see human affairs as if from a contemplative height. But Lear's indifference to politics extends even to an indifference to his own freedom, and hence he seems happy to endure what formerly would have struck him as the ultimate humiliation: to be imprisoned by his enemies. Lear is now content to live like a bird in a cage; as attractive as this image may seem, there is something demeaning about it as well: the majestic lion of a king has been reduced to a tame house pet.[16] As if to remind us that Lear may be indifferent to politics but cannot escape its power, Shakespeare punctuates the king's lyrical fantasy with Edmund's curt and peremptory order: "Take them away" (5.3.19). We may applaud Lear's rising above his earlier conventional devotion to political life, but the fact is that his indifference to power in this scene is about to lead directly to the death of Cordelia. If basically decent men like Lear renounce political life, however justified they may be in their contempt for corruption in high places, no one will be left to defend the Cordelias of this world. Thus if Lear comes to understand the supreme worth of Cordelia, he cannot simply abandon political life to men like Edmund, who will ruthlessly stamp out all that Lear legitimately has come to value in the realms that transcend politics.

It is thus characteristic of the complexity of the movement of *King Lear* that Shakespeare has Lear at least partially rediscover the value of political life just before his death. Lear does not go to the grave still believing that there is no difference between a human being and an animal; on the contrary, he powerfully asserts the superiority of Cordelia to other forms of life: "Why should a dog, a horse, a rat, have life, / And thou no breath at all?" (5.3.307–8).[17] Recapturing his sense of human excellence, the man who in act 4 could see no reason to punish any malefactor, returns in act 5 to his role as judge and executes the subordinate sent by Edmund to eliminate Cordelia: "I kill'd the slave that was a-hanging thee" (5.3.275). With his unique grasp of psychology, Shakespeare chooses just this moment for Lear to recapture a bit of his old pride and anger, and at the same time to recall his youth, as he responds to the confirmation of his surprisingly valiant deed: "I have seen the day, with my good biting falchion / I would have made them skip" (5.3.277–78).

This is a fascinating moment, as we finally get the briefest glimpse of the young King Lear. Nearing the end of his life, Lear thinks back presumably to the earliest days of his political career, remembering what he forgot in his plan for dividing the kingdom, that the ability to do justice must ultimately be backed up by the sword. Lear's execution of the man who killed Cordelia tells us as much about the nature of justice as his speeches about the hollowness of authority back in act 4, scene 6. It is not that his final act cancels out the truths he articulated earlier; it is only that his deeds bring out the partiality of his speeches. To get at Shakespeare's understanding of justice, we cannot identify it with any single statement by his characters, but must take into account the pattern of the whole play, both deeds and speeches.

The fact that Lear thinks back to his youth at the conclusion of the play provides a clue to its structure; as Edmund's line "The wheel is come full circle" (5.3.175) suggests, the end of *King Lear* harks back to the beginning. At the start of the play the British regime, like Lear himself, has grown old. At the end of the play, the regime renews itself. Like Lear recalling the powerful sword strokes of his youthful arm, the regime must get back in touch with its foundation in the ultimate guarantor of political right: military force. At the beginning of the play, as a result of Lear's peaceful reign and his unquestioned authority, his regime has lost touch with political reality and he himself thinks that he can maintain control even while turning military power over to his children. Act 5 takes us back to the brute facts of political life and reminds us that in the end the deepest political divisions can be settled if not healed only by war.

This consideration explains why the trial by combat of Edmund and Edgar figures so prominently in act 5. Edgar has an airtight legal case against Edmund and one might imagine that their conflict would be settled in a court of law, where a juridical process could establish Edmund's guilt unequivocally. But Shakespeare shows a more primitive form of justice, trial by combat, because the thrust of act 5 is to keep reminding us that angels may dispense with violence in settling their disputes, but human beings cannot. The point is not that might makes right; we have seen the limitations of that savage principle in the destruction of Cornwall, Regan, Goneril, and now finally Edmund, whose careers in evil all go to prove the self-defeating and self-destroying character of a purely low-minded conception of justice.[18] But what Edgar's resort to the sword shows is that right cannot be entirely divorced from might. It is not that the good cause always triumphs in battle, only that if the good cause is to triumph, it ultimately must be in battle (recall that Lear must resort to force in this scene as well).

Edgar has had to learn how to turn some of the weapons of evil men and women against them in order to protect what he values in life.[19] Starting the play as a naive young man, untutored in the deceptive ways of the world, Edgar has had to don one disguise after another in the course of the play to come to terms with the evil in the world. Though he remains almost comically scrupulous in dealing with his enemies,[20] the Edgar at the end of the play can at least no longer be called naive. When Edgar kills Edmund in combat he establishes his right to rule in the realm, and seems to have absorbed whatever was best in his enemy, much as Prince Hal does when he defeats Hotspur.

The fact that Edgar can stake out a claim to rule only with a sword reminds us of the violence at the basis of politics, and we have more confidence in the capacity of this temperamentally mild man to maintain political order once we have seen that he can answer the savagery of evil antagonists with some brute force of his own. But it would be a mistake to fall into a totally cynical reading of the end of *King Lear*, arguing that the good party has had to become as savage as the evil in order to overcome it. The Edgar at the end of the play is not the same Edgar we saw at the beginning, but he has not become an

Edmund. In general, in the end the good characters maintain their distinction from the evil, in part because they have been spared the necessity of descending to the barbaric level of their antagonists by the fact that the evil characters have largely destroyed each other. Edgar and Albany never display the lust for power that is the hallmark of their counterparts Edmund and Cornwall. At most they have learned the need for political action to counter the machinations of their enemies, but that means that they resort to morally dubious actions with a marked reluctance. Unlike Edmund, Edgar never takes pleasure in deceiving others, and he never glories in evil deeds. Hence the end of the play forms a sharp contrast to the beginning:

Albany: Friends of my soul, you twain
Rule in this realm, and the gor'd state sustain.
Kent: I have a journey, sir, shortly to go:
My master calls me, I must not say no.
Edgar: The weight of this sad time we must obey,
Speak what we feel, not what we ought to say:
The oldest hath bourne most; we that are young
Shall never see so much, nor live so long.
(5.3.320–27)

At the beginning of *King Lear* we are in a world where many of the characters, though not all, are hungry for power; at the end we see characters who apparently cannot wait to hand over power to others. The course of the action has evidently been a sobering experience for decent men like Albany, Kent, and Edgar. No one of them is Plato's philosopher-king—Edgar perhaps comes closest—but they have developed some of his reluctance to rule. As Edgar acknowledges in the final lines, even his experience cannot match the journey Lear went through in the course of the play,[21] but the way in which he accepts rule as a duty imposed on him and not something he eagerly sought shows that he has come to share some of Lear's doubts about political life. Because of his consciousness of the limits of power, Edgar will presumably rule more moderately.

After a period of political chaos, we see a regime refounded at the end of *King Lear*. Like all regimes, its foundation may ultimately be traced back to an act of violence, but given the character of its founders, we may reasonably expect that it will not be a violent regime. All signs in fact point to the inevitability of entering a diminished and tamer world. The precondition for refounding the regime has been the elimination of the evil extremes of humanity who threatened all conventional order. But the extremes of good in Britain have been destroyed as well; Lear, Cordelia, and the Fool are dead, and Kent apparently does not have long to live. A political regime tends to compress the range of humanity, trying to force people into conventional molds, to moderate their passions, to move them toward a comfortable center. The world Edgar will rule will be a safer world, but it will be a world without Lear's grandeur or Cordelia's beauty. That is another way of saying that it will no longer be a heroic or a tragic world. The moderation—one might even say the mediocrity—of the characters left standing at the end of the play is the truest measure of the greatness of King Lear and the tragic nature of his story. No ending of a Shakespeare play captures more perfectly the fundamental contrast at work in tragedy between the ordinary human beings who are content to stay within the limits of the conventional world and the heroic souls who try to go beyond them.

Notes

1. In his *Shakespeare Our Contemporary*, trans. Boleslaw Taborski (Garden City, N.Y.: Anchor Books, 1966), 130, Jan Kott makes explicit what many critics assume about Lear: "He does not see or understand anything. . . . Lear is ridiculous, naive and stupid."

2. The classic statement of this view is to be found in A. C. Bradley, *Shakespearean Tragedy* (1904; rept. New York: Meridian Books, 1955), 258–60. See especially Bradley's attempt to state the moral of the play on p. 260: "The good are seen growing better through suffering. . . . The judgment of this world is a lie; its goods, which we covet, corrupt us. . . . Let us renounce the world, hate it, and lose it gladly. The only real thing in it is the soul, with its courage, patience, devotion. And nothing outward can touch that." For a similar view of *King Lear*, see G. Wilson Knight, *The Wheel of Fire* (1930; rept. New York: Meridian Books, 1957), 195–201, and Reuben A. Brower, *Hero and Saint: Shakespeare and the Graeco-Roman Heroic Tradition* (New York: Oxford University Press, 1971), 415. For a more recent statement of this position, see Barbara Everett's essay, "*King Lear*: Loving," in her *Young Hamlet: Essays on Shakespeare's Tragedies* (Oxford: Clarendon Press, 1989), 59–82.

3. See, for example, Knight, who speaks of "the absurdity of the old King's anger" in the first scene, describes him as "cutting a cruelly ridiculous figure" and as "selfish, self-centered," and characterizes him as "a tremendous soul . . . incongruously geared to a puerile intellect" (*Wheel of Fire*, 161–62).

4. Letter to Gummo Marx, June 1964, in Groucho Marx, *The Groucho Letters* (New York: Simon & Schuster, 1967).

5. Knight says that *King Lear* "resembles a Hardy novel" (*Wheel of Fire*, 202). Shades of Groucho, Knight remarks: "It is, indeed, curious that so storm-furious a play as *King Lear* should have so trivial a domestic basis" (161). So curious that one might question whether the basis is really trivial or domestic.

6. Harry V. Jaffa, "The Limits of Politics: *King Lear*, Act 1, Scene 1," in Allan Bloom, *Shakespeare's Politics* (New York: Basic Books, 1964), 113–45. This essay was originally published in *The American Political Science Review* 51 (1957): 405–27. Briefly stated, Jaffa's thesis is that the intent of Lear's original plan was to give Cordelia the bulk of his kingdom (the middle portion), while giving Goneril the extreme northern and Regan the extreme southern portion, regions their husbands already controlled as feudal lords. Lear intends to marry Cordelia to the Duke of Burgundy, a foreign power strong enough to give her support but not strong enough to conquer and absorb Britain (as the King of France might). Jaffa is the only critic of the play to have articulated the strategy of Lear's original plan, but he was not the first to note that Lear enters act 1, scene 1 with a division of the kingdom already worked out (after all, maps have been drawn up and Lear's counselors Gloucester and Kent are evidently already aware of the details when the play opens). See Samuel Taylor Coleridge, *Shakespearean Criticism*, ed. Thomas Middleton Raysor (London: J. M. Dent, 1960), 49–50, Bradley, *Shakespearean Tragedy*, 202–3, and Kenneth Muir, *Shakespeare: King Lear* (Harmondsworth: Penguin, 1986), 32, 55. For a further elaboration of Jaffa's analysis of Lear's plan, see David Lowenthal, "*King Lear*," *Interpretation* 21 (1994): 393–96.

7. "Nature and Convention in *King Lear*," to be published in Joseph Knippenberg and Peter Lawler, eds., *Poets, Princes, and Private Citizens: Literary Alternatives to Postmodern Politics* (Lanham, Md.: Rowman & Littlefield, 1996).

8. Compare Apemantus's criticism of Timon of Athens: "The middle of humanity thou never knewest, but the extremity of both ends" (4.3.300–1).

9. All quotations from Shakespeare are taken from G. Blakemore Evans, ed., *The Riverside Shakespeare* (Boston: Houghton Mifflin, 1974).

10. On the significance of clothing in act 3, see Lowenthal, "*King Lear*," 403.

11. For a similar analysis of Lear's speeches in act 4, scene 6, see Lowenthal, "*King Lear*," 407–9.

12. See, for example, Knight, who speaks of Lear "penetrating below the surface shows to the heart of human reality" here (*Wheel of Fire*, 192), or Derek Traversi, *An Approach to Shakespeare* (Garden City, N.Y.: Anchor Books, 1969), vol. 2, 164, who sees Lear revealing "the true state of man" in this scene.

13. The idea of breaking with the conventional parent-child relationship and

replacing it with something more "natural" is presented earlier in the play in demonic form when Cornwall tells Edmund after he betrays Gloucester: "thou shalt find a dearer father in my love" (3.5.24–25). Here the conventional bond between father and son is replaced by a bond of pure self-interest between villains; in the case of Lear and Cordelia, the conventional bond is replaced by a higher bond of spiritual love.

14. One must be very careful in formulating one's estimation of King Lear. Even as perceptive a critic as Bradley, who has a better feel for what is tragic in *King Lear* than almost anyone else who has written on the play, gets carried away with his own rhetoric: "there is no figure, surely, in the world of poetry at once so grand, so pathetic, and so beautiful as [King Lear]" (*Shakespearean Tragedy*, 228). It is very difficult to be grand and pathetic *at once*. What is precisely characteristic of Shakespeare's portrayal of King Lear is that he shows a grand political man at the beginning of the play, who becomes a figure of great pathos in his reunion with Cordelia. The dramatic movement of *King Lear* is so extraordinary, the contrast between Lear at the beginning and at the end of the play is so great, that we must be wary of making statements that conflate what I might refer to as the public and the private Lears.

15. See my essays "Shakespeare's *The Tempest*: The Wise Man As Hero," *Shakespeare Quarterly* 31 (1980): 64–75 and "Prospero's Republic: The Politics of Shakespeare's *The Tempest*," in John Alvis and Thomas West, eds., *Shakespeare as Political Thinker* (Durham, N.C.: Carolina Academic Press, 1981), 239–55. For a brief but insightful comparison of *King Lear* and *The Tempest*, see Lowenthal, "*King Lear*," 416.

16. Bradley is aware that a change has occurred in the Lear of act 5; of his utterances toward the end of the play, Bradley writes: "We feel in them the loss of power to sustain his royal dignity" (*Shakespearean Tragedy*, 234). But Bradley blurs the issue by trying to redefine magnanimity in Christian terms: "what remains is 'the thing itself,' the soul in its bare greatness" (234).

17. On this point, see Lowenthal, "*King Lear*," 413.

18. This outcome fulfills Albany's ominous prediction at 4.2.49–50. For the self-destructive character of evil, see Lowenthal, "*King Lear*," 409.

19. For a different view of what Edgar learns in the course of the play, see Joseph Alulis, "The Education of the Prince in Shakespeare's *King Lear*," *Interpretation* 21 (1994): 373–90.

20. Consider, for example, Edgar's hesitation in opening the letter from Goneril to Edmund when it falls into his hands (4.6.259–61).

21. I take "the oldest" in Edgar's speech to refer to Lear; some critics feel the words refer to Kent. This suggestion seems unlikely; usually at the end of a Shakespearean tragedy, the highest-ranking character surviving speaks of the tragic hero of the play. In any event, the closing lines round out the play effectively. The play opens with a discussion of how the difference between two men has been obscured in a political settlement. It closes with lines stressing the way in which one man is distinguished from his fellows; moreover

the criterion by which he is distinguished is the depth of his experience, more specifically how much he has been able to "see." Edgar's respect for wisdom is reflected in the fact that he values age (with its greater experience) over youth; at the beginning of the play, Edmund spoke out for youth over age. (On the issue of youth vs. age in the play, see Lowenthal, "*King Lear*," 399.) Finally, in the first scene of *King Lear* hypocrisy governed the court; at the end Edgar is calling for a new honesty when he enjoins: "Speak what we feel, not what we ought to say." In sum, Edgar's final words manifest a new regard for truth.

10

The Relation of Thought and Action in *Macbeth*

Timothy Fuller

Macbeth begins as does *The Tempest* in the correlation of time and storm.[1] "When" appears centrally three times in the first four lines. These are attended by repeated references to the confusion of foul and fair weather in the first ten lines, and the riddle of confusing winning and losing in line 4. The images of "lost" and "won," sunrise and "set of sun," "foul" and "fair," suggest revolution round and round, and temporality—the intimate connection of time and storm, the soul and the world.

In the second scene Macbeth is introduced as "disdaining Fortune," which is both his strength and his weakness. The scorning of fortune is the basis of Macbeth's "bloody execution" (1.2.17–18). King Duncan admires this (1.2.24). Macbeth is likened to the eagle hunting sparrows and Banquo as the lion to the hare (1.2.35). They doubled and redoubled their battle strokes until it seemed to the captain that they relished violence as an end in itself. The king is not detained by that thought but responds positively both to the report and to the sight of the reporting captain's wounds (1.2.43–44). The king sees the violence as honor. This is reinforced by his remark that what the Thane of Cawdor has lost, Macbeth has won. Yet as far as we can tell Macbeth does not yet know of the honors that are to come to him. Perhaps Macbeth is only latently ambitious and we might wonder whether here violence is not self-forgetful, in a way at odds with ambition. The irony is carried out in that Macbeth becomes Cawdor, i.e., he conquers the one in revolt only to become the one in revolt. Perhaps King Duncan is himself so enthralled by violence that he cannot distinguish its ambiguous possibilities by reflective judgment. Macbeth in becoming Cawdor is the winner becoming the loser and the loser the winner, and the king lends legitimacy to this by acknowledging himself to be at one with both loser and winner. The patriot becomes the revolutionary.

These confusions are borne out by the witches' speeches (1.3.1–26) where the shipman is drained dry, where there is no sleep night or day and where increase and decrease rule:

> Weary sev'nights, nine times nine,
> Shall he dwindle, peak, and pine.
> Though his bark cannot be lost,
> Yet it shall be tempest-tost. (22–25)

And Macbeth's next line is: "So foul and fair a day I have not seen" (1.3.38).

Banquo in noticing the witches sees that they are of uncertain sex (1.3.45) and thus inaugurates another of the fundamental dramatic confusions of the play. They say Macbeth is twice thane and also king, and Banquo wonders why Macbeth is startled by something that sounds so fair. Then the witches foretell that Banquo will be both lesser and greater (1.3.65). Banquo will beget kings and thus live through fortune's cycle—Macbeth will beget nothing. But the witches, too, only seem corporal and melt as "breath into the wind" (1.3.82). Banquo wonders whether the vision of the witches is caused by eating "the insane root / That takes the reason prisoner?" (1.3.84–85). Banquo and Macbeth then try to reconstruct the dream to remember exactly what happened (1.3.86–89). And Banquo opines that

> . . . oftentimes, to win us to our harm,
> The instruments of darkness tell us truths,
> Win us with honest trifles, to betray's
> In deepest consequence. (1.3.123–26)

Evading providence is both hope and danger. Macbeth reflects that this "supernatural soliciting / Cannot be ill, cannot be good" (1.3.130–31). He wonders at his own fear in the face of the prophecy and he sees that thoughts engendered by that prophecy must be murdered to maintain any orderly existence. As it is, his capacity to function is subdued by his own surmise and he fixes his attention such that what is not is what is real to him—both the witches and the kingship. The honor in battle was won by unthinking, patriotic gore, disrupted by the witches' prophecies. Macbeth must think how not to think. In this condition, Macbeth is "rapt" (1.3.142).

Nor is Duncan in any more thinking a condition. When Malcolm announces the execution of Cawdor, the king remarks, "There's no art / To find the mind's construction in the face" (1.4.11–12), and immediately responds to Macbeth's protestation of loyalty by feeding Macbeth's ambition: "I have begun to plant thee and will labor / To make thee full of growing" (1.4.28–29). He then acknowledges Banquo's equal merit, and it is Banquo who says what Macbeth might have been expected to say: "There if I grow, / The harvest is your own" (1.4.32–33). One might wonder, given equal merit, why the superior Banquo is not rewarded ahead of Macbeth. In the providential sense, of course, he will be. The irony is carried through to the end of act 1, scene 4. Macbeth is already growing in ambition, aiming to overleap Malcolm, newly ordained as Prince of Cumberland, heir to the throne, and Duncan refers to Macbeth as his "peerless kinsman" (1.4.58).

Enough has now been said to establish the atmosphere of the play, and it need only be remarked for present purposes that the themes of confusion are only carried deeper and deeper in the progress of the action. In discussing the progress of the play from this point on, I propose to concentrate on a central aspect of Macbeth's character already alluded to: The intense conflict between thought and action, or, to put it another way, the necessity for Macbeth to reject thought in order to act in the manner he wishes to act. As I see it, the argument of the play is not that thought and action are opposed, but that for a man like Macbeth they must be opposed. Furthermore, there are only a very limited number of circumstances in which action that abandons thought can be justified. There is one such occasion dramatized for us in *Macbeth*: In act 4, scene 3, in the concluding exchanges between Macduff and Malcolm, Macduff could spend time lamenting his terrible loss and he could spend time bragging about what he might do for revenge: "But, gentle heavens, / Cut short all intermission. Front to front / Bring thou this fiend of Scotland and myself" (4.3.231–33). For Macduff it must be action now with no intervening thought. And Malcolm responds, "This tune goes manly" (4.3.235), because, as in the opening scenes of the play with Duncan, Macbeth, and Banquo, there is no doubt in any of them that manliness is greatest in the self-forgetfulness of action.

In the case of Macduff, in contrast to Macbeth, the issue of righteous wrath seems to redeem the warrior's virtue from all ambiguity. Infinite ambition is compelling but purposeless and cannot sustain itself if it is recalled by reason. Righteous revenge, on the other hand, is exhausted in the completion of the retributive action. It has, one might say, a natural limit that operates even if the action is carried out in opposition to further thought and deliberation. Infinite ambition, however, is unnatural; it has no natural limit and, therefore, must depend on reason or self-limitation as opposed to natural limitation. This is implied in the necessity of Macbeth and Banquo to try to recollect exactly what transpired in their initial encounter with the witches. The incorporeal, melting, dreamlike world is where the natural limits are transgressed—where dreams permit or even encourage the extreme. Here we have an imagistic as well as an intellectual connection to *The Tempest* and to *Sonnet 129*:

> Th' expense of spirit in a waste of shame
> Is lust in action; and, till action, lust
> Is perjured, murd'rous, bloody, full of blame,
> Savage, extreme, rude, cruel, not to trust;
> Enjoyed no sooner but despised straight;
> Past reason hunted, and no sooner had,
> Past reason hated as a swallowed bait
> On purpose laid to make the taker mad:
> Mad in pursuit, and in possession so;
> Had, having, and in quest to have, extreme;
> A bliss in proof, and proved, a very woe;
> Before, a joy proposed, behind, a dream.
> All this the world well knows; yet none knows well
> To shun the heaven that leads men to this hell.[2]

Let us then descend briefly into the details of the portrayal of Macbeth with respect to thought and action: act 1, scene 7 begins with Macbeth's, "If it were done when 'tis done, then 'twere well / It were done quickly" (1.7.1–2). This is followed by a most remarkable exposition of the theme we are discussing.

If Macbeth's assassination of Duncan could complete the action not only in its immediacy but in its consequences, then the act itself would be the be-all and the end-all and we could risk the salvation of our souls. I interpret this as meaning (1.7.2–5) that an act with no subsequent implications would be an invisible act, and an invisible act requires no thought. It is not the act that requires thought but rather the act undertaken in a world engaged in seeing and responding to and interpreting the act—an act in context—that demands thought. A visible act requires justification therefore; an invisible act does not. Here we have a Shakespearean version of the Ring of Gyges' ancestor story in Plato's *Republic*. In both cases the confusion of dark and light is related to the confusion of what is visible and invisible. Equally in each case the question of the foundation of morality is at stake. Macbeth is saying that invisibility, or release from the fatal chain of consequences, is the release from scruples. Release from thought is like release from time that preserves in remembrance actions long after they are literally over and done with. Release from remembrance or recollection would also be release from time. Release from remembrance before the act would facilitate the act—i.e., to forget the unforgivingness of time and the autonomous ability of the world to assess for itself spurs ambition. Release after the act eliminates remorse if we can avoid remembrance of things past. Similarly, to be armed with the Gyges' ring would mean escape from thought, memory, remorse, inaction.

But the point both for Plato and Shakespeare is that this is a vain hope in a magical device. In fact, there is a structure or moral universe in reality, that asserts itself against these vanities which have their reality only in dreams. Or, if one wishes, it could also be said that Macbeth's nihilistic end is dictated by his inability to find any satisfactory alternative to his vain and empty dreams that require him to deny a real moral universe were real. Thus, finally, it is not Macbeth's tale told by an idiot that is the last word, but the consequences of his actions, which are the last word as he foresees in act 1, scene 7.

As Macbeth says:

> We still have judgment here, that we but teach
> Bloody instructions, which, being taught, return
> To plague th' inventor. This even-handed justice
> Commends th' ingredience of our poisoned chalice
> To our own lips. (1.7.8–12)

And he admits his only spur is "Vaulting ambition, which o'erleaps itself" (1.7.27). His ambition, in short, extends into the celestial sphere—it seeks equality with the universe and thus violates the boundaries of human place. Macbeth must set in motion what he cannot later control. What begins as the attempt to leap over all measure and rule must abandon all standards of measure and rule. Caithness says in 5.2.15–16, "He cannot buckle his distempered cause / Within the belt of rule.'' His rule is a fraud and thus only the dream of rule. Macbeth can extend his dream to infinite power, but symmetrically as he does so his real rule diminishes. Angus says,

> Those he commands move only in command,
> Nothing in love. Now does he feel his title
> Hang loose about him, like a giant's robe
> Upon a dwarfish thief. (5.2.19–22)

He is a little man clothed in brief authority.

The contrast between ambition reaching, in dream, to the starry vault and the dwarfish thief is unmistakable. As Banquo sees in act 1, scene 3, ''New honors come upon him, / Like our strange garments, cleave not to their mould / But with the aid of use'' (144–46). Banquo's speech may be seen as playing on ''habit'' in its two senses: there must be a fit between custom and the character of the man—but in Macbeth this could never be. Habit bespeaks settledness and repetition—one might call it the congealed reflectiveness of convention—and as such is a barrier to unrestrained action. Failing the natural limit of righteous wrath, the imaginative limit of sober reflection, and the combination of elements of the natural and the reflective limits that produce conventionality, we have Macbeth.

In the action from scene 5 to scene 7, Lady Macbeth deepens the confusion of the action. She fears Macbeth's nature (1.5.14–18), because he is too full of the milk of human kindness. She fears, in short, the femaleness of Macbeth or femaleness in general. It might also be said that Macbeth is a failure for her insofar as he is pregnant with thought—presumably the milk of kindness relates reflectiveness to the female as opposed to the violent, unreflective life of the warrior-king. She wishes to be unsexed to achieve ''direst cruelty'' (1.5.41). And this includes the appearance of kindness without the substance of it. She wants Macbeth to ''look like th' innocent flower, / But be the serpent under't'' (1.5.63–64). And she illustrates this by greeting the newly arrived king with: ''All our service / In every point twice done, and then done double'' (1.6.14–15), which describes assassination in the form of hospitality. In scene 7, when Macbeth is nearly ready to settle for enjoying the current high opinion in which he is held, she chides him for fearing ''To be the same in thine own act and valor / As thou art in desire'' (1.7.40–41). She wants Macbeth to unify desire and act.

Macbeth tries to put her off by asserting, ''I dare do all that may become a man'' (1.7.46). This is suitably ambiguous in that what is becoming to a man and what a man is able to become are in tension here. It is what a man is able to become that interests Lady Macbeth and she engages to try to alter what a man is: ''What beast was't then / That made you break this enterprise to me?'' (1.7.47–48). She thinks he was more a man when a beast in his first thoughtless enthusiasm. The confusion of beast and man follows when there is the subsumption of the female into the male, so that all becomes male. She says, ''When you durst do it, then you were a man; / And to be more than what you were, you would / Be so much more the man'' (1.7.49–51). The more the beast—this transsexual being—the more the man. The culmination is in her rejection of the mother's role, the final dissolution of clear categories.

Lady Macbeth then urges boldness and lays the plan to drug the king's chamberlains so ''That memory, the warder of the brain, / Shall be a fume, and the receipt of reason / A limbeck only'' (1.7.65–67). They will then descend into ''swinish sleep.'' Lady Macbeth is now a Circe. To this Macbeth replies: ''Bring forth men-children only; / For thy undaunted mettle should compose / Nothing but males'' (1.7.72–74). In the context, Lady Macbeth does exactly that by bringing Macbeth forth—a male producing a male. She is composing Macbeth, producing an order that is in reality a disorder.

Act 2, scene 3 is, throughout the interchanges of the Porter, Macduff, and Lennox, an essay on confusion in both nature and in man. This culminates with Macbeth acknowledging the killing of the king's attendants out of pretended righteous wrath. He turns the injustice of action that overtakes thought to a pretext for seeming justice: ''The expedition of my violent love / Outrun the pauser, reason'' (2.3.106–7). Is there an ambiguity here that might be called the thoughtfulness of thoughtlessness? Do we not have the subduction of reason to passion so that the ''pauser reason'' is inverted to become the rationalization of unreason, the use of reason to dispel reason?

From the very moment of Duncan's murder the rest of the play proceeds to work out the inevitable consequences that time brings forth. Macbeth, in further and further frenzied action, cannot fend off the reassertion of reality against his dream. On ''this bank and shoal of time'' Macbeth has risked his eternal soul and has done so even knowing that his acts are in danger of becoming visible (1.7.6). He recognizes this and the two ways in which Banquo is superior to him.

Banquo is superior to him first because he, like Macbeth, has a ''dauntless temper'' that allows him to dare much, but also, ''He hath a wisdom that doth guide his valor / To act in safety'' (3.1.52–54). In the second place, Banquo has true descendants. On Macbeth's head has been ''placed a fruitless crown.'' Macbeth has a ''barren sceptre'' and it will be ''wrenched with an unlineal hand,'' that is, the descendant of Banquo, not of Macbeth (3.1.61–63). Macbeth in doing all for himself has done only for another. Memory of past actions brings only remorse and the inevitable reassertion of consequences against action taken in the hope of invisibility. What utter irony that a king should see triumph in darkness. Lady Macbeth offers her usual remedy: stop ''Using those thoughts which should indeed have died / With them they think on . . . Things without all remedy / Should be without regard. What's done is done'' (3.2.10–12). The remedy of this darkness is even more darkness. Macbeth continues in the brooding vein and Lady Macbeth repeats insistently, ''You must leave this'' (3.2.35).

Macbeth cannot leave it. His conspiracy against Banquo is undermined by the escape of Fleance. The contingency of reality has shattered the dream of perfection. The man of ''vaulting ambition'' who would have perfected himself to become ''As broad and general as the casing air'' is now ''cabined, cribbed, confined, bound in / To saucy doubts and fears'' (3.4.23–25). Suitable accommodations for a dwarfish thief. It shows the fatuity of Lady Macbeth's remedy. We are the beings of time. As such, we can long for the eternal. Or we can long for the instantaneous, hoping to diminish to the point where consequence vanishes and thus the substance of the chain of time. But neither is our proper province here and now. Macbeth has murdered sleep and thus has destroyed the balance of sleep and waking or of nonthought and thought. He has tried to think himself into the beastly and then tried to forget that he has thought himself into beastliness. Now he can neither perfect his beastliness, nor return to what he once was:

> I am in blood
> Stepped in so far that, should I wade no more,
> Returning were as tedious as go o'er. (3.4.136–38)

In seeking the sleep of reason, he has achieved only unnatural, continual sleeplessness. Lady Macbeth says, ''You lack the season of all natures, sleep'' (3.4.141).

There is no alternative now for Macbeth but to play out the course of action he has chosen. He rededicates himself to immediacy of action so that no separation of purpose and deed may appear:

> The very firstlings of my heart shall be
> The firstlings of my hand. And even now,
> To crown my thoughts with acts, be it thought and done. (4.1.147–49)

And without further ado he sets off to surprise Macduff's castle and to commit crimes even more heinous than those against the king and Banquo.

There follows in act 4, scene 3 the curious exchange between Malcolm and Macduff where Malcolm casts himself as lower than Macbeth in respect to his "voluptuousness," the "cistern of my lust" (4.3.61, 63). According to Malcolm, wives, daughters, matrons, and maids, none would be safe. Macduff's prescription for this is secret lust with "willing dames" and the maintenance of a publicly cold appearance (4.3.73). Malcolm then confesses to "stanchless avarice" (4.3.78), and Macduff counters with an optimistic assessment of the riches Malcolm will derive from his own Scottish property when he becomes king (4.3.87–90). Then Malcolm denies he has any kingly graces and asserts he will "confound / All unity on earth" (4.3.99–100).

Thus, Malcolm finally forces Macduff to reject him and to lament the fate of Scotland. This certifies Macduff's patriotism to the satisfaction of Malcolm and he reveals his rectitude, remarking on the way that "modest wisdom plucks me / From over-credulous haste" (4.3.119–20). And the last word is given to Malcolm who "will perform in measure, time, and place" (5.8.73).

What Macbeth and Lady Macbeth suffer from is a disease of the soul, the destruction of the proper balance between thought and action. When the doctor tells Macbeth that his Lady "is troubled with thick-coming fancies / That keep her from her rest" (5.3.38–39), Macbeth demands he cure her:

> Canst thou not minister to a mind diseased,
> Pluck from the memory a rooted sorrow,
> Raze out the written troubles of the brain,
> And with some sweet oblivious antidote
> Cleanse the stuffed bosom of that perilous stuff
> Which weighs upon the heart? (5.3.40–45)

And the doctor responds: "Therein the patient / Must minister to himself" (5.3.45–46). Macbeth receives this prescription by gathering himself for one last assault on thoughtfulness: "Throw physic to the dogs, I'll none of it! / Come, put mine armor on" (5.3.47–8). By contrast Malcolm and Macduff put on "industrious soldiership" (5.4.16).

Macbeth's frenzied, warrior's ending returns us to the play's beginning with the difference that we now see the virtues of Macbeth in radically altered and deepened perspective. Manliness is now beastliness. As Birnam Wood now moves, he is trapped: "They have tied me to a stake. I cannot fly, / But bear-like I must fight the course" (5.7.1–2). And Macbeth's alternatives are reduced to death in combat or "to be the show and gaze o'th'time," a rare monster, "Painted upon a pole" (5.8.24–26).

Notes

1. Alfred Harbage, ed., *William Shakespeare: The Complete Works* (New York: The Viking Press, 1977).
2. Harbage, *Complete Works*, 1475.

11

Courage and Impotence in Shakespeare's *Macbeth*

Michael Davis

I

First impressions are important. Even if not always correct, they are the stuff out of which our later opinions are fashioned. They may be confirmed, altered, or rejected, but in each case they must be explained. It is for this reason that our first glimpses of Shakespeare's major characters are invariably instructive. The description we first hear of Macbeth may or may not be accurate, but the very anonymity of the Captain who utters it as a report to the king of the battle against the rebel Macdonwald, coupled with the fact that the king readily believes it, is an indication that the description is a fair rendering of what Macbeth is generally reputed to be.

> For brave Macbeth—well he deserves that name—
> Disdaining Fortune, with his brandished steel,
> Which smoked with bloody execution,
> Like valor's minion carved out his passage
> Till he faced the slave; (1.2.16–20)[1]

Three things strike us immediately. Macbeth is characterized as brave: courage is his signal, and perhaps his single virtue. Second, his courage comes to the fore in a situation in which he defies Fortune—not just chance, but chance deified. Finally, Macbeth is contrasted to the slavish Macdonwald. Courage is the virtue not of slaves but of masters.

Macbeth's courage has something to do with his capacity to master a chancy situation.[2]

Courage is the central issue of the play.[3] This becomes clearer once we see the connection among courage, bravery, and valor on the one hand, and the staggering frequency of references to manhood, being a man, not being womanly, etc., on the other. Shakespeare writes in a tradition in which courage is the manly virtue par excellence. This tradition has its roots in the literature and philosophy of Greek antiquity in which the word for courage, *andreia*, also means manliness, and in which among the fundamental cosmic principles of opposition we find male and female.[4] The former is the active principle, the latter passive—so much so that the female body is thought to provide only the raw material for nourishment and growth of the fetus. The male sperm provides everything else. In Aristotle the existence of an ordered cosmos is owing to the imposition of form (the male principle) on matter (the female principle)—something purely potential, purely passive.[5] To say that Macbeth is courageous, then, means that he takes matters into his own hands, that he seizes opportunities—potentialities—that he does not passively let fortune guide him but disdains it with his brandished steel.

The deeper implications of *Macbeth* require an understanding of the meaning of courage and manliness within the play. A variety of possibilities come to the fore. "I dare do all that may become a man; / Who dares do more is none" (1.7.46–47).[6] At the beginning Macbeth holds a very classical notion of the nature of courage. There are limits placed on human action. To cross these limits means to become something nonhuman—whether subhuman or superhuman. At the same time, he shows a grudging admiration for his wife who is not put off by the prospect of crossing these limits. "Bring forth men-children only; / For thy undaunted mettle should compose / Nothing but males" (1.7.72–74). This strange woman is the first to emphasize the connection between courage and being the most manly of males, but it is a view shared by Macbeth. After Duncan's body has been discovered, when Macbeth wishes to give the appearance of strength and virtue he suggests that those present meet again after they have "put on manly readiness" (2.3.135). And later he taunts the murderers into agreeing to attack Banquo by suggesting that if they do not avenge themselves they are less than men:

> *First Murderer*: We are men, my liege.
> *Macbeth*: Ay, in the catalogue ye go for men;

As hounds and greyhounds, mongrels, spaniels, curs,
Shoughs, water-rugs and demi-wolves, are clept
All by the name of dogs: the valued file
Distinguishes the swift, the slow, the subtle,
The housekeeper, the hunter, every one
According to the gift which bounteous nature
Hath in him closed, whereby he does receive
Particular addition, from the bill
That writes them all alike: and so of men.
Now if you have a station in the file,
Not i' th' worst rank of manhood, say't,
And I will put that business in your bosoms
Whose execution takes your enemy off,
Grapples you to the heart and love of us,
Who wear our health but sickly in his life,
Which in his death were perfect.
Second Murderer: I am one, my liege,
Whom the vile blows and buffets of the world
Hath so incensed that I am reckless what
I do to spite the world.
First Murderer: And I another
So weary with disasters, tugged with fortune,
That I would set my life on any chance,
To mend it or be rid on' t. (3.1.91–114)

Manhood is thus not simply generic; it does not simply distinguish one class of beings from another. It does this, but it also provides the basis for a hierarchy among men.[7] To be a real man is to be more than a mere man, and to be a real man means above all to take one's fate and one's honor into one's own hands even to the point of being reckless enough "to spite the world" and risk death.

This understanding of the connection between manhood and courage is confirmed in what follows in the play with one interesting exception. Upon hearing of the death of his wife and children at the hands of Macbeth, Macduff is told by Malcolm to "dispute it like a man." He replies, "I shall do so; / but I must also feel it as a man" (4.3.220–21). In other words, he must suffer it like a man; he must be passive for a time in order to place his actions in the proper context. This exception deserves some attention. It is the one moment in the play when the identity of courage and manliness is explicitly questioned. And yet in this context Macduff's passivity is perceived by Malcolm as a weakness. And Macduff himself, after letting "grief / Convert to anger" (4.3.228–29), characterizes his grief as womanly, although he does not for that reason regret having shown it. In other words, this exception is seen as an exception. Feeling grief like a man means acting like a woman. Shakespeare chooses to abstract from this more moderate and sensible view of human life as some mixture of manliness and womanliness, of activity and passivity; he does so because he wishes to teach us something about manliness by showing us its most extreme, and at the same time most consistent, form. For this reason the dominant view of manliness remains fairly expressed in the speech that announces the death of the young Siward.

> Your son, my lord, has paid a soldier's debt:
> He only lived but till he was a man;
> The which no sooner had his prowess confirmed
> In the unshrinking station where he fought,
> But like a man he died. (5.8.39–43)

Young Siward's manliness consists in facing almost certain death, knowing it, and still "to spite the world" continuing.

That Macbeth is under the spell of this view of courage is clear from the last scene. Having just learned that Macduff is not of woman born Macbeth says, "it hath cowed my better part of man"; that is, it has momentarily deprived him of courage (5.8.18). Courage is the better part of man. Macbeth's last words are "And damned be him that first cries 'Hold enough!' " (5.8.34). Damnation, and so salvation, apparently have to do primarily with one's conduct in battle.[8] The worst of all sins is to say "uncle."

Macduff too is an advocate of courage. "[F]ront to front / Bring thou this fiend of Scotland and myself; / Within my sword's length set him. If he 'scape, / Heaven forgive him too!" (4.3.232–35). Malcolm's reply to this declaration is "This time goes manly" (4.3.235). Should Macbeth prevail in battle, Macduff, whose wife and children have been brutally slaughtered, is willing to see their slaughterer forgiven. We have already seen Malcolm call upon Macduff to cure his grief with revenge like a man. We also see that Siward, the old soldier, hears of his son's death, and can only think to ask whether he received his wounds in front like a man or behind like a coward (5.8.46). But the most striking statement of this cult of manliness comes from a woman, Lady Macbeth.[9] First she taunts her husband with the charge of cowardice in order to persuade him to murder Duncan. "And live a coward in thine own esteem, / Letting 'I dare not' wait upon 'I would' " (1.7.43–44). And shortly thereafter: "When you durst do it, then you were a man; / And to be more than what you were, you would / Be so much more the man'' (1.7.49–51). This view of courage as the highest of human possibilities is held at least in part by all the major characters in *Macbeth* save the one singled out for her womanliness, Lady Macduff, and the one singled out for his saintliness, Edward, the pious king of England. Our first impression is that the play is a great praise of the virtue courage. Macbeth more consistently than anyone else takes his bearings by the reduction of human virtue to courage that is implied in the identification of courage and manliness. Why then is the tragedy his? Macbeth may be justly punished for his excess, but this excess is rooted in his consistency.

If *Macbeth* is, as its full title suggests, a tragedy, then there ought to be something redeeming in the man Macbeth. He cannot be simply cruel, ambitious, bloodthirsty, and tyrannical. *Macbeth* is in the deepest sense a tragedy because it presents us with a man who does possess a virtue but of such a kind and to such a degree that he dares do all that may become a man and as a result ends up less than a man. We are presented with the spectacle of one virtue pushed to such an extreme that it ceases to be virtue. Macbeth's tragedy is the tragedy of courage. To make this claim plausible requires that something be said about the peculiar structure of courage.

Courage is the virtue of action, of nonpassivity, of taking one's fate into one's own hands. At the same time, however, it is a reactive virtue. It is not possible to be courageous unless one is in some sense threatened. As a virtue the purpose of which is conquest, its success is simultaneously its failure. It is not accidental that this play almost begins with the famous lines, ''Fair is foul and foul is fair.'' The goal or end toward which courage tends is victory, but victory creates conditions under which there is no longer any outlet for courage. Courage is the martial virtue. But, as Aristotle puts it, ''War is for the sake of peace.''[10] In war every effort is made in the name of victory, but this very victory deprives the warrior of his pre-eminence.

To say that courage is reactive and at the same time the virtue of action is to say that human action is at its best reactive. It is always geared to the overcoming of obstacles. All of this is quite interesting but not as yet particularly tragic so long as we make war in order to enjoy peace. But for Macbeth whose essence is his courage, this structure portends an unceasing drive to overcome obstacles, which, because they are finite, must cease to be obstacles as soon as they are overcome. His courage thus requires that he seek out ever new obstacles, obstacles, which once overcome, are recorded for us by the train of dead bodies he leaves in his wake. He is first concerned only to kill Duncan, thereby becoming king. But he is not content with having the throne; he must have it so securely that it cannot be wrested from him. This desire for security takes the form of attempting to prevent even death from causing him to lose the throne. Macbeth thus seeks to secure the kingship for his offspring. This was so far from being a part of his original ambition that the very prophets who assured him he would be king also assured him that his sons would not be. Macbeth's concern for his children cannot be understood as a natural paternal desire to assure the well-being of his offspring. There are as yet no children, or at least if there are they are so minimized as individuals that they are never mentioned in the play even by this worried father.[11]

Macbeth is a man in search of a foe. With each success he becomes less content. Had he simply desired the throne he could have made his reign relatively secure in the way taken by the Macbeth of the source for this play, Holinshed's *Chronicles*.[12] That is, he could have ruled more justly, or at least more moderately.[13] The real Macbeth ruled for seventeen years, ten of which were wholly untroubled. No, our Macbeth desires more than the throne. He seeks an obstacle so great that he will not have to seek another, but that must mean one so great that, while ensuring the continuance of his manliness, it will thwart his victory.

We are confronted with a dilemma. If it is the core of our natures to attempt to overcome obstacles, either they can be overcome, in which case we will have nothing left to do—we are unmanned; or they cannot be overcome, in which case we wonder why we should make an attempt—we are again unmanned. In either case, we, who wish to be courageous, are rendered impotent. What may perhaps save us is that we do not know—cannot know—whether victory or defeat awaits us.

The play that is concerned with courage is also concerned with tyranny, and not accidentally. Shakespeare is not the only one to have seen the tyrannic impulse as the extreme version of the desire to be master of one's fate. Nor is he the only one to have seen the tragic implications of tyranny.[14] Xenophon's *Hiero* teaches that the tyrant will be less free to do what he wills than most men; he will be hated, and so his freedom of movement will be restricted from fear of assassination, and, because he will be envied he will be in no position to distinguish real friends from artful flatterers. The tyrant will be able to trust no one.[15] Hegel also illustrates the self-defeating character of the tyrannic impulse. We seek to master others, to enslave them, because we seek their recognition. But what we really want is their recognition freely given. Our very acts of conquest, while ensuring recognition, at the same time, by enslaving opponents, makes their recognition worthless.[16] Here, too, fair is foul.

But Shakespeare goes deeper. One might reply to Xenophon as Machiavelli would have. If a tyrant is clever enough, he need not be hated.[17] And one might reply to Hegel that tyranny is only tragic if what is desired is recognition and not mastery for its own sake. Shakespeare wants to show that tyranny is necessarily tragic because, as the extreme form of courage, it is what it is by virtue of overcoming obstacles. Its complete success would put it out of business.

Shakespeare does not mean to suggest that this most extreme form of tyranny is possible. For it to be so, more than other human beings would have to be mastered. Yet because he does wish to proceed for a time with the pretense of its possibility, he is forced to enlist the aid of preternatural beings on Macbeth's behalf. This is instructive for two reasons. First, it enables us to see that if courage could be pushed to its extreme form, it would prove tragic. Second, by introducing conditions for this extreme form of courage that are on the one hand necessary and on the other admittedly impossible, Shakespeare shows us just why complete mastery is impossible. With that it is necessary to turn to the role of the witches in the play.

II

Courage may consist in disdaining fortune, but Macbeth places trust in fortune-tellers. He is aware early on that: "If chance will have me King, why, chance may crown me, / Without my stir" (1.3.143–44). From the moment he entertains this possibility, the manly Macbeth begins his submission to the "powers of darkness" and is unmanned. There is a great temptation to interpret the witches away—to understand them as a powerful, if subliminal, force in Macbeth's psyche. To surrender to this temptation is to miss the point. The immediate evidence of the play is that the witches are independent of Macbeth, not in his soul. The witches always precede Macbeth on stage. They appear to Banquo as well as Macbeth. There are certainly examples of visions which appear to Macbeth alone, and which are therefore intentionally of uncertain status. Both the dagger of act 2, scene 1 and the ghost of Banquo in act 3, scene 4 are clearly meant to be taken in this ambiguous fashion. The witches are not. It is their very independence and their connection to fortune (Holinshed hints that they may be the goddesses of destiny) that set up the crucial tension between Macbeth and fortune. A fully adequate analysis of the play would require a complete interpretation of the witches. In lieu of that, it will be helpful to concentrate on what the witches bring to the play, prophecy, and its connection to the problem of courage.

On the surface, one who disdains fortune should have no truck with fortune-tellers. Macbeth feels this tension, and so his attitude toward the witches is throughout the play equivocal. On the one hand, he acts out of the belief that what they say is true; on the other hand, he acts on his own in order to be doubly sure. Having just heard that he cannot be harmed by any man of woman born, and taking that to mean that no man can harm him, Macbeth nevertheless resolves to kill Macduff to "make assurance double sure, / And take a bond of fate" (4.1.83-84). This attitude is certainly understandable—no use taking chances. At the same time, however, it is patently ridiculous. To know one's fate is to neutralize chance. To think that prophecy needs assurances is to doubt that it is prophecy. In Macbeth's case this means to call into question all of the motives for what he has done and for what he plans to do. Macbeth decides to murder Banquo because the witches have foretold that Banquo's heirs will rule Scotland. He believes them enough to worry about Banquo, but not enough to give up all attempts to forestall the future they predict. He doubts and does not doubt that what they say about the future is correct. As Macbeth's attitude toward the prophecy is equivocal, it is poetic justice that the prophecy itself should turn out to be equivocal.

The question of equivocation, mentioned explicitly only twice, deserves closer scrutiny. Its occurrence late in the play is fairly straightforward. Having just seen Birnam Wood beginning to move toward Dunsinane, Macbeth says: "I pull in resolution, and begin / To doubt th' equivocations of the fiend / That lies like truth . . ." (5.5.42–44). An equivocation appears to speak with one voice but really speaks with two. Birnam Wood, not actually moving to Dunsinane, is still sort of moving to Dunsinane. The prophecy is ambiguous. (There is, of course, a more serious difficulty with Macbeth's view of prophecy. He traffics with preternatural beings, beings who do things no man can do, and yet it does not occur to him for a moment that, having defied the ordinary course of nature in one respect, they might well be able to do so in other respects. If you put part of your faith in preternatural beings, it does not seem very clever to put the rest of it in natural laws. Beings who can foretell the future might just be able to make trees move.)[18] The crucial word here is equivocation. To understand what Shakespeare has in mind when using it we must turn to act 2, scene 3, a scene often noticed for its humor, but too seldom for its meaning.

Shakespeare draws our attention to a parallel between prophecy and drinking. Both equivocate. The equivocation is not spelled out with regard to prophecy, but it is spelled out with regard to drinking. The drunken porter tells Macduff that drink is notorious for three things—nose painting, sleep, and urine, but:

> Lechery, sir, it provokes and unprovokes; it provokes the desire, but it takes away the performance: therefore much drink may be said to be an equivocator with lechery: it makes him and it mars him; it sets him on and it takes him off; it persuades him and it disheartens him; makes him stand to and not stand to; in conclusion, equivocates him in a sleep, and giving him the lie, leaves him. (2.3.31–38)

Drink provokes desire and at the same time causes impotence.

Prophecy has a similar structure. It plants desire in Macbeth, and at the same time makes it impossible to fulfill this desire. Both drink and prophecy arouse and emasculate, and do so not by dint of any easily resolved ambiguity in their natures. It is not that part of drink, or prophecy, arouses, and part emasculates. No, the very same thing that heightens our desire renders us unable to achieve the object of our desire. Drink and prophecy are not part fair and part foul but simultaneously fair and foul.

To tell Macbeth that he will become king is to tell him that regardless of what he does he will become king. In the meantime, however, he still has to act. He is alive. The choice of letting himself be crowned without his stir is not a real choice. Since he must do something, not stirring is not a real alternative. But this man of action, of manliness, has been placed in a situation in which, whatever he does, his fate is sealed. Accordingly, he cannot think of himself as taking his fate into his own hands. To be favored by fortune is fine, but to be favored by fortune and told about it in advance is an insult to his manhood. Courage is the virtue of action, but to be worthy actions must have some consequence. It might seem ideal to know in advance what the consequences of one's actions will be. Yet to know in advance what the future holds, and at the same time know that a variety of courses of action appear open, must lead to the conclusion that one's particular choice of action is inconsequential, and if inconsequential not worthy, and if not worthy not virtuous. Foreknowledge, which appears to ensure courage, in the end makes it impossible to consider oneself courageous.[19] Macbeth is indeed "valor's minion." He who appears to be the favorite of courage is in fact the slave of courage.[20]

Faced from the beginning with the prospect of enslavement, the manly Macbeth is bound to rebel. Because the witches are agents of his enslavement, they are the targets of his rebellion, a rebellion at first only partial but in the end total. Macbeth has two choices. He may accede to the prophecy, that is, to emasculation, or he may fight what he knows from the outset to be a losing battle. He chooses the latter.

> I 'gin to be aweary of the sun,
> And wish th' estate o' th' world were now undone.
> Ring the alarum bell! Blow wind, come wrack!
> At least we'll die with harness on our back. (5.5.49–52)

And his last words:

> Though Birnam Wood be come to Dunsinane,
> And thou opposed, being of no woman born,
> Yet I will try the last. Before my body
> I throw my warlike shield. Lay on, Macduff;
> And damned be him that first cries "Hold, enough!" (5.8.30–34)

Hecate, the top witch, has seen this coming all along:

> And, which is worse, all you [the other witches] have done
> Hath been but for a wayward son,
> Spiteful and wrathful; who, as others do,
> Loves for his own ends, not for you. (3.5.10–13)

And so she punishes Macbeth, but the raw materials for that punishment are already available in human nature.

> And that distilled by magic sleights
> Shall raise such artificial sprites
> As by the strength of their illusion
> Shall draw him on to his confusion.
> He shall spurn fate, scorn death, and bear
> His hopes 'bove wisdom, grace, and fear:
> And you all know security
> Is mortals' chiefest enemy. (3.5.26–33)

Security is mortals' chiefest enemy because only when threatened by insecurity can mortals exert themselves, and only by exerting themselves can they fulfill themselves. Yet paradoxically, mortals treat security as though it were their greatest friend, and must do so. "To be thus is nothing, but to be safely thus—" (3.1.48). All exertion is directed toward security, the very thing that makes exertion unnecessary. This thought is unwittingly expressed by Macbeth himself when asking the murderer about the success of the attack on Banquo and Fleance: "Banquo's safe?" (3.4.26). In the context, to be safe is to be dead.

Macbeth's rebellion began early. His very action to gain and hold the kingship secure is in its way a rebellion. What has only been implicit, however, becomes explicit in his second go-around with the witches. At the beginning of act 4 Macbeth appears as one accustomed to command. He who ought to be the supplicant acts imperiously. Macbeth attempts to command the return of the first apparition, and having asked the witches, not very politely, to tell him whether Banquo's heirs will ever rule in Scotland, he meets their response, an apparition, brusquely. "Thou art too like the spirit of Banquo. Down!" (4.1.112). Macbeth attempts to regain control over his own future by commanding the fortune-tellers. Earlier in act 3 he had responded to the prospect of Banquo's heirs ruling with the following words. "To make them kings, the seeds of Banquo kings! / Rather than so, come, fate, into the list, / And champion me to th' utterance!" (3.1.70–72).

Macbeth challenges fate and, of course, fails. Knowing that damnation consists in giving up the fight, renouncing courage and ceasing to consider oneself master of one's own fate, Macbeth sees only one way of avoiding it—"damned [be] all those that trust them! [the witches]" (4.1.139). But Macbeth has trusted them. If he had not, and did not continue to do so, his wrath against them would be unintelligible. Only because he believes what they say does he find it necessary to challenge them. Macbeth's attitude toward the prophecy is to the end equivocal, and necessarily so.

III

Macbeth is a tragic figure for two reasons. His virtue, courage, when pushed to its extreme is self-annihilating. And his belief in the prophecy is incompatible with his courage, and so with his self-esteem. Still, it is legitimate to ask why courage need be pushed to the extreme, and why we need worry about things like prophecy. A play that touches us so deeply must be based on a foundation more accessible and more generally applicable than the prophecy of witches. It is therefore necessary to find some means of connecting the questions of prophecy and courage in such a way as to show that the essence of the tragedy of courage is displayed most clearly by means of a consideration of the effects of prophecy. The means will be time, and in particular what it means for human beings to be temporal beings.

Prophecy turns the temporal order topsy-turvy. Lady Macbeth, upon receiving a letter from her husband describing his first meeting with the witches puts it very well. "Thy letters have transported me beyond / This ignorant present, and I feel now / The future in the instant" (1.5.57–59). To say that the present is always ignorant is only to say the commonplace. The specifics of our futures may at times seem very probable, but we are never really sure that some chance event might not intervene to frustrate our hopes and ambitions. This precariousness of human life generally is not exactly caused by the fact that we are temporal creatures; it is rather part of what it means to be a temporal creature. Hope, anxiety, ambition—these are signs that we are never sure of our fates. Prophecy would destroy the open-endedness of the future present in the instant. The problem of time enters with the witches. The play literally opens with the word "when," and the first problem the witches set for themselves is a temporal problem. Perhaps more instructive is the manner in which they initially present themselves to Macbeth.

> All hail, Macbeth! Hail to thee, Thane of Glamis!
> All hail, Macbeth, Hail to thee, Thane of Cawdor!
> All hail, Macbeth, that shalt be King hereafter! (1.3.48–50)

This is not simply prophecy; it is not concerned only with the future. The first two salutations are emphatically addressed to Macbeth rather than being descriptions of him. They represent his past and his present. He is addressed as Glamis, which he has been for some time, and as Cawdor, which he has just become, but only rather matter of factly described as the king he will be. While the first two salutations may be understood as according to Macbeth the customary respect due his titles, the last leaves some doubt whether the respect due the person of a king is something to which Macbeth is entitled. Macbeth is certainly more taken with the prophecy. (He of course takes the salutation as Thane of Cawdor as a prediction because he is as yet unaware of what Duncan has done. This is itself important, since we are always in a sense unaware of the present until we have reflected upon it, and by then it is past.) But the implications of the prophecy do not escape the more sober Banquo.

> If you can look into the seeds of time,
> And say which grain will grow and which will not,
> Speak then to me, who neither beg nor fear
> Your favors nor your hate. (1.3.58–61)

The witches must represent time past, present, and future because the future is not independent of the past. Time has seeds. Events done in the present grow in the soil of past events and have consequences for the future. Macbeth grows to understand this better as the play progresses. "Come what come may, / Time and the hour runs through the roughest day" (1.3.146–47). And later in act 1:

> If it were done when 'tis done, then 'twere well
> It were done quickly. If th' assassination
> Could trammel up the consequence, and catch,
> With his surcease, success; that but this blow
> Might be the be-all and end-all—here,
> But here, upon this bank and shoal of time,
> We'd jump the life to come. (1.7.1–7)

The "life to come" can, but need not, mean the life to come after this life. It may also mean that actions in the present have consequences. They shape the possibilities open to us in our futures. It is not so easy to "Let every man be master of his time" (3.1.40).

The entire play subsequent to the regicide may be described in terms of Macbeth's struggle against the consequences of his earlier actions. His battle is not so much a battle for a specific future as a battle against the past. And yet his every attempt to right the situation sinks him deeper into enslavement by the past. Since Macbeth's actions are reactions to situations growing from his previous actions, his attempts to free himself—to assert his independence and manhood—bind him to the past even more slavishly.

Lady Macbeth realizes the impossibility of the situation long before Macbeth.

> Nought's had, all's spent,
> Where our desire is got without content:[21]

> 'Tis safer to be that which we destroy
> Than by destruction dwell in doubtful joy.
> How now, my lord! Why do you keep alone,
> Of sorriest fancies your companions making,
> Using those thoughts which should indeed have died
> With them they think on? Things *without* all remedy
> Should be without regard: what's done is done.
> (3.2.4–12)[22]

That there are things without remedy, and in particular that these are paradigmatically the things of the past, flies in the face of Macbeth's own understanding of his manliness. The final and overwhelming obstacle to Macbeth's courage is the past, and its apparently commonsensical rule uttered by a madwoman, "What's done cannot be undone" (5.1.71).

Macbeth's flirtation with prophecy is first a symptom of his desire to overcome the fundamental insecurity of not knowing what the future holds for him. He wishes to be master of his time, but this means that he must seek to overcome his nature as temporal. Security, which is "mortals' chiefest enemy," is at the same time the object of mortals' chief desire, a desire that can only be satisfied if it is possible to be sure of the consequences of one's actions. Security is mortals' chief enemy, however, because to be mortal is to be in that precarious and endangered position of being threatened, and so attempting to gain security. Life consists in the activity of reacting to this threat. When the threat is gone, so is life understood in this way. If courage is the paradigmatic human virtue, then it is the human plight to pursue an object all the while knowing that if the pursuit is successful, all that is desirable in human life vanishes with the victory.

Macbeth's equivocation is thus not simply the result of a fantastic and imaginary situation. While prophecy is at most a very unlikely matter of concern for us, the mere consideration of its possibility leads us to see that the temporal conditions necessary for an act of the most extreme courage, an act that attempts to overcome the source of human insecurity, would require an attack on *the* condition of this insecurity, time. Such an attack must fail because the attempt to assure our futures at the same time makes us prisoners of our pasts. Put most simply, if courage is virtue, human life is tragic. In *Macbeth* we see this tragedy acted out. It can only be acted out if the impossible—prophecy—is made possible, if "nothing is / But what is not" (1.3.141–42). It may be unlikely that a real human being will ever run out of obstacles to overcome, but real human beings can think through this tragedy, and so realize that life understood in terms of courage is tragic. Courage, in principle, leads to impotence, or in more familiar language, to nihilism, that state in which, because everything is permitted, nothing is desired.

Nietzsche describes nihilism as the resolution rather to will nothing than not to will at all.[23] Macbeth fits this Nietzschean description. Pressed by his wife to forget the past since "what's done cannot be undone," Macbeth refuses to submit to this law of time. He tries to compel fortune by compelling the fortune-tellers, and when this fails, he defies fortune knowing it will mean his death. He wills nothing rather than not will at all—a final effort to assert his manliness in a world that can only mock the attempt.[24]

> Tomorrow, and tomorrow, and tomorrow
> Creeps in this petty pace from day to day, . . .
> And all our yesterdays have lighted fools
> The way to dusty death. Out, out, brief candle!
> Life's but a walking shadow, a poor player
> That struts and frets his hour upon the stage
> And then is heard no more. It is a tale
> Told by an idiot, full of sound and fury
> Signifying nothing. (5.5.19–28)

Epilogue

We are still left to ask what all of this has to do with us. We are not terribly tempted to speak of courage as the paradigmatic virtue. Indeed, we are tempted not to speak of virtue at all. Shakespeare's *Macbeth* is of importance to us because we are heirs to a tradition that understands man as enveloped in a hostile atmosphere, alienated from the world, and at his best in the battle to overcome this estrangement. If this battle is in principle capable of being won, then either man will no longer be at his best, or he will no longer be man.[25] If the battle against a hostile nature is in principle not capable of being won, it is not at all clear why it ought to be fought. To take our bearings by attempting to overcome a hostile nature is inevitably to be caught between Scylla and Charybdis. If we cannot win we lose, and if we can win we lose. It is appropriate that the first scene of Macbeth should contain the line "When the hurlyburly's done, / When the battle's lost and won." If life is understood as a battle, winning is losing.

Two options seem open to us if we are to understand human life as other than tragic. One is suggested by Shakespeare. There are two kinds of prophecy in Macbeth. One comes from the "powers of darkness"; it is satanic and tempts Macbeth to be more than a man, to be like a god. The other is a "heavenly gift" (4.3.157) and is practiced by Edward of England. This passing reference to Edward, coupled with the fact that it is Edward who supports Malcolm in restoring Scotland to normalcy, is an indication of an alternative understanding of man as not confronted with a hostile nature but as living within a beneficent nature. The appropriate response, then, is not courage but something like piety. Put less gracefully, it is not so bad to be a slave. To fill out this suggestion would require another reading of the play, keeping in mind that the alternative to manliness is womanliness and that the two need not be understood as incompatible.

The alternative was understood most powerfully by Friedrich Nietzsche. Nietzsche, on the one hand understanding the necessity of some fixed and eternal standards for our action (security) and on the other hand understanding the tragic implications of such standards for our non-fixed and non-eternal lives (security is mortals' chiefest enemy), sought to elaborate a doctrine that combined the eternal and the temporal and thus satisfied both human needs—the need for security and the need for insecurity. Nietzsche did this by attempting to make the sequence of temporal events itself eternal in the sense of eternally recurring. His solution intentionally violates that temporal law according to which "what's done is done" without sacrificing its other formulation "what's done cannot be undone." By reinterpreting the rigid separation of past, present, and future time, Nietzsche attempts to make it possible to overcome our enslavement to the past. By willing our future we are simultaneously willing our past and so, in a paradoxical manner, determining what we have already become.[26] Difficult as it is, Nietzsche's teaching of the eternal return is not lunacy. It is a bold attempt to avoid the tragic implications we have seen sketched out in Shakespeare's *Macbeth*, not by rethinking the importance of courage but by rethinking the structure of time.

But perhaps there is a third way—a combination of the manliness of Macbeth and the womanliness of Edward. Uncovering the underlying conditions of human life in which we have no choice but to acquiesce requires a certain boldness. Understanding this togetherness of moderation and madness would help us to take the measure of our most philosophical poet.

Notes

This essay, in a slightly different form, was originally published in *Essays from the Faculty*, Sarah Lawrence College (February 1979). It owes a great deal to Jose Benardete's fine article "Macbeth's Last Words" (*Interpretation* 1 [Summer 1970]: 63-75), as well as to several conversations with Richard Kennington on the question of equivocation in *Macbeth*. I would also like to thank my daughter Jessica Davis for her help in preparing the typescript.

1. All references from the play are to *The Tragedy of Macbeth*, ed. Sylvan Barnet (New York: New American Library, The Signet Classic Shakespeare, 1963).

2. Compare this with Niccolò Machiavelli's advice to princes in chapter 25 of *The Prince:* "fortune is a woman; and it is necessary, if one wants to hold her down, to beat her and strike her down" (trans. Harvey C. Mansfield, Jr. [Chicago: University of Chicago Press, 1985], 101).

3. See Samuel Johnson's notes on the play in Barnet, *Macbeth*, 159-60.

4. Aristotle *Metaphysics* 986a26.

5. Aristotle *On the Generation of Animals* 730a-b.

6. For other instances of the connection between manliness and courage see 2.3.111; 3.4.59, 66, 74, 80, 100, 109; 4.2.66, 76; 5.2.4, 11; 5.3.6; 5.5.6.

7. Compare with Plato *Republic* 474b-476a.

8. See Benardete, "Macbeth's Last Words," 63-65.

9. The importance of Lady Macbeth for the meaning of the play must be clear to any interpreter. She is especially important in an interpretation based on the distinction between manliness and womanliness. Like the witches, who appear to be female and yet have beards, Lady Macbeth has an ambiguous sexual status. She explicitly unsexes herself (1.5.42). That the statement of the cult of manliness should come from an unsexed being is of some interest. It may well point to the instability of manliness or courage. To be manly is always on the way toward being something else. Benardete suggests that "if Lady Macbeth unsexes herself, Macbeth may be said to dehumanize himself" ("Macbeth's Last Words," 71).

10. Aristotle *Politics* 1333a35. For the extreme modern view see Nietzche's *Thus Spoke Zarathustra*, "On War and Warriors," where Zarathustra says, "it is the good war that hallows any cause" (*The Portable Nietzsche*, ed. Walter Kaufmann [New York: Viking Press, 1954]), 159.

11. There would be little doubt that there are no children were it not for what Lady Macbeth says at 1.7.54–55—"I have given suck, and know / How tender 'tis to love a babe that milks me." At 4.3.216 Macduff says of Macbeth, "He has no children." The apparent contradiction does not really weaken the

point here. Even if Macbeth does, or did, have children, his silence about them makes it clear that he is not thinking about them in any but the most abstract of ways when he plans to murder Banquo.

12. Barnet, *Macbeth*, 145.

13. Compare this with the discussion between Macduff and Malcolm in act 4, scene 3, where Shakespeare makes it clear that he is aware of, and has thought through, the possibility of a more sober variety of tyranny.

14. Compare the account of tyranny in books 8 and 9 of Plato's *Republic* as well as *Gorgias* 471aff.

15. For this see the whole of the *Hiero*, and the interpretation of it by Leo Strauss in *On Tyranny* (Glencoe, Ill.: Free Press, 1963).

16. Hegel, *Phenomenology of Spirit*, B.4.A.33, the section on master and slave, and also Alexandre Kojève, *Introduction to the Reading of Hegel* (New York: Basic Books, 1969), ch. 1.

17. See chapter 19 of Machiavelli's *Prince*.

18. That Macbeth knows this is obvious from 3.4.124.

19. Compare Aristotle *Nicomachean Ethics* 1116a1–25.

20. See Benardete, "Macbeth's Last Words," 74.

21. Note the double entendre.

22. Emphasis mine.

23. Nietzsche, *On the Genealogy of Morals*, 3.1 and 3.28.

24. The speech is made on the occasion of the death of Lady Macbeth. Her death is announced by Macbeth's servant, Seyton, pronounced as Satan.

25. Despite their obvious differences, two of the great prophets of the nineteenth century, Marx and Nietzsche, see the problem of modern man in terms remarkably similar to these. For Nietzsche man is at a crossroads and must become either more (*der Uebermensch*) or less (*der letzte Mensch*) than he has been. In Marx, postrevolutionary man is necessarily radically different from prerevolutionary man since the latter is what he is by virtue of the class struggle, which is abolished by the revolution.

26. Compare this with the subtitle of Nietzsche's *Ecce Homo*—"*Wie man wird was man ist*," or "How one becomes what one is." The attempt to eternalize the sequence of temporal events is an attempt at once to maintain and to deny the distinction between being and becoming.

12

"With Himself at War": Shakespeare's Roman Hero and the Republican Tradition

Dennis Bathory

"We make out of the quarrel with others, rhetoric, but of the quarrel with ourselves, poetry."

—William Butler Yeats

Shakespeare's challenge to Roman republicanism suggests that the political virtue upon which Rome rested was well suited to Rome's imperial foreign policy but was less well suited to its domestic politics. Honor not justice provides the political foundation of the Roman Republic. The Roman tradition had led time and again to the forging of internal peace in time of domestic crisis by going to war with a foreign enemy. This strategy, Shakespeare suggests, failed to educate either Roman leaders or citizens in the most important lessons of politics—the arts of sustaining a regime while simultaneously sustaining the virtue of its citizens. Shakespeare knew that Rome was touted as a model worthy of emulation, and he was clearly skeptical. His examination of the virtues and vices of the Roman Republic is most clear in two plays, one set at the very beginning of the Republic and one set near its demise—*Coriolanus* and *Julius Caesar*.

Julius Caesar was written first, near the end of the Elizabethan era; *Coriolanus* was written a decade later, at the dawn of the Jacobean era. Thus Shakespeare, not, I think, coincidentally, writes of dramatic Roman transitions in the midst of transitions equally dramatic in his own world.[1] Shakespeare's sophisticated skepticism reaches to the heart of the Roman Republic as he describes the central character in Julius Caesar. "Brutus, with himself at war" (1.2.46) provides us with a remarkably contemporary look at the dilemmas of the political reformer/revolutionary.[2] Shakespeare in his development first of Brutus and later of Coriolanus tells us of the danger of such internal, psychic warfare, not simply to frame the tragedy that befalls each, but to introduce as well the problems that all republican leaders have to face in times of rapid change and crisis. They have need (always, but especially in such times) of resources that Rome could not provide.

The need for solace and strength, and even more, for self-examination and self-evaluation on the part of leaders of republics in the midst of change and crisis is profoundly central to Shakespeare's stories. Confronted with the problem of republican virtue, many, including Niccolò Machiavelli, would attempt to substitute institutional arrangements for virtue as a support for the republic. For Shakespeare, Rome's lesson led to a call for a better political virtue, one based on self-reflection. Self-reflection permits a public language that introduces the possibility of accommodation among the various conflicting parts of the city. The danger in Rome, Shakespeare understood, was that, having defeated all foreign enemies, Caesar would, and Augustus did, forge Roman unity by denying Roman freedom. For Shakespeare, the person and the torment of Brutus frames the discussion. Brutus fails in his efforts to save the Republic because he does not understand the need to educate Rome to a better political virtue. Rome had offered little instruction in such education and for all his republican spirit, Brutus had little alternative save to exercise the sound but limited and ultimately self-defeating strategy of joining the conspiracy to assassinate Caesar. These powerful lessons, important for Shakespeare's audience, are no less important for contemporary audiences.

Shakespeare offers us a "mirror of republics" to replace the medieval "mirror of princes." What is needed, he suggests, is not only a place for reflection removed from the chaos of rapidly changing public opinion, but also the means to engage in that reflection consistent with obligations to the common good. If the problem of the leader's ability to get good advice is ancient and common to all cultures, so is the problem of the leader finding time to himself to reflect. The need for self-examination even, or especially, in the face of extreme pressure, deadlines, and crises has never been more obvious. The need for leaders to confront public opinion and to offer wise counsel to those whom they lead seems to be ever more difficult. These plays address such problems and offer wisdom to our age as well as Shakespeare's.

They suggest that poets and storytellers may have much to offer us as well. Western political science has always known this, but it has not always acted on what it knows. We need stories about politics, but we need to tell them to one another in ways that facilitate understanding across times and cultures.

Political Knowledge and Knowledge of the Self

Shakespeare's teaching about Roman politics in *Julius Caesar* and *Coriolanus* addresses the relationship between self-knowledge and political knowledge. The inability of major characters in each play to come to terms with their *selves* leads them to make critical, self-defeating, ultimately tragic political errors. This is particularly true of Marcus Brutus, whose role in the conspiracy against Julius Caesar masks a fundamental lack of self-knowledge, and of Coriolanus, whose lack of self-reflection leads to unthinking action that destroys his political opportunity. In each case, the Roman hero,[3] as portrayed by Shakespeare, "confronts" inner turmoil or self-doubt by turning to decisive external action that masks internal tension and uncertainty.

Shakespeare thus develops in these and other characters a parallel between their personal crises and Rome's centuries-old tradition (habit) of turning to foreign warfare—both conquest and defense—to mask domestic faction. In this pattern, domestic politics was continually challenged by disorder, and order was reclaimed by the discipline required in time of war or by an emerging Roman legalism. The relationship between domestic and foreign politics was thus dominated by the foreign and external; domestic politics was left on unsure footing for the Republic and for its leaders. Shakespeare asks us to reflect on the relationship between the internal and the external through his portrayal of individual characters, who turn to the "outside" to solve their individual, internal problems. The inability of individuals to recognize the important link between self-knowledge and political knowledge leaves internal strife unaddressed and makes political life sometimes difficult, sometimes tragic, and always confused. The relationship between the internal and external—both for the individual and the state—is thus dramatized in these plays and presented as a central political problem.

Marcus Brutus, leader of the conspiracy against Julius Caesar, the "noblest Roman of them all" (5.5.68)—Brutus, "with himself at war,"—is the central political figure in Shakespeare's Roman plays.[4]

Well respected by Romans of all classes, Brutus reveals both the politics of Rome in crisis and Shakespeare's understanding of that politics. Yet, if this is so—and if as some have suggested, the Romans were the "greatest political people who ever lived"[5]—what is Shakespeare's teaching about politics, Roman and otherwise? Brutus—"with himself at war"—makes a number of critical errors of judgment and surely fails in his stated goal of saving the Republic. If "the noblest Roman of them all" could not save the Republic, then who or what could have? Had Roman republican politics run its course? Is this simple and obvious teaching the core of Shakespeare's tragedy, and, thus, of his understanding of Roman politics?[6]

Brutus *is* central to Shakespeare's teaching, but he must not be judged, simply, through Mark Antony's praise, words that must, after all, be filtered through Antony's own prism.[7] Brutus's speeches provide a more apt point of departure. But, Brutus's "war" with himself is complex. To be sure, Shakespeare invites us to consider the obvious source of this psychological "war." Torn *between his* loves for Caesar and Rome, Brutus reports that the reason he conspired against Caesar was "not that [he] loved Caesar less, but that [he] loved Rome more" (3.2.21–22). Resolved to overcome his personal, internal civil war, Brutus takes the lead in planning the assassination. His *words* frame the *deed*. The conspirators must be "sacrificers, but not butchers," he counsels, so that it will be the "spirit of Caesar" that is assaulted, not his body (2.1.166–67). His self-deception will haunt him throughout the play. To save Rome he must change Rome, not just Caesar's power over Rome. His war with himself as a Roman requires a change of Rome that would, as well, require a change in Brutus. Before he can change Rome he must change himself, and before he can change himself he must "see" himself.

Shakespeare's teaching of Roman politics begins with Brutus because he understands that Brutus's confusion is Rome's. To a great extent Rome was always (at least in times of peace) with *itself* at war. Roman politics—both external warfare and party politics at home—depended on an understanding of conflict, latent and manifest. The failure of Shakespeare's Roman heroes to understand the subtlety of that conflict is common to both the beginning and the end of the Republic, to his portrayal of Roman politics in both *Julius Caesar* and *Coriolanus*. Coriolanus, at war with the "many-headed multitude" (2.3.15) of Rome, was equally "with himself at war." The Roman world, in which he sought honor, had changed. Like Brutus he failed to understand the extent of the change and the need to change himself in the face of these changes. Political judgment requires, Shakespeare teaches, self-awareness. Complex and difficult under any circumstances, the Roman world made the process of self-examination even more difficult.

From its origin, recorded in myth and history, Rome's was a heterogeneous and syncretic culture.[8] Incorporating different languages and cultures and conflicting religious practices, Rome was from the very beginning a centrifugal society, threatening always to fly apart from the center. A turn inward—to Rome's origins, to its original disorder—was always difficult, potentially fragmenting. Roman conquest exacerbated the centrifugal tendencies making self-examination at once more difficult and more dangerous—difficult because Rome constantly changed, dangerous because it highlighted the tenuous connection any one individual had to *romanitas*.[9] The temptation to look outward for "solace" was powerful and almost always overwhelmed an invitation to self-examination.[10] The republican transitions emphasized in each play exacerbate the problem from Shakespeare's vantage point.

Through the intervention of family and friends, fellow patricians and soldiers, Shakespeare seems to urge the protagonists to look more carefully at their politics and themselves.[11] All lessons about the relation of the self to the community, the noble individual to the broader *res publica*, fail. In part this is the result of life in the city, which must be plural, conflicting, faction ridden. The "conquest" of this disorder may be beyond human capacity. An acceptance of its limitations *and* an ability to work within those limits are, however, necessary. Politics is of the city, and being of the city, Brutus and Coriolanus are, willy nilly, political and must confront conflict. However, they must also understand the internal implications and reflections of that conflict.

The self in Shakespeare's Roman construction is ridden with "faction." But how does Shakespeare suggest confronting that factional division? The alternatives are three: 1) Attempt to overcome "war" with the self by turning one's attention away from internal conflict and artificially "unifying" the self through confrontation with an external enemy. This solution, Shakespeare implies, involves the self-delusion that haunted not only Brutus and Coriolanus but Caesar, Antony, and others as well. 2) Escape internal conflict by escaping politics. That alternative—one Thomas Hobbes would promote in England later in the seventeenth century—was one that Octavius, become Caesar Augustus, would embrace in Rome. Shakespeare's coolness toward Octavius is clear in both *Julius Caesar* and in *Antony and Cleopatra* so that he seems to have rejected the Augustan alternative.[12] 3) Accept the enduring reality of conflict, both external and internal, and fashion an accommodation to it. This last, which Shakespeare seems to recommend, requires careful instruction and the creation of a perspective that his Roman heroes lack.

While instruction in "policy" and "process," in rhetoric and political tactics is, of course, found within the plays, the perspective required for self-examination is that of the poet. Shakespeare addresses the problem of faction, internal and external, not to offer a solution to the Roman republican dilemma but to make his audience aware of issues that the Roman ear could not, or would not hear.

Brutus and Cassius: At War with Rome

"[P]oor Brutus, with himself at war, / Forgets the shows of love to other men," says Brutus to Cassius (1.2.46–47). He has been with Julius Caesar. Now, alone with Cassius, he is distracted. This is not, he says, due to anything that Cassius has done, but "I turn the trouble of my countenance / Merely upon myself" (1.2.38–39). The problem, as Cassius makes him understand, is that he cannot see himself, "for the eye sees not itself, / But by reflection, by some other things" (1.2.52–53). But, who or what will reveal Brutus to himself? Cassius "modestly" offers to be his "glass," to "discover . . . / That of [himself] which [he] yet know[s] not of" (1.2.68–70). But Cassius's needs and those of Brutus are different and Cassius's instruction will prove wanting.

Cassius's "Epicurean" opinion offers little thoughtful "policy" to Brutus's "Stoicism" (5.1.77–106).[13] Brutus steadfastly defends "honor" and the "general good," but he wonders at Cassius: "wherefore do you hold me here so long? / What is it that you would impart to me?" (1.2.83–84). He would not, it appears, impart anything about Brutus. Cassius's "glass" reflects himself (Cassius), *not Brutus*. Brutus learns something of the case that Cassius puts before him. He is moved by Cassius's summary report of Caesar's ingratitude and injustice. Politically, Brutus is challenged; indeed, he says:

> Brutus had rather be a villager
> Than to repute himself a son of Rome
> Under these hard conditions as this time
> Is like to lay upon us. (1.2.172–75)

But, of himself, he has learned little. The war raging inside needs a weighing of the "hard conditions" that is more thoughtful than that to which he is led by Cassius's "mirror."

"Noble Brutus" is needed by Cassius and his words are meant to pull the "warring" parts of Brutus together in the service of the conspiracy, not to bring "peace" to Brutus's internal war, certainly not to make him "well in health" (1.3.141 and 2.1.257). Cassius is, of course, successful and Brutus's resolve delivers him "wholly" to the conspirators, though it does not make him whole. Cassius notes that "three parts of him / Is ours already," his search for "the man entire" (1.3.154–55) is a search for an accomplice, one whose nobility will legitimate their cause; he is not concerned for Brutus's inner well-being. Brutus's malaise, all the while, grows. He compares the "state of a man" to "a little kingdom" that suffers "the nature of an insurrection" and describes his waking hours as a "hideous dream" (2.1.65, 67–69). Aware of the task that awaits he urges "smiles and affability" lest his inner turmoil betray a "monstrous visage" (2.1.81–82). But he *appears* focused as he directs the conspiracy and defines its spirit. There is no need to include Cicero he insists, nor to punish Mark Antony (2.1.150–61). The conspirators need not swear an "oath" among themselves, given the strength of what he calls the "even virtue of our enterprise" (2.1.114, 133). Again, they will be "sacrificers," not "butchers." Ironically, his recently expressed fear of Caesar—that "Th' abuse of greatness is, when it disjoins / Remorse from power"—is lost, masked in his carefully chosen, but self-deceptive words (2.1.166, 18–19).[14]

Theirs is a "purely" ordained enterprise, though it must be undertaken with the skills of "Roman actors." The dilemma, as Shakespeare conveys it, is still apparent: Caesar has become Rome and Rome must be saved from itself, but will Rome consent to be "saved"? Brutus wars *with* Rome and *against* Rome as he leads the conspiracy and, so, as a noble Roman is still "with himself at war." It is Portia who recognizes the "actor" and his "act" and "some sick offense within [his] mind" (2.1.268). She is his "glass," the mirror he needs to reflect his discontent, to anticipate and appreciate the consequences, still unrecognized and clearly unanticipated. Portia sees what Brutus cannot or will not. Unlike Cassius who seeks to manipulate his discontent, Portia seeks the source of his "sickness." The "right and virtue of [her] place" requires that she know his secret. Though "I am a woman," she persists, I am "well reputed" and presumably well able to help (2.1.269, 294–95). Brutus has, however, turned his attention away from the "domestic." Like Rome in time of crisis, this "little kingdom," suffering from "insurrection," turns its attention to the outside. The answer to his enduring illness, he says to Ligarius after Portia has left, is "A piece of work that will make sick men whole" (2.1.327). But, like Rome's centuries-old politics, the turn to external warfare leaves internal conflict unresolved. Brutus's anxiety reemerges as he meets with Caesar and the final pieces of the conspiracy are assembled. Caesar compels Brutus to consider the full scope of his role as a "Roman actor." "We (like friends) will straightway go together," says Caesar to the conspirators (2.2.126). Brutus, uneasy with his deception, replies in an aside: "That every like is not the same, O Caesar, / The heart of Brutus yearns to think upon" (2.2.128–29). But little thought is given. Shakespeare makes it clear that Brutus's only true "mirror," Portia, with "a man's mind, but a woman's might," is unable to encourage Brutus's self-examination (2.4.8).

The result is self-delusion as Shakespeare reveals in act 3, scene 2. The assassination plot accomplished, Brutus turns to the plebeians gathered in the forum. Restless, they await explanation of the murder of the man to whom they would, so recently, have given a crown. Brutus's eloquence marks both his position and his naiveté (as well as Shakespeare's poetic genius as he sets up Antony's speech to follow). It is "not that I loved Caesar less," he says, "but that I loved Rome more" (3.2.21–22). For a moment the crowd is appeased, but Brutus has sorely overestimated them. They do not share his "nobility," as Antony's ironic defense of Caesar's "ambitions" makes clear. He cleverly appeals to the greedy "ambitions" of an audience he knows far better than Brutus does. Whipped into a frenzy with promises of a "rich legacy" bequeathed to them by Caesar, the crowd is quickly turned against Brutus. The task of Brutus and the conspirators was far greater than the "mere" assassination of Caesar.

Caesar's "spirit" had a monetary value far greater to this Roman audience than Brutus's noble sentiments about Rome and Roman freedom. It was this "spirit," which Brutus obviously did not anticipate and apparently did not understand, that threatened Rome as surely as Caesar's impending dictatorship. The question for the conspirators, for Rome, for Shakespeare and for Shakespeare's audience was the same: How to conquer that "spirit"? Brutus was right to say that it was the "spirit" of Caesar that had to be conquered (2.1.167), but the "spirit" of the people in the streets of Rome was as well a product of Caesar's "spirit." The task of the Roman republican patriot was to educate or reeducate the people of Rome. Brutus's internal warfare blinded him to the most important challenge to his Roman nobility—the education of the Roman citizenry in the face of the changes that were, indeed, threatening the Republic that he loved. Whether or not such education was possible in the Rome of his day is less the issue than his blindness to the need for it. In a world in which foreign war could less easily provide either a common enemy around which warring domestic factions could coalesce or the booty with which to bribe the audience of Brutus and Antony, such education was necessary for the continuation of the Republic. Brutus's story is the story of Rome. Brutus is at war with himself because he fails to understand the proper nature of the relation between the parts of the community—both the community of the soul and the community of the city. He requires an understanding of both, if he is to be an effective republican leader.

Shakespeare urges us to consider the parallel between Brutus's internal war and Rome's—both turn to the outside but leave the sources of internal conflict unresolved. The result, as Jan Blits points out, is a "conception of the common good [of Rome which] lacks a public or republican spirit."[15] Shakespeare invites us to pass judgment on this shortsightedness both in *Julius Caesar*, and ten years later, when he turned to the beginning of the Republic in *Coriolanus*.

Coriolanus: At War with Himself and Rome

In turning to the beginning of the Republic in the *Tragedy of Coriolanus* Shakespeare continues his examination of Roman politics with a study of another major transition. The Republic is in its infancy, the tribunate only recently created. Caius Martius (Coriolanus), a heroic figure in the overthrow of Tarquin's tyranny, confronts the transition, as Brutus did his, with confusion and uncertainty. Again this is a world *with itself at war*. Most obviously, the plebeians are upset with the patricians. A shortage of corn has exposed class distinctions, differences that for the plebs are most clearly represented by the arrogance of Caius Martius (Coriolanus) (1.1). Yet, Caius Martius's role in the overthrow of tyranny has made the Republic possible in the first place, and the citizens know this. More, they understand the gratitude they owe him. He has only to recognize the changes in Rome and the "honor" that he craves will be granted, for, they understand, "there was never a worthier man" (2.3.36–37).

As with Brutus,[16] the problem for Coriolanus lies not only with understanding Rome's transformations but also how those changes affect him. As Rome's upheavals in the reign of Julius Caesar required Brutus to reexamine his very "self," so Rome's changes in the early days of the Republic required the same of Coriolanus.

A "worthy" man whose "chiefest virtue" is "valor," Coriolanus is a hero "by his rare example," even a man of generous spirit (2.2.35, 81–85, 102; 1.9.82–86).[17] He shuns flattery—both as flattered and flatterer. He resists the new "custom" that requires that he "speak to the people" (2.2.133), if he would be consul. He asks that he might "o'erleap that custom" (2.2.134) rightly fearing, as Shakespeare plays it out, that the public is fickle and easily manipulated. More, he articulates a suspicion of custom itself, which left unexamined can, like "the dust on antique time," lie "unswept" and leave a "mountainous error . . . too highly heaped / For truth t' o'erpeer" (2.3.114–16). Ironically though, it is the very dust of an older custom, patrician custom, that Coriolanus cannot himself "o'erpeer."

Rome has changed; it will not do to return to still older customs, especially, if he "would be consul" (2.3.126). He recognizes the danger of a political order without "purpose" (3.1.148–49), an order manipulated by the winds of public opinion that "With every minute . . . do change a mind" (1.1.177). Yet, if he would lead the new Rome, he must look inside himself and discover new resources required for a new political order. To do so, however, he, like Brutus, will need assistance.[18]

Shakespeare gives Coriolanus three "mirrors": Menenius, patrician and friend to Coriolanus; his wife, Virgilia; and, most crucially, his mother, Volumnia. None of these, however, is able to bring him face to face with himself. Menenius's teasing (and sometimes effective) rhetoric preaches "patience" to both plebeians and tribunes. His "fable," a variation on the medieval organic analogy, cleverly sets the plebeians to consider the difficulty the Senate has in meeting the needs of the "weal o' th' common" (1.1.146). His tale is at least in part successful. With words carefully crafted for their ears, he convinces the plebeians that the Senate, the "belly" in his unusual account, looks out for their interests, distributing goods even to "the great toe of this assembly" (1.1.150). It is the tribunes, however, that are his real concern. Again, his use of words is important both for *his* audience and Shakespeare's. He confronts the two tribunes, Sicinius and Junius Brutus, directly. Their power, though derivative, is great. Their "pride," however, masks "infant-like" behavior. In fact, he says, "you know neither me, yourselves, nor anything" (2.1.34–37, 62–63), and this is precisely why they are dangerous.

Menenius himself knows a great deal. Through his rhetoric he conveys and uses his knowledge to significant effect. His effectiveness is, however, limited by his position. Though his audiences respect him, he is not destined for leadership. Coriolanus's "valor," his "chiefest virtue," has made him ripe for "honor" and so for the position of leadership the Senate seeks to convey. Menenius is a shrewd analyst and has the tools, as Coriolanus's friend, to be an excellent counselor, but Coriolanus must first learn to listen. This, for all Menenius's skill, he apparently cannot teach. Menenius is direct in his counsel: " . . . go fit you to the custom and / Take to you, as your predecessors have, / Your honor with your form" (2.2.140–42).

Coriolanus will not or cannot hear him. Incapable of a "gentler spirit" Coriolanus rages at the tribunes. "Not now, not now," Menenius urges, but Coriolanus does not listen (3.1.55, 63). Failing at directly influencing him, Menenius will turn his rhetorical skills back directly against Coriolanus's antagonists. He pleads with the tribunes to "proceed by process" (3.1.313), lest they threaten the very Rome they claim to serve:

> Lo, citizens, he says he is content.
> The warlike service he has done, consider; think
> Upon the wounds his body bears, which show
> Like graves i' th' holy churchyard. (3.3.48–51)

Coriolanus's petulance continues and so prompts Menenius:

> Consider further,
> That when he speaks not like a citizen,
> You find him like a soldier. Do not take
> His rougher accents for malicious sounds,
> But, as I say, such as become a soldier,
> Rather than envy you. (3.3.52–57)

But the game is lost, for it is Coriolanus whom Menenius must engage. He cannot overpower Coriolanus's antagonists without Coriolanus's assistance, and that assistance cannot be forthcoming until Coriolanus confronts himself. But Coriolanus's pride will not permit him. Rather, his own flagrant, violent use of words deafens Coriolanus to his friend's plea. Instead, the self-destructive nature of his language ironically leads a senator to beseech: "No more words" (3.1.75).

In need of words to claim his honor, in need of words to know Rome, and in need of words to know himself, Coriolanus is instead conquered by his own "deeds." Words "debase / The nature of our seats," he says, when "deeds" should "speak" for themselves. (3.1.135–36). His understanding of the Roman world is based on "deeds." The plebeians and their tribunes are portrayed as incapable of such "deeds" and thus must have recourse to words—words that, for Coriolanus, merely flatter and deceive. To be sure, words *can* flatter and deceive and Shakespeare gives us many examples in this play. But words can also instruct and reveal. Coriolanus has not been taught this wiser use of words. In the Roman fashion he lets action speak for itself.

Rome defines itself in large part externally. Roman heroes like Brutus's "little kingdoms" define themselves externally as well.[19] The domestic "mirrors" of Caius Martius Coriolanus, like those of Brutus, are unsuccessful in their attempts to bring him face to face with himself. His wife and mother are no more able to instruct Coriolanus than was Menenius. Virgilia's traditional support of her husband reinforces all of his intransigence. Her role is to "support" him. She tells Volumnia that she will "not over the threshold till my lord return from the wars" (1.2.71–72). Her "affection" will never turn him in on himself. Her "lord and husband" is distant. She supports him but primarily "to keep [his] *name* / Living to time" through the son she bore him (5.3.37, 126–27).[20] His mother is another story.

In some ways Coriolanus is as much Volumnia's creation as he is Rome's. She taught him to "seek danger where he was like to find fame" (1.3.12–13). When he returns from battle with the Volscians, she proudly asserts: "O, he is wounded; I thank the gods for't" (2.1.113). She wants him to have fame, honor and power, but she has done her work too well. His pride in all of its excess is, in part, her creation as well. His anger, uncontrolled, lacks her "brain that leads [her] use of anger / To better vantage" (3.2.30–31). She rebukes him for being "too absolute" and counsels a combination of "honor and policy" (39, 42). He has understood that deception is necessary in time of war; she says to him:

> If it be honor in your wars *to seem*
> The same you are not . . .
>   how is it less or worse,
> That it shall hold companionship in peace
> With honor, as in war . . . . (3.2.46–50)[21]

How indeed? If those he addresses in peacetime in Rome are, like his enemies in war, deceived, then they are like his enemies. Yet, they are by the *new* "custom" a part of Rome and so to war with them is to war with Rome and for Coriolanus to war with himself. However debased they may be, however contemptible, they cannot be deceived as one would deceive an enemy in war.[22]

Volumnia's advice to combine "honor and policy" is, in general, not dissimilar from that of Menenius. In its particulars, however, it is quite different. Menenius's fable creates a space for discussion of the Senate's concern for the common good. Volumnia's analogy implies civil war. Shakespeare quickly helps us to understand the source of her problem. She too prefers "deeds" over words. "Action is eloquence," she proclaims, "and the eyes of th' ignorant / More learned than the ears . . ." (3.2.76–77). Hers is not an effort to return to the organic analogy of Menenius's fable, but rather to describe a pestilence to be overcome. They are his "enemy," these common people of Rome. The only difference between them and Aufidius is that they must be flattered.[23] None of this counsel will Coriolanus hear, however, perhaps because he is too proud, perhaps because her words have been preceded by action that render them meaningless. Of the latter we can only guess, though we are later shown his reaction to his mother's action as she kneels to her now traitorous son. That she finally reaches him is clear:

> What is this?
> Your knees to me? to your corrected son?
> Then let the pebbles on the hungry beach
> Fillip the stars! Then let the mutinous winds
> Strike the proud cedars 'gainst the fiery sun,
> Murd'ring impossibility, to make
> What cannot be, slight work. (5.3.56–62)

She responds: "Thou art my warrior; / I holp to frame thee" (5.3.62–63). She has helped create a "warrior" but not a consul of Rome. Volumnia's Coriolanus lacks "purpose" save that which demands enemies and this, Shakespeare teaches, is a long-standing Roman dilemma that makes domestic politics and peace difficult.

Republican Rome can be governed neither by Coriolanus's arrogance nor by the people's "multitudinous tongue." When they stand in opposition to one another, their mutual impotence is apparent and, more, the manipulative tribunate is empowered. How then is that manipulation to be quelled? In the first place, given the fact that Rome is changing, Rome's past has to be accommodated to the new reality of the Republic and so there must be a new foundation for public authority. In this story Coriolanus becomes a representative of that past and stories of his exploits and ancestors are central to the political story that Shakespeare tells. First, Cominius, his commanding general who has named him in honor of his conquest of Corioli, speaks of Coriolanus's "deeds," of his "rare example" in fighting the tyranny of Tarquin (2.2.102). Praised as someone who in defeating Tarquin helped give rise to the Republic, his action at Corioli only confirms prior deeds and makes him clearly worthy of the consulship. In the very next scene, his recent exploits now ignored, the tribunes portray him in contrast to his illustrious ancestors (2.3.233–40). As Shakespeare plays the scene, arrogance is pitted against ignorance, and the tribunes, at least for the moment, emerge victorious.

Sicinius and Junius Brutus at once commend Coriolanus's heritage and condemn the pride that is "descended" from that very same lineage.[24] Still, their audience is beguiled, the tribunes' message has been artfully delivered. They have at once praised the past[25] (of which their Roman clients are proud) and attacked its progeny. Coriolanus is attacked as a representative of the patrician class even as that class is apparently, implicitly praised. The result for Rome is confusion, the very coin of the tribunate in this play, and the perpetuation of the world without "purpose" that Coriolanus will soon criticize.[26] But the tribunes' words have hit their mark. The citizens change their mind again, confirming both Coriolanus's analysis and the tribunes' power.

Coriolanus's republican successors will have to find their way among these portrayals of Rome's past, holding on to that which still defines Rome, while still learning to "o'erpeer" the past and the "antique dust" that clings to it. The purpose of Rome is not as easily identified as it might seem to be. It is surely beyond Virgilia's domestic support for her warrior, and Volumnia's apparent move beyond Virgilia's traditionalism does not offer the "foundation" that is needed. Moreover, republican institutions, Shakespeare insinuates, require more than Cominius's love of "valor." The question that must be asked is *the* republican question: What is the city? The tribunes respond too easily, "the people," but that begs the question, for the people are clearly muddled, in need of leadership and education (1.1. and 2.3). The tribunes manipulate and in turn risk being outmanipulated, for they manipulate without "purpose." Coriolanus cannot learn from any of these "teachers," but his successors must, if they are to be the definers of the broad "public weal" Rome requires.[27]

The dilemma is that the "public weal" will continue to be founded in part on the virtue of men like Coriolanus. The heroic ideal is still critical.[28] The hero stands for Roman honor and represents *romanitas*; but heroic action is by definition rare and exceptional, distant from ordinary citizens, whose participation in the "spirit" of Rome is generally vicarious, distant, and indirect. The problem for the Republic then is always to find leaders whose stature helps redefine *romanitas* while still making contact with the people whose greater good and glory they must represent. Such leaders must, Shakespeare seems to suggest, confront warfare—not simply warfare with external enemies, not simply the "warfare" among Roman factions in time of peace, but also the "warfare" within.[29] Rome's republicanism dictates that each of these battles continues.[30]

Rome artfully used external warfare to forge internal unity throughout the republican era. Shakespeare frames this practice from the earliest scenes of *Coriolanus* to the end of the Republic and *Julius Caesar*. Caius Martius applauds the Volscian threat to Rome: "I am glad on 't. / Then we shall ha' means to vent / Our musty superfluity" (1.1.220–21). Julius Caesar's Rome, on the other hand, has nearly used up this strategy.[31] The factional politics of the age of Caesar were not overcome by Caesar's military victories; quite the contrary.[32] Caesar's conquering majesty makes recourse to external war superfluous and unavailable; his subjection of the external "world" eliminates the "vent," which Coriolanus and many of those who followed used with great success. Lacking that vent, the "superfluities" of Roman internal politics explode. The dilemma for Marcus Brutus, Cassius, and their fellow conspirators is on one level not unlike that which Volumnia describes to her son. They, too, must combine "honor and policy." "Process" and "policy" are required, Menenius says, "lest parties . . . break out / And sack great Rome with Romans" (3.1.313–14). And from the very beginning of *Julius Caesar*, it is clear that this very problem is infecting Julius Caesar's Rome.

Several questions remain unaddressed by the Romans whether early or late in the Republic: Is shrewd political calculation enough? If it is, where will it come from, who will offer it? Of what does this calculation and advice consist? Menenius attempts to persuade his friend, but Coriolanus remains "untaught."[33] Coriolanus knows himself only in the "Senate House" (2.3.143). His mother's advice would, he says, have him be "false to [his] nature" (3.2.15). Similarly, Brutus cannot hear Portia. "Honor and policy" do not easily combine in domestic politics. Brutus's lack of "policy" is in its way, as glaring as Coriolanus's, though again Shakespeare points to a more basic dilemma. Perhaps, having killed Antony in the plot would have aided the conspirators' "purpose"[34] (3.2.147); perhaps, Cicero's oratory would have helped their cause. Shakespeare hints at both possibilities, but the fundamental problem lies elsewhere: The city requires more than "honor and policy." The pride that both accompanies honor and leads to it makes the proud and honorable reluctant to engage in "policy" and disdainful of "process." Indeed, the proud and honorable are not predisposed by "nature," Shakespeare suggests, to "policy" and "process" within the city. The justness of their common cause leads time and again to honorable victory over external enemies. Justice, within the city and in the soul of the Roman hero, is, however, more difficult to discover.

Times of crisis such as those portrayed in both plays merely emphasize problems endemic to the Roman republican world. With themselves at war, Shakespeare's Roman heroes find tragic ends. Merely to adapt, cunningly, to the times is inadequate. As Aufidius ironically notes, "Our virtues lie / In th' interpretation of the time" (4.7.49–50). The virtue of Shakespeare's Roman hero is not well suited to peacetime. Honor, not justice, is the hallmark of Rome. Coriolanus's crudeness would be cosmetically hidden; Roman leaders would learn to flatter and be flattered, but they would not come to know themselves as leaders of the Roman public in peacetime. Rome could not teach these lessons; Shakespeare could and did.

The citizens of Rome, both at the beginning and at the end of the Republic, required more than flattery. Republican virtue could be manipulated, even subverted, by rhetoric's flattery. Coriolanus was right to be suspicious.[35] It is, however, one thing to be aware of the limits, and even the corrupting dangers, of rhetoric and another to dismiss the Roman public because of its need to flatter and be flattered. Shakespeare understands that rhetoric is needed to make contact with that public—to educate it as well as to manipulate it. He knew of the temptation to misuse rhetoric and explored the narrow line between education and manipulation. He suggested that the leader must proceed with great caution or risk his own undoing. Neither Brutus nor Coriolanus understood the self-defeating consequences of their "deeds." At war with themselves they were unable to establish a relationship with Rome that successful leadership required. Neither flatterers nor educators, their political efforts were destined to fail.

The Roman military-political strategy was a brilliant one, enduring for centuries; but Roman politics was, as Shakespeare's Roman plays invite us to consider, radically incomplete. The Roman hero at once contributed to that incompleteness, was a victim of it, and was symptomatic of a broader Roman political dilemma. With deeds that turned attention away from internal strains, the hero unwittingly lets those strains fester, offering a powerful palliative—but a palliative nonetheless. Also victimized by his very distance, the Roman hero had both to be an exceptional individual and to subordinate himself to the greater good of the Republic, which included, throughout the Republic's long history, an appeal to those intimidated by and often jealous of his "deeds." In the end Shakespeare insinuates a tragedy beyond that of his hero. Rome itself is the victim, for republican Rome, defined by the hero, is defeated by the hero's success—the success of Julius Caesar. The problem is constant: the force of the "lion's" honor can only be masked, cosmetically hidden, by the "fox-like" cunning of "policy." The combination of the lion and the fox is, for Shakespeare, incomplete. It is not enough for Coriolanus to learn to be cunning, nor for Brutus to learn political tactics. The greatness of the Romans reveals lessons that only the philospher or the poet can complete. The Romans lacked both philosophic and poetic spirit. There was little room for either in their public world.

Shakespeare offers to his England, and perforce to us, what seemingly could not be offered to Rome. What Portia could not accomplish with Brutus, what Menenius and Volumnia lacked the capacity to convey to Coriolanus, Shakespeare introduced to his English audiences. Shakespeare thus becomes a mirror for an audience he hopes will look into its own "eye" as it learns to listen to words that counsel self-examination.

Conclusion: Shakespeare's "Mirror of Republics"

Shakespeare's language is in some ways an antidote to republican Rome's self-destructive words. Stephen Coote argues that in *Coriolanus* "language—which should be the bond of civil community—has been used as an instrument to tear it apart."[36] Shakespeare's brief is for more than "policy" and "process" and the rhetoric they require. The people, whose corruption is the key to these plays, require more than the palliative of Menenius's fable. Still in need of education at the close of the Republic, the Romans are unable to hear either their tribunes or Marcus Brutus. They listen to Mark Antony's artful deception, but his rhetoric lacks the requisite nobility, at least insofar as that "nobility" is meant to create "the bond of the civil community."[37]

The modern state, following Machiavelli's lead, lowered the stakes of honor and raised "policy" to new heights. Shakespeare resists the shift even as he criticized the excesses of "honor." It was never enough simply to temper the "lion's" honor with the "fox's" cunning. Shakespeare does not applaud Octavius's Roman solution. Shakespeare presents Caesar Augustus, Bloom writes, as a man who was "no hero [but] a dry opportunist with the capacity for neither loving nor fighting."[38] Whatever his success in Rome, Octavius gets no commendation from Shakespeare. It is, of course, Octavius who puts Brutus's nobility in perspective when, immediately following Antony's praise of the "noblest Roman of them all," Octavius closes the play by replying: "According to his virtue let us use him . . ." (5.5.76). New modes and orders were introduced by Caesar Augustus, but they are not endorsed by Shakespeare. As the "stillness of the Augustan peace" approaches, Shakespeare reveals, as Michael Platt has argued, a world "as stale and motionless as a 'gilded puddle.' "[39]

For Shakespeare's own more positive message, we must return to Aufidius's reminder that "our virtues / Lie in th' interpretation of the time . . ." (4.7.49–50). Shakespeare would have his audience reexamine Roman republicanism in order to reevaluate it on its own terms and theirs. Rome's was a great politics, but it was a politics that absorbed itself. Fatally limited, its example taught lessons crucial to late Elizabethan and early Jacobean audiences. *Coriolanus*, Shakespeare's last tragedy, addresses an audience well aware of the advantages and of the difficulties of "mixed government."[40] This was, however, an audience undergoing profound social changes, and Shakespeare's teaching reminds them subtly of the way in which they might evaluate the "virtues" appropriate to their "time."

Shakespeare's use of Roman history for this purpose is in sharp contrast to that of his Renaissance predecessor, Niccolò Machiavelli. Shakespeare offers a searching treatment of "antique Rome," but his "purpose" was quite different from that of Machiavelli. Though confronted with republican ideas, Shakespeare is not an uncritical republican enthusiast.[41] By the time he wrote *Coriolanus* he had begun to hear of James I's unflattering descriptions of puritans as "Tribunes of the people."[42] Yet Shakespeare's Roman plays cannot be labeled defenses of monarchy—Roman, "divine right," or otherwise. Not a "modern" in the sense that he believed that significant progress in the human condition was either immanent or for that matter possible, not a republican after the fashion of Rome or Machiavelli, Shakespeare nonetheless offers counsel to an audience for whom republican images would be increasingly important. Bloom has argued that, "Shakespeare indicates that he himself possesses a spirit of acceptance. That is the way things are, and there is no hope of reforming humanity."[43] Still, his treatment of Roman republicanism is critical for the education of his audience and for others to follow.

If, as Bloom further suggests, Shakespeare's Roman hero stands out as a "public example of virtue . . . necessary for civil society,"[44] that example must convey its "virtue" to the "public." For Shakespeare the vehicle for the conveyance of public honor in Rome was complex and ambiguous, an uncertain model for his world (and so it remains). Still, for all his skepticism, his is not a Hobbesian rejection of poltics. Though his audience and that of Thomas Hobbes nearly overlap, Shakespeare's analyses both of human nature and politics are far less dire. To be sure, violence is everywhere apparent in Shakespeare's republican Rome. Indeed, one might argue that the rise of Octavius is in part the result of the very exhaustion that Hobbes postulates as the result of the "fear of (violent) death."[45] A ruler, like Octavius, who in many ways relieves Romans of their *political* obligations and imposed a dry but effective Roman peace[46] on their heretofore chaotic and violent existence does, in fact, have a strikingly Hobbesian "countenance." Shakespeare seems, however, unwilling to settle for, let alone to advocate, such an undignified end to political virtue. Roman virtue created problems for Shakespeare's Roman hero not so much because political virtue and politics generally are dangerous but because they revealed particular weaknesses that Rome could not overcome. And Roman failure, Shakespeare hoped, might provide for English political education.[47]

In his way, Shakespeare is as devious in his teaching about Rome as Machiavelli but his "purpose" is quite different. Unlike Shakespeare's, Machiavelli's lessons were not, in the first instance, directed at the soul of the audience. On the contrary, Machiavelli seeks to promote "policy" and "process" in ways that avoid self-examination. He develops, as a recent commentator has suggested, a politics based on the "calculating deference and sensational performance of the elected official who relishes the opportunity to advance his ambitions. . . ."[48] Machiavelli's politics is in the end an "institutional politics," which "relies on institutions rather than virtue."[49] This offers a sharp contrast indeed with the renewal afforded Rome by the virtuous actions of its exceptional individuals.[50]

This was a more subversive "policy" than Shakespeare could accept. For Shakespeare, the inadequacy of Roman virtue rightly learned, pointed to a better understanding of political virtue and its limits, and especially, to the necessity of self-reflection. In Shakespeare's teaching, the soul remains at the center of politics. He invites us to reconsider the relationship between self-knowledge and political knowledge in at least three ways. In the simplest sense internal conflict can fog political judgment and lead to rash, self-defeating, even tragic decisions. In a second, and more complex case, when internal conflicts are directly related to political conflicts as is the case with both Brutus and Coriolanus, the possibilities for confusion and imprudence are greater. Finally, if internal conflicts are symptomatic of broader political problems (as again seems to be the case in these plays) the danger is even greater. In this situation one finds a repression of the internal and domestic. The internal is private and secondary in this more extreme rendering, and so is all the more difficult to confront; soulful reflection is a sign of "weakness" and, therefore, rejected out of hand, no matter how necessary and therapeutic it may be. Shakespeare's message is clear. Look at yourself and see what your "external" actions reflect of that self. Avoid, thereby, some of the unseen, unanticipated, and unintended consequences of action carried out for its own sake or action carried out to avoid other more painful, more private reflection.[51] Not as optimistic as Machiavelli, Shakespeare had no new science, but his poetry offered an enduring way of examining the challenges and changes of political life.

William Butler Yeats said that "We make out of the quarrel with others, rhetoric, but of the quarrel with ourselves, poetry." Unable to fathom the quarrel within themselves, poetry was unavailable to most Romans of the republican era.[52] Rome's alternative—rhetoric—was obvious, for Rome's quarrels were defined externally, they were with "others." Not of themselves aware, they were destined to be "with [themselves] at war." Shakespeare provided a "mirror" to his audience with his Roman plays, a "mirror of republics" that was in its way a successor to the "mirror of princes."[53]

Notes

I am grateful for the careful reading given this manuscript by my friends and colleagues Carey McWilliams, Gordon Schochet, and Susan Lawrence, and by my daughter, Eleanor Bathory, and for the thoughtful and encouraging suggestions of Joseph Alulis and Vickie Sullivan.

1. Paul Cantor stresses the importance of these transitions in *Shakespeare's Rome: Republic and Empire* (Ithaca: Cornell University Press, 1976), 12.

2. Quotations to the plays are drawn from Alfred Harbage, ed., *William Shakespeare: The Complete Works* (New York: The Viking Press, 1977).

3. See, for example, Jan H. Blits, *The End of the Ancient Republic* (Lanham, Md.: Rowman & Littlefield, 1993), 73 for a discussion of Shakespeare's concern with Roman heroes and heroism.

4. Michael Platt, *Rome and Romans According to Shakespeare* (Lanham, Md.: University Press of America, 1983), 204–5.

5. Allan Bloom makes this point in "The Morality of the Pagan Hero," in *Shakespeare's Politics* (New York: Basic Books, 1964), 78.

6. The self-consuming nature of Roman republican politics has been the subject of many commentaries on this play: both Bloom and Platt make a strong case in this regard. J.G.A. Pocock finds a civic virtue in Rome that is strikingly different from that which Shakespeare discusses (*The Machiavellian Moment: Florentine Political Thought and the Republican Tradition* [Princeton: Princeton University Press, 1975]).

7. Antony's rhetoric is dominating but his motives are mixed at best. His manipulation of the people of Rome, far from "noble," his manipulation of the Roman political scene in the months and years that follow suggest a person whose judgment is often faulty. This is not to say that Brutus's nobility is called into question, but that its full scope is not revealed by Antony.

8. See, for example, Fustel de Coulanges, *The Ancient City* (Garden City, N.Y.: Doubleday Anchor, 1956).

9. Roman culture, of course, demanded that the self and Rome be closely identified. See, for example, Stephen Coote, *Coriolanus* (London: Penguin Books, 1992). For Shakespeare, the problem was that the "self" revealed in Rome was far too limited.

10. The failures of Portia, Calpurnia, and Volumnia to counsel Brutus, Caesar, and Coriolanus are indicative.

11. Shakespeare does not use these interventions to counsel either noble Roman to be at "peace" with himself. He understood that service to the city necessitated uncertainty, even turmoil. Indeed, to be utterly at peace would, for Shakespeare, seem to require separation from the city and so would in a sense be seditious. Shakespeare's counsel is not seditious. On the contrary, he seeks sound political judgment. Such judgment requires, for Shakespeare, knowledge of both political circumstances and of the self. Brutus's failure to examine more fully his internal conflict leads him to a series of poor political judgments. Most significantly, he misjudges the Roman people and so fails them as a leader and a patriot.

A more careful self-examination would surely not have brought him peace, but might have permitted him to understand better than he did the complex interaction between political knowledge and knowledge of the self. This would be a problem not only for Brutus but for Coriolanus, Caesar, and Mark Antony as well. Indeed, it may be a problem endemic to Rome, symptomatic of Rome's internal crises. Shakespeare warns that self-knowledge must precede political knowledge, and so, effective political leadership.

12. See Cantor, *Shakespeare's Rome*, 204.

13. See David Lowenthal, "Shakespeare's Caesar's Plan," *Interpretation* 10 (1982) for a discussion of the Epicureanism and Stoicism of Brutus and Cassius.

14. Brutus is unaware of his own great power in these circumstances and so "disjoins" power from remorse, though in a manner quite different from Caesar's.

15. See Blits, *Ancient Republic*, 51ff.

16. Of course, the worlds of Brutus and Coriolanus are dramatically different. The tribunate, for example, greedy and self-serving in *Coriolanus*, are thoughtful and public spirited in the beginning of *Julius Caesar* (see Bloom, "Pagan Hero," 82). But, for all of the differences, Shakespeare still draws our attention to a set of common underlying themes.

17. His generosity, however, is limited. He forgets the name of the man of Corioli whom he would save.

18. See Blits, *Ancient Republic*, 3–20. See also Wilson Carey McWilliams, "Lyndon Johnson and the Politics of Mass Society," in *Leadership in America: Consensus, Corruption and Charisma*, ed. P. D. Bathory (New York: Longman, 1978), 190–91. McWilliams discusses friendship and the lack of friendship as a central component in the understanding of American political leadership, especially in the presidency of Lyndon Johnson.

19. Indeed, in the very scene in which Coriolanus rages about "deeds" and "words" he receives news of Aufidius. "Spoke he of me," asks Coriolanus (3.1.127). He apparently defines himself not only by his martial actions but also, ironically, through and by his opponents' words. A turn inside, a meeting with himself may be unnecessary in such a situation; perhaps it is even dangerous.

20. There is none of the support of the sort that Portia gives, or attempts to give, Brutus. Emphasis supplied.

21. Emphasis supplied.

22. The danger here is crucial and that Volumnia does not recognize it any more clearly than her son is telling in Shakespeare's political story.

On the relation between "war" and domestic politics see Arlene Saxonhouse, "An Unspoken Theme in Plato's *Gorgias*: War," *Interpretation* 11 (May 1983): 139–69. Saxonhouse argues that in this dialogue Callicles looks outside the city to relations between cities and the inclination to war among states as a model that he will use to justify the actions he would like to take within the city. That action is based on a "law of nature," which justifies inequality. In some ways the Roman "way" is similar to that of Callicles, though it is clothed in rhetoric that masks its true intention.

23. Coriolanus will soon flatter Aufidius, however, as his treachery begins. Ironically, this comes more easily than flattery of his own Romans. The *Gorgias*, again, provides an important point of reference, as Socrates' discussion of rhetoric and its reliance on flattery serves as an interesting complement to Shakespeare's analysis of Coriolanus.

24. As a descendant of Numa, however, Coriolanus can hardly be expected to bow to the plebeians with abject flattery.

25. This is presumably important to the Roman identity of these people whom Coriolanus earlier describes as liking neither "war nor peace," the one making them afraid, the other proud (1.1.175).

26. The people had forgotten the advice of the tribunes—the lessons they had been taught about Coriolanus's insolence—and have accepted Coriolanus as consul. The tribunes here try, successfully, to undo the "damage." Again the difference between the tribunate here and in *Julius Caesar* is considerable.

27. The danger here is much like that discussed by Plato in the *Gorgias*. Relying solely on rhetorical manipulation and "flattery," the tribunes risk being outmanipulated by a better rhetorician. Compare, for example, *Julius Caesar*, act 3, scene 2, and Antony's speech to the people of Rome.

28. Coote commenting on Coriolanus's conquest of Corioli suggests: "The stature of the hero and his worth to the community could hardly be made more nobly clear. The reappearance of the living Martius, covered in blood and fighting the enemy, is thereby made all the more amazing and welcome. Communal joy raises new energies and we are presented with a . . . vivid military encounter: 'They fight, and all enter the city.' Rome and *romanitas* have triumphed."

29. Of course, such warfare is defining of Roman republican history, however, and continues throughout to be the setting for Roman honor and heroism. See also Cantor, *Shakespeare's Rome*, 72–98 for a fascinating discussion of Coriolanus's understanding of republican politics and his reluctance to participate in it.

30. Compare Platt, *Rome and Romans*, 53, for a slightly different take on this issue.

31. Bloom, "Pagan Hero," 79.

32. See, for example, Lily Ross Taylor, *Party Politics in the Age of Caesar* (Berkeley: University of California Press, 1961).

33. Quoted in Coote, *Coriolanus*, 18.

34. The lack of "purpose" is as important in *Julius Caesar* as it is in *Coriolanus*, at least insofar as unanticipated and unintended consequences occur in each, consequences that could have been planned for.

35. See Antony's speech in *Julius Caesar*, act 3, scene 2 and Plato's *Gorgias*.

36. Coote argues that it is only Coriolanus whose "native language"

preserves "the ideal of a speech in which language and intention are one" (*Coriolanus*, 55). The problem is, of course, with Coriolanus's intention, and that problem, Shakespeare wants us to understand, is not simply a matter of the lack of "temperance" of the early Republic. Though the price of "civil survival" may have been "compromise, dishonesty and deceitful language," as Coote says, Shakespeare sees another problem.

37. Coote, *Coriolanus*, 55.

38. Bloom, "Pagan Hero," 79.

39. Platt, *Rome and Romans*, 313.

40. C. C. Huffman charts the course of these plays and understands *Coriolanus* to represent a return by Shakespeare "to an overtly political concern" last raised a decade earlier in *Julius Caesar* (C. C. Huffman, *Coriolanus in Context* [Lewisburg, Penn.: Bucknell University Press], 170). As before, he asserts: "Shakespeare relied on the more cultivated to use their knowledge of a wide range of political opinion, made possible by contact with the classics and with Italy, to consider the dramatized situation and the normative standards for civic virtue which the play proposes. If honored, they would yield continued honorable political and moral existence."

41. Platt, *Rome and Romans*, 313.

42. Huffman, *Coriolanus in Context*, 74.

43. Bloom, "Pagan Hero," 84.

44. Bloom, "Pagan Hero," 103.

45. Thomas Hobbes, *Leviathan* (Oxford: Basil Blackwell, 1960), 83ff.

46. Hobbes, *Leviathan*, 112.

47. The standpoint of the poet was unavailable to the Roman hero because he could not look inside. The poet might, however, make the lessons of his virtue and his vices available to Elizabethan England and to us.

48. Harvey Mansfield, Jr., *Machiavelli's New Modes and Orders* (Ithaca: Cornell University Press, 1979), 301.

49. Mansfield, *New Modes and Orders*, 301. See Niccolò Machiavelli, *The Discourses on the First Ten Books of Livy* (New York: The Modern Library, 1950), 297–302. In the process Machiavelli solves the problem that would nag Hobbes. Machiavelli moves beyond the need of the fear of violent death by reintroducing, via sensational punishments "every ten years," a memory of that anxiety that made the Leviathan state possible and attractive in the first place.

50. My colleague Carey McWilliams reminds me that for Machiavelli the prince's only real concern should be war and that Machiavelli's doctrine suggests that foreign policy is a matter of external conflicts, at least in the first instance. Shakespeare, in my account, returns to the classical view that domestic politics and the soul have at least equal primacy.

51. If, like Plato, Shakespeare is investigating the self and politics as "mirrors" for one another, if justice in the city is related to justice in the self, then it is crucial to permit an inward-looking musing of the sort that Shakes-

peare finds lacking in his Roman heroes. It may be that Rome's inability to look inside makes justice difficult for Rome. But, if such a standard of judgment is unavailable to Romans themselves, it is surely not unavailable to those commenting on Rome (see, for example, St. Augustine, *The City of God Against the Pagans*, and Montesquieu, *The Greatness of the Romans and Their Decline*, for two very different examples). Shakespeare's use of Rome and Roman history employs such a standard of judgment, one available *to* and *for* his audience.

52. Of course, rhetoric is crucial to politics, and these "quarrels" with others are inescapable, but it is possible to imagine a politics for which rhetoric is a means to a broader public good.

53. The suggestion is not that Shakespeare, advocating republican government, held a "mirror" of ideal republics to England which would permit them to perfect their putative republicanism. Rather it suggests that there are republican sentiments in late Elizabethan and early Jacobean England and that Shakespeare wanted his audience to examine those sentiments with great care.

Shakespeare was not, it has been argued, willing to give up "political virtue." He educates his audience about the limits of Roman heroic nobility, which seemed so profoundly and deeply associated with Roman republicanism, in order to expose and explore what he understood to be the complex, sometimes paradoxical nature of republican government.

Index

About the Contributors

Joseph Alulis teaches political science at North Park College. He also teaches in the Basic Program of the University of Chicago. He has published essays on Shakespeare, Tocqueville, and Lincoln and is the coeditor with Peter Lawler of *Tocqueville's Defense of Human Liberty* (Garland Press, 1993).

Dennis Bathory teaches political theory at Rutgers University where he is also vice chair for graduate studies. He is currently at work on a new edition of his book on St. Augustine, *Political Theory as Public Confession*.

Paul A. Cantor is professor of English at the University of Virginia and a member of the National Council on the Humanities. He is the author of several essays and books on Shakespeare, including the *Hamlet* volume in the Cambridge Landmarks of World Literature series. He is currently working on a book-length study of *King Lear*.

Christopher Colmo is associate professor of political science at Rosary College in River Forest, Illinois. He has published articles on Alfarabi and on Leo Strauss.

Michael Davis has taught philosophy at Sarah Lawrence College since 1977 and teaches political philosophy in the graduate program in political science at Fordham University. He is the author of *The Politics of Philosophy: A Commentary on Aristotle's Politics* (Rowman & Littlefield, 1996), *Aristotle's Poetics: the Poetry of Philosophy* (Rowman & Littlefield, 1992), and *Ancient Tragedy and the Origins of Modern Science* (Carbondale: Southern Illinois University Press).

Timothy Fuller is professor of political science and dean of Colorado College. He works on British thought from Hobbes to Oakeshott. He has previously published essays on Shakespeare's *Measure for Measure* and *The Tempest.*

Pamela K. Jensen teaches political philosophy and politics through literature at Kenyon College. She has published several other essays on Shakespeare's plays and is currently working on a study of the place of poetry in the philosophy of Rousseau.

David Lowenthal is a professor of political science at Boston College. He has written on Shakespeare and has been teaching courses on Shakespeare's moral and political thought for thirty-five years.

Tim Spiekerman recently received his Ph.D. from the University of Chicago's Committee on Social Thought. He has taught in the college at the University of Chicago and at Kenyon College.

Vickie Sullivan is an assistant professor in the political science department at Tufts University. She has also taught in the government department at Skidmore College. She is the author of *Machiavelli's Three Romes: Religion, Human Liberty, and Politics Reformed* (Northern Illinois University Press, 1996).

Barbara Tovey is associate professor emeritus of philosophy at the University of New Hampshire in Durham. Prior to her retirement in 1994, she taught a course on philosophical literature. Shakespeare was among the authors she treated. She has previously published interpretative essays on *The Merchant of Venice* and *The Tempest.* She is currently preparing a manuscript on philosophical themes in the writings of Boccaccio and Chaucer.

Michael Zuckert is Congdon Professor of Political Science at Carleton College. Among other works he has published on seventeenth-century political thought is *Natural Rights and the New Republicanism* (Princeton, 1994). He is also the author of *The Natural Rights Republic* (Notre Dame, 1996).